Negotiating Procurement Contracts

Learning The Knowledge To Negotiate

John C. Tracy

Copyright © 1995-2011 John C Tracy

All rights reserved.

ISBN:1461128250
ISBN-9781461128250

TO MY WIFE JUDITH, THANK YOU FOR YOUR PATIENCE AND ENCOURAGEMENT.

Table of Contents

	Acknowledgments	i
1	Building Negotiation Knowledge	1
2	Understanding Cost	7
3	Understanding Cost In Contract Terms	21
4	Understanding Procurement Risks	33
5	Understanding Contracts	65
6	Limits of Liability	69
7	Structuring Contracts To Drive Behavior and Performance	81
8	How Companies Operate	83
9	Standard Terms – Why Are They There?	97
10	Negotiation Basics	113
11	Using Pre-qualification To Prepare To Negotiate	117
12	Negotiation	123
13	The Remaining Phases Of Negotiation	137

14	Buyer's and Supplier's Negotiation Goals	141
15	Communications In Negotiation	145
16	Avoiding Enforceability Problem Costs	151
17	How Supplier Attempt To Manage Liability	163
18	Buyer's Management of Risk and Liability	181
19	Contract Negotiation Example	183
20	Negotiating Concessions	191
21	Negotiating Cost	195
22	Discounts	215
23	Negotiating Delivery	221
24	Negotiating Quality, Managing Quality Costs	227
	Glossary of Procurement And Contract Terms	239

CHAPTER 1 BUILDING NEGOTIATION KNOWLEDGE

To be successful in negotiating you need three things:
1. The appropriate **negotiation strategy or strategies** for the leverage you have and relationship you want to establish or maintain.
2. The right **tactics** to help get what you need.
3. Significant **knowledge** about what you are negotiating, including all the terms.

If any one of these is missing, there's a high probability that you won't be successful.

You can learn negotiation tactics a number of ways and one of the things that helped me was a course on negotiation by Dr. Chester Karrass. If you every get a chance to attend one of his company's seminars I'd highly recommend it. If you can't, read his books. Herb Cohen's book "You Can Negotiate Anything" also is good for understanding power in negotiations. You can learn about negotiation strategies, especially win/win strategies if you read any books that have been written by individuals from the Harvard Negotiation Project such as "Getting to Yes" by Fisher and Ury.

I quickly discovered that negotiations don't operate on tactics and strategies alone, and for the tactics and strategies to really work; you need to know more about what you are actually negotiating and the environment you're negotiating in. It's easy to say that the supplier "needs to do better" as a tactic, but it's far more effective when you can explain exactly why they need to do better and the impact it will have if they don't. In a course on "Total Cost" given by Dennis Kudrna, I learned part of the "why", and understanding and using "Total Cost" is an important part of procurement knowledge.

Each different style of procurement (production, MRO, administrative, services) has different issues. Even within the same style of procurement such as production, different commodities present different challenges and opportunities to learn because of the dynamics of the suppliers and marketplaces. This means that you can't always go back to the same playbook of tactics and strategies and expect to win. What I found was that the more complex the item you negotiate to procure, the more frequently you'll draw on pieces of knowledge you learned. For example, if you purchased a complete product for resale under your brand name, your negotiation would need to address manufacturing, service and resale issues all as part of the one relationship. Most procurement knowledge is portable and many of the issues are the same irrespective of the industry. Each industry has certain nuances that are unique and must be learned.

The best way I can start to describe what you need to know to successfully negotiate is to share three things: 1) the negotiation process. 2) The steps in the procurement process leading up to the negotiation. 3) The types of knowledge you need to negotiate. The **negotiation process** is built up of a number of individual sub-processes: The first three are totally controlled by the supplier.

| Conceptual Planning | Product & Service Development | Marketing & Prospecting |

For most standard products and services the negotiation really starts when the supplier is in the **conceptual planning phase.** In the conceptual planning phase the supplier tries to determine what the market needs or wants and what product or service features they will include to make their product unique. Their goal is to differentiate themselves from other suppliers to potentially reduce competition from other suppliers that don't have those features.

During the **product and service development** phase the supplier will establish how they want to sell the product, what they will price it at, what discounts they will provide to different types of customers such as OEM's and what different selling tiers they will maintain. For example, if they determine that they will sell their product exclusively through distribution that determines the company you have to negotiate with. It usually determines the terms you can potentially get. The discount model the supplier provides to distributors will also impact your price.

During the **marketing and prospecting** phase the key negotiation activity that is occurring is the sales person is trying to understand the problems you have, your needs and preferences to compare against their product or services features. The more they know that you need or want their product, or that their product has features that are unique to them that you need of want, the less leverage you may have in the negotiation. Frequently much of this is occurring before procurement is involved so procurement needs to educate their customers on how to manage initial discussions with suppliers to maintain leverage. The buyer controls the next three phases of negotiation.

Knowing how to qualify a supplier and understanding what to look for in the qualification is important tool in preparing for a negotiation. **Qualification** isn't to just understand whether the supplier can perform the work. That's only one aspect of qualification. Other aspects are being able to look at what the supplier does and how they do it to understand their costs and the cost impact of their processes and materials. This is very important for long-term supplier relationships as you consider whether you will be able to drive their price down. A third aspect of pre-qualification is to note what you see that you can use in the negotiation or that may require you to add certain terms or requirements to your contract. I'll discuss more about this later.

The **bid / quote / proposal** phase of negotiations is a tool that you can use in a number of ways. It can set expectations of what you want and what it will take to win. It can include "anchors" for the negotiation. For example if you include your contract as part of the request and require the supplier to identify any assumptions or exceptions, your contract is the anchor that they now have to negotiate off. The bid / quote / proposal phase also allows you to explore a number of options to understand the potential schedule or cost impact of certain requirements.

The **proposal review, negotiation preparation** phase does two things. You can have preliminary negotiations in the form of asking the supplier to clarify their proposal and ask questions about any exceptions or assumptions they included. The negotiation preparation aspect involves establishing a number of things such as the plan, strategy, tactics, goals, minimums etc. that will be used and the roles of any team members.

The **negotiation** stage is where all the advance planning, strategies and tactics are implemented in an attempt to reach agreement on the terms and contract. The output is the execution of the purchase order, license or contract.

After the execution of the contract there may still be five more phases in the negotiation process.

Mobilization is the period of time from execution of the contract to the time performance commences where the supplier may be requesting changes or substitution of materials, equipment, etc. For example, if your specification required a specific item, they might request an alternative be approved because of lead times or opportunity to reduce cost. This is a negotiation and it's important to make sure that if what they propose is of less value or cost, you need to make sure that you are getting appropriate reductions in price for that reduced value.

The **production delivery, changes and performance management** phase is supplier management. It's making sure that you get what was promised.

The **contract close out** phase will vary greatly depending upon what you are purchasing. Most of the contract close out activity involves ensuring that all deliverables that the supplier was to provide under the contract have in fact been provided and are acceptable before there is final payment. For example, has the supplier provided all the documentation, training, manuals, drawings etc. that they were obligated to provide?

The **warranty** phase of negotiations is simply managing the supplier to ensure they meet all their warranty obligations under the contract. This can include correction of problems that require warranty replacement or service or it can also include correction of any of the other warranties that the supplier made under the contract that may have been breached.

The **claims** phase involves negotiating the settlement of any open claims that either the supplier or buyer may have under the contract. To effectively negotiate any potential claims as part of the management of the contract you may need to establish what actions each party took and when, or what changes occurred and when to be able to specifically identify who is responsible. For example if a problem occurred with a product that was manufactured during a specific period of time, you may need to establish what the specifications were at that time. For something to be defective you normally would look to whether the product met the agreed specifications that were in effect at the time of purchase.

Building knowledge.
To be the best, you must invest. In that I mean that if you want to negotiate procurement contracts, you need to invest in building substantial procurement knowledge. For example to effectively prepare for a negotiation, you or someone else needs to have accomplished all the procurement steps leading up to the negotiation which means knowledge is needed on how to conduct each of the following sub-processes:
1. Gather internal information on requirements. What do we need, when do we need it, how do we

need it?
2. Qualify potential suppliers. Does the supplier have the capability and capacity to do the work? What did I uncover that I can use in the negotiation. b) Will anything I discovered impact cost? Did I identify anything that's potential risk I need to address?
3. Analyze suppliers and supplier risks (especially financial risks).
4. Select the appropriate contract template to use and modify as needed.
5. Assemble specifications and requirements.
6. Prepare bid / quote / proposal document.
7. Solicit RFQ. RFI / RFP or bid.
8. Analyze and clarify responses.
9. Assemble the negotiation team.
10. Establish roles and ground rules for the team.
11. Identify negotiation strategy.
12. Identify tactics.
13. Identify goals and minimums.
14. Prepare the negotiation plan.

A negotiator of procurement contracts needs substantial knowledge in a number of areas to be successful:
- General business knowledge
- Communication skills
- Language skills
- Project management skills
- Computer and computer software skills such as being able to create and manage spreadsheets
- Knowledge of company tools, processes and policies
- General knowledge of the commodity for the product or service you will be negotiating
- Knowledge of the supplier
- Knowledge of the specific product or service including how it is made or performed, and all that's involved in managing the product or service from initial demand to delivery.
- Contracts knowledge.
- Knowledge to be able to analyze needs and motivation of both your company and the supplier.
- Knowledge of the types of supplier relationships so you can determine the type of relationship you are trying to establish
- Knowledge or power or leverage so you can assess the leverage of the parties to help determine the strategies and tactics to use
- Knowledge of the different negotiation strategies and when to use them
- Knowledge of negotiation tactics so you can determine what tactics to use and when
- Knowledge on how to manage the negotiation team
- Knowledge on how to conduct and manage the negotiation

As you can see from the above lists, strategy and tactics are only a small portion of what is needed to successfully negotiate procurement contracts. If you are going to negotiate contracts you need to understand that contract terms are all about managing cost and risk. So you need to have a thorough understanding of the costs and risks associated with procurement. Contract terms fall into one of seven general categories that each tie back to cost.

1. The tasks or work to be performed or the products or services to be delivered. All of these tie to the cost you should pay for the product or service.

2. Specific performance requirements and what rights or remedies the parties may have if performance is not met. These deal with the ability to recover some, if not all, of the costs you will incur from non-performance.

3. The responsibility for certain costs in the relationship such as what's included in the price, what party pays for delivery, what party bears what costs associated with the warranty. The scope of each is part of determining the cost of the relationship.

4. The administrative processes by which the relationship will be managed such as ordering, re-scheduling, cancellation, warranty returns, rejection of defective products or services, payments, termination processes, etc. These terms drive either direct costs or indirect costs.

5. Responsibilities for various risks that may occur and the standard of performance for managing the risks being assumed. These tie to the potential liability and resultant cost if the risk materializes. These can include things like a third party claim where whoever owns the risk will have the cost of defending against the claim and the responsibility of paying for costs and damages awarded.

6. Legal terms that cover the obligations of the parties and the interpretation and enforcement of the contract such as what law will apply, and where will the dispute be heard. While these may not have a direct cost impact, they may impact your ability to enforce the contract and recover costs and damages as a result of the other party not meeting their obligations.

7. Where you haven't been able to transfer the risk or cost to the supplier, you need tools built into contracts to help manage performance against those costs and risks. For example many contracts have a number of terms to help manage against the potential cost of quality problems.

Over time I've developed a number of materials on negotiation that I want to share with you to make you a better negotiator. The delivery approach, simply because of the volume of materials, is split between this book and my blog that can be found at **http://knowledgetonegotiate.blogspot.com**.

At the back of this book is a glossary of terms that you may encounter in procurement negotiations or that may be used in this book. It's important to understand the language of procurement and procurement contracts as a large part of negotiation is communicating. You need to make sure you and the supplier both understand each other. If a term is used in the book or blog that you don't understand, check the glossary to see if it has been described.

A number of the materials and examples are focused on production procurement, but don't let that discourage you and as a majority of the issues, concerns and suggestions apply irrespective of what you buy. Since buyer / supplier negotiations are all about cost, that's where we'll start.

John C. Tracy

CHAPTER 2 UNDERSTANDING COST

2.1 Types of Costs

In every procurement relationship you will have:

1. Direct costs that you will pay the supplier.
2. Direct costs that you will assume because of the terms that you agreed.
3. Indirect costs that are driven by the supplier's performance.
4. Indirect costs that are driven by the terms you agreed.
5. Costs that are associated with certain risks that may occur that either you or the supplier will be responsible for depending upon the terms and limitations you agreed.
6. There are costs and risks that you can limit or avoid by the terms.
7. There are costs or risks that you try to manage through the terms.

Here's an example of each:

An example of direct costs would be charges that you pay the supplier such as price you pay, any premium costs, costs that are reimbursable such as if you agreed to have them ship something to you freight pre-paid.

An example of a direct cost that you will assume because of the terms that you agreed would be the cost of delivery and insurance for items while in transit and any duties if you purchase a product under origin based delivery terms (such as ex-works). Origin based delivery terms also create a risk as the buyer assume the responsibility for delivery to your location.

An example of an indirect cost that is driven by performance would be things like increased inventory cost driven by supplier delivery or quality problems.

An example of an indirect cost that is driven by the terms you agreed would be things like increased inventory levels because of terms that forced you to purchase more inventory than you need. An example of this is minimum order quantities or limitations on rights to cancel or reschedule product deliveries or services.

An example of a cost that is associated with certain risks that may occur would be things like the legal cost to defend against a third party claim for intellectual property infringement or other types of third party claims. It could also include having to bear the damages awarded if the supplier didn't or wasn't able to defend against those claims.

An example of costs that you can limit or avoid by the terms would be the limitation of liability that both limits the types of damages a buyer or supplier may recover against the each other (as limiting the types of damages limits the potential cost). It can also include any limitation in the amount of the damages they may collect, which would be expressed as a cap on liability.

An example of costs that you try to manage through the terms would be quality costs and the ways to manage quality cost will be in a number of areas of your contract where you either transfer the cost and risk to the supplier or include controls to try to manage the risk as a way of managing the potential cost. Those controls for managing potential quality costs would include things such as limiting modifications or changes to the product or service, control over assignment and sub-contracting by the supplier to third parties.

In writing and negotiating contracts you need to manage your ability to enforce the terms of the contract and get recovery from the supplier for non-performance, otherwise that adds to your cost.

Most contracts and contract negotiations are about basic two things.

1) Attempting to transfer the cost and risk to the other party, and

2) For costs or risks that can't be transferred, it's making sure that you have the tools needed to help you manage the costs or risk that you've assumed.

For example, if you agreed to purchase an item under ex-works delivery term that means that you have taken possession at the suppliers dock. What that also means is you have agreed to assume the cost and risk involved in having the item delivered from that point to your location. To manage against the potential risk, you could specify how the item will be packed and packaged to reduce the risk of damage. You could specify the specific carrier and freight lanes to be used as that may reduce the risk of loss or theft of the item. You may also purchase insurance to cover you against the potential loss or damage to the item. If you purchased the item ex-works the supplier's dock and let the supplier control all of it, you can wind up having the item damaged or lost, and at best have a claim against any insurance you may have. Insurance covers the cost of the item, but not the cost impact of not having it when needed.

In a negotiation your primary goal is to have the costs and risks be the responsibility for the party that can best manage them. If you assume the responsibility for costs and risks that you can't manage by the terms you agree upon, you have no control over the potential resulting cost. If you require a supplier to assume responsibility for costs or risks that they can't manage, odds are they will include a contingency in their price to cover the risk. If the risk happens, the contingency covers the cost. If the risk never materializes, it becomes extra profit for the supplier at your expense.

In every negotiation always ask yourself who is more capable of managing this cost or risk? If the answer is the supplier, then the terms you agree upon should reflect that and the supplier should be bearing the majority, if not all, of the cost and risk for that issue. If it's the buyer, you should be assuming it. If neither party has control over the cost or risk you may need an alternative approach. One area that frequently requires alternative approaches is currency exchange risks.

For the most part costs will involve either a direct payment, or they will add additional cost to the relationship due to the cost of money, cost of delivery, cost of inventory, cost of performance, cost of quality, or the impact on the ability to recover cost. All of these fall under the concept called total cost. In addition to total cost many negotiations require you to look at the cost of total supply chain and the total life cycle cost for the purchase. Cost is not just the purchase price you pay.

2.2 Costs in a supplier relationship

Your real cost in a supplier relationship or your total cost of ownership includes or will be impacted by the following:

Price. What's included in a supplier's price (less discounts, plus any incremental charges)?

Administrative costs required by the supplier's processes. This would include all your resources required to expedite issues if the supplier's order-fulfillment processes are cumbersome, bureaucratic or routinely cause problems. This would also include incremental costs required to manage return material authorizations.

Cost of money, time value of money, cost of inventory, obsolescence and net present value for terms such as payments, reimbursement of costs, etc.;

Design qualification or re-qualification cost. This includes the cost to qualify the supplier and the part originally and the costs to re-design products to replace a part if a supplier or part doesn't perform. It may include the cost to re-qualify the item if there have been any changes.

Demand is a cost if the activity drives demand for support, services, and inventory. For example: low quality levels drive demand for more inventories to offset expected failures. A weakness in a supplier's administrative processes like invoicing drives a demand on the buyer's resources to deal with those weaknesses and that has a cost associated with it. For many areas, design, and standards clearly drives demand and cost.

The **"effective date"** for when the price changes. How long does it take for a new lower price to really impact the price you pay is a cost? If it isn't instantaneous, that's a cost.

Enforcement of contract rights. This includes the cost of things like managing enforcement of warranty obligations to reduce internal costs and investment in spare parts inventory.

Field costs and risks - defects, epidemic defects etc. quality and reliability is a huge potential portion of cost, and the scope and length of the warranty, warranty exclusions and the cost of field failures or replacements is high in the list of cost drivers. Service and support costs (warranties, reliability, warranty limitations, spare parts and repair costs, forced end of life purchases, support costs, no problem found (NPF) charges all are part of field costs)

Hidden costs created by third parties. This frequently occurs in outsourcing where standards have not been set on terms and the risk /cost flows back to the buyer. It also occurs where the outsourced supplier's different requirements or terms (which are usually designed to reduce their cost) actually drive up the price you may pay in the long term. For example a vendor managed inventory (VMI) program with suppliers will reduce a contract manufacturer's inventory and the costs associated with that, but driving the cost of the inventory back to the supplier may impact their future pricing or size of price reductions as a result of that cost.

One-time charges (non-recurring engineering (NRE), tooling)

Landed costs includes the price, acquisition costs (such as delivery, duties, material acquisition costs), brokers fees, taxes

Lead-time. Can drive cost if lead-time has an impact on inventory levels; buy quantities and the impact that inventory have the other potential cost of risk of loss or obsolescence?

Manufacturability costs includes issues of design for manufacturability or the cost of introducing the item into the manufacturing process such as whether the items are packed or packaged for manufacturing, or it can also include the impact the design has on how it must manufactured such as requiring hand versus machine placement.

Operational management costs. You may pay higher prices or assume more cost if:
- Contracts are not managed and are allowed to expire when product is still needed.
- Contracts are renewed late and the new contracts offer a price advantage.
- Time demands or lack of a planning calendar provides too little time to prepare & negotiate the best contract.
- You don't track and manage cost over time, such as track and manage activities where costs have been amortized into the pricing.
- You don't track and mange things like quality performance.

Packing or packaging (If billed separately)

Part management costs. There is a to administratively maintain parts information current.

Performance cost. Includes the cost of quality problems, cost of inventory associated with quality, delivery, reliability, defects, along with the costs of managing quality performance because of the supplier's quality performance such as the need for incoming inspection, higher levels of testing etc. It also includes order fulfillment problems that require increased costs of expediting, rush production, expedited delivery. It can also include increased costs to suppliers caused by lack of predictability or wide swings in demand.

Recurring charges (set-up, tooling maintenance, calibration)

Serviceability costs includes whether the item was designed for repair (keeping repair time at minimum levels),

Service life cycle costs include the cost of spare parts, repairs, Mean time to repair (MTTR), the frequency of failures measured by mean time between failures (MTBF) and the impact warranty related service costs has profitability.

Supplier Relationship Costs. This is the investment of resources required to manage the relationship because of the character of the supplier and the demands required to manage them and deal with their administrative processes.

Supply chain costs are based on the supply chain structure and the impact that has on all of the other costs. Different supply chain models such as vendor managed inventory can have substantial impact on costs such as inventory, reschedules and cancellations, obsolescence, etc. Supply chain costs can also include down stream costs in moving product to the end customer.

Supplier sales model. Every step in the sales chain adds cost. Where you buy from within the supplier's structure or channels will clearly impact the price you can negotiate and the value of terms you get. For example, if a supplier will not deal with you direct, there will be a clear impact on the price you pay because:
- The channel will be both limited the discounting they can do,
- The channel adds their overhead and profit.
- The channel can't provide the same value to you in contract terms

Terms, risks and costs assumed by the contract terms. The vast majority of terms in any contract either define who is responsible for performing specific tasks (and their associated costs), or who bears what risks (and the costs associated with those). This includes the cost of contractual risks assumed or excluded such as warranty terms, cost of field re-calls for epidemic failures, cost of patent indemnification risks/costs, costs associated with cancellation and flexibility provisions, etc. Throughout any purchase contract there are risks that are assumed by one party or the other such as problems with loss or damage to materials in transit, warranties, indemnities, etc. If these risk materialize that represents an added cost. For example, if you buy FOB, supplier's Dock, you are assuming all the costs of shipping, risk of loss for damage in transit, the cost of purchasing insurance, duties, broker's fees etc.

Total Cost of the relationship includes landed costs plus costs that are driven by the structure of the relationship and costs that are driven by the supplier's performance including:
- Quality and returns management, including receiving, inspection
- Delivery (performance related costs of delivery problems, expediting)
- Inventory (safety stock, lot or order quantity, lead time reschedule or cancellation impact on inventory)
- Cost of money, cash flow costs (payment terms, forced inventory investments, currency exposure, hedging cost

Total life cycle costs includes total cost, plus all the costs associated with operation, use, maintaining, servicing, and disposal of the product, less any residual or salvage value. For example, when you license software you pay an initial license fee, but life cycle costs involved in that decision may include annual maintenance fees, requirements to purchase upgrades, customization costs, and any costs associated or driven by that decision. If you purchase a piece of capital equipment the life cycle costs can include not just the costs of using the equipment (such as spare parts, maintenance, repairs, consumable supplies, etc.) but also other costs such as utilities cost, cost of operators, etc. A great example of a life cycle cost is if you bought a Gillette™ razor, it forced you to buy Gillette™ razor blades.

Selling Location and Taxes. Profits are taxed based upon the location of sale. Sellers want to manage the location of sale to manage their taxes and profit. Asking a supplier to sell in a different location will impact the price you will pay if it impacts the taxes the Supplier must pay. For example if you asked a supplier to set up a local stocking hub in another country a number of things occur. They need to be legally registered to conduct business in that location, they become subject to that country's laws and they becomes subject to taxes on the income they make from the sale. If they will do that it will impact your price.

2.3 Key Ingredients of Cost

Excluding the risks you assume and the price, there are five main cost ingredients that get negotiated or that are impacted as part of the terms you agree upon.
- Cost of money / and impact to cash flow based on the time value of money.
- The cost and risk of delivery.
- The cost of inventory,
- The cost of quality.
- The cost of warranty.

Cost of money / impact to cash flow based on the time value of money

Any term that forces you to buy more than you need or buy it earlier than needed is adding cost. For example, if a supplier has a minimum order quantity or minimum order amount and that is forcing you to purchase more than what you need then it's forcing you to make an investment in inventory. Terms that limit your ability to cancel or reschedule orders or that force you to pay cancellation charges are forcing you to make an investment in inventory. Things such as extended lead times will force you into carrying higher inventory levels. Long response times for things like replacement of defective product or replacement of product under warranty will drive you to invest in carrying higher inventory levels. All of these are requiring you to make an investment of your available cash which either prevents it from being used elsewhere where it could provide a return on the investment or it is costing you to borrow the money needed to pay for it. In large companies the value from a cost of money perspective of being able to pay suppliers in sixty days versus thirty or forty-five days is huge. If you can have that amount of money for an extra 30 or 15 days and invest it, think about how much it would be worth!

The cost and risk of delivery

The cost and risk of delivery will be determined by the specific delivery point and delivery term that you agree upon, For example, if you were to purchase a product under Ex-Works terms at a supplier dock in China and your point of use is New York City, by agreeing to that term the costs that you have agreed to assume are:
- Carriage from the supplier's dock to the port of exportation
- The costs of any export charges or fees including customs brokers
- The cost of air or ship transfer to the port of importation
- The costs of any import charges or fees including duties and customs brokers charges for importation.
- The cost of air or surface shipment to New York City.
- In addition to these costs by that term you also assumed the risk of loss or damage to the product while it was in transit, and
- To protect against the cost of loss or damage you may have also purchased insurance on the product.

If the purchase failed to get to there or was delivered damaged, you could also sustain internal costs, lost revenue or profits by not having it or damages by not being able to fulfill a customer order that required it. The cost of delivery can apply not just to delivery of the product, but also the return of defective product, and the return of products under warranty.

The cost of inventory

The cost of inventory in made up of a number of factors. One is the cost or value of the money that was involved in purchasing it. It also includes the cost of managing it, and facility costs to store it such as the cost of the space, heat, light, and insurance. It will include other things such as the cost of potential loss or damage and other costs if it is held too long such as obsolescence. Some products have a limited life and deterioration over time such may occur with aging date coded products or products with limited shelf life is a cost. Anything that forces you to buy inventory before you need it, buy it in larger quantities than you need or forces you to increase your inventory as a protection against potential failure of the supplier to perform will carry an inventory cost. For example, if the supplier ships defective products, you will most likely carry a higher level of inventory. If the supplier's delivery performance is spotty, you will most likely carry a higher level of inventory. If the supplier's products have increased failure levels, you will most likely carry higher levels of spare parts or field replaceable unit (FRU) inventories.

The cost of quality

The cost of quality is made up of a number of factors:

Supply chain. If you have a supplier that has quality problems it will create additional handling and stocking locations as you couldn't ship directly to a customer, that additional handling, inspection and inventory adds to your cost.

Inspection. If you have a supplier that ships you defective materials on a regular basis that forces you to maintain higher degrees of inspection and the resulting inspection costs and it adds to your cost as you need to do increased levels of return materials management.

Inventory related costs. Frequent or significant problems with quality will cause: increased investment in inventory; increased handling costs; increased storage cost as that's related to the volume of the inventory; increased insurance costs as that's related to the value of goods being insured; increased risk of obsolescence and write offs of the material; risk of loss, damage while in inventory; and risk of deterioration of inventoried product / date code issues.

Correction of the Defect Cost. This includes replacement costs such as returns management cost; premiums to procure elsewhere when critical; re-work costs associated with the removal of the defective product and the replacement it with a good product; and increased investment in service inventory to deal with increased failures.

The cost of warranty,

When there is a problem with a product or service, the cost usually involves the cost of labor to remove or correct the problem and the cost of materials required for the repair or replacement of the item. For products that fail that have been made part of another product, the cost may also include what's called the cost of rework which is the cost to remove the defective item and the cost to replace it with a good item. It can also include the cost of scrap if the items can't be repaired of replaced. The things that impact the cost of warranty are:
    The length of the warranty or warranty term.
    When the warranty period is started (shipment, delivery, installation, acceptance).
    What's included in the warranty (parts, labor, both).
    Any exclusions or limitations to the warranty.

In many product purchases, suppliers only want to provide coverage for the buyer for the cost of the item (repair or replace). Many buyers will try to manage their cost of warranty by negotiating in terms such as epidemic defects, where after an agreed threshold of defects has been exceeded, the supplier has to begin to pay some of the buyers other costs related to defective products or services or unacceptable reliability. That way the supplier begins to assume labor costs associated with repair or replacement at the point of use and other costs such as rework.

2.4 Understanding the concept of Total Cost.

To effectively negotiate you need to think about all the terms from a cost and risk perspective and understand the "Total Cost" of the relationship. In understanding Total Cost here are some simple definitions:

- **Price** is what you pay.
- **Landed cost** is the Price plus all distribution cost, duties, and other fees required to get the product to the point of use.
- **Total cost** is a method by which you allocate the costs of the supplier relationship. Total cost is the landed cost plus additions or deletions based upon the impact of the contract terms and supplier's performance.
- **Total life cycle cost** is the total cost, plus all future costs associated with the purchase over the useful life of the item. As these are future costs, they need to be calculated on a net present value basis. Total life cycle costs would include things like spare parts, repairs, consumable supplies, differences in operating hours, yields, consumption of energy, residual value, etc.
- **Total supply or value chain cost** adds the fulfillment cost parameters to the concept of cost. It looks at not just the cost of getting the items to you, but the cost of getting the item to the end user. This cost includes the total life cycle cost, plus the transactional costs for remainder of supply chain. For example, if one supplier could perform direct fulfillment and another couldn't, the comparison of the total supply chain costs would be their cost plus your costs of fulfillment against the cost of the supplier providing the turnkey operation.

These costs include both direct and indirect costs. The majority of indirect costs are made up of the cost of money, the cost of inventory, the cost of quality and the cost of warranty / reliability in some combination. To do a form of total cost calculation, you allocate costs (both positive and negative) to many of factors that exist in a supplier relationship. The sum is the total cost of the supplier relationship. Total cost brings in costs that are driven by the contact terms; the supplier's performance or supplier practices into your sourcing decision, negotiation or cost management process. Here is an example of the types of cost factors that could be used in calculating the total cost or to highlight when a supplier is adding to your cost in a negotiation

Reductions to cost:	Additions to cost:
Discounts	Advance Payments
Extended payment terms	Non-recurring engineering costs
Retained Payments	Set up costs
Quantity Discounts	Tooling Costs
Estimated Cost Reductions	Packaging Costs
Learning Curve Reductions	Price Fluctuations (Increases)
Price Fluctuations (Decreases)	Raw Material Adders and Surcharges
Positive Currency Fluctuations	Negative Currency Fluctuations
Tax Credits Available	Taxes
Investment Credits	Tooling Maintenance
Residual Tooling Value	Duties
Export Credit (Duty Drawback)	Lead time
Poor Performance Credits	Delivery Performance
Vendor Stocking	Order/expedite costs
Credits for Freight Problems	Risk of loss

Loss Recovery	Freight Cost and Insurance
Freight Quantity Discounts	Delivery Time
Value of Extended Warranties	Delivery related Performance
Credits for Quality Problems	Quality Problems
Extended Reliability	Warranty limitations
Packaging Re-use savings	Premiums for Maintenance Cost
	Premiums for Spare Parts
	Premiums for Repairs
	Inventory cost for Minimum Order Qty.
	Technical Assistance Charges
	Internal Support Required
	Re-schedule premiums
	Cancellation charges
	Design Change Premiums
	Test Equipment

For an item to be a reduction to the price, it needs to be a firm commitment (such as cost reductions or committed learning curve improvements), and it must provide value to the buyer. For example, if the supplier offers an extended warranty, that alone may not provide value to the buyer if the buyer will not use or get the benefit of the extended warranty. For an item to be an addition to the price it needs to add to the price, the buyer's costs or risks.

In day-to-day decision-making we each do a form of "total cost" evaluation. For example, in searching for the best source to purchase a toy for a birthday you might check out sites on the Internet and scan all of the newspaper ads in the Sunday paper to find the best price. You find three potential sources for your purchase. The Internet price is $22.95 plus $5.95 for shipping and handling. A local specialty store (5 mi. from your home has them available for $24.95. A discount store 40 miles from home in another state with no sales tax has them has them available for $20.00. In a simple total cost calculation the respective costs would be:

	Specialty store	Discount Store	Internet
Price	$24.94	$20.00	$22.95
Sales tax	$1.25	$0.00	$1.25
Mileage cost	10mi x .36 = $3.60	80mi x .36= $28.80	0
Ship & Hand	0	0	$5.95
Total Cost	$29.79	$48.80	$30.15

This is Total Cost in its simplest form.

Cost items may be one time, recurring, or may not apply to all units. Where items are a one-time cost, in determining the total cost you spread those one-time costs over the total estimated purchases to determine the impact of that one time cost. Included in one-time payments are items such as non-recurring engineering or design charges, initial set up costs, tooling cost, and unique test equipment or other charges that are in addition to the price and are not repeat costs. For these one-time costs you may need to evaluate whether it is better to amortize the costs into the purchase price or pay it separately. As not all costs are immediate, as part of this type of calculation you need to you need to look at the cost from an investment perspective and do calculations of net present value or discounted cash flow.

2.5 The time value of money *(Net Present Value (NPV) and Discounted Cash Flow)*

Net present value looks at what a future cost is worth in today's dollars. Discounted cash flow looks at how much of an investment would need to be made today to make a payment or investment in the future. Net present value takes into account the fact that the other party will have the benefit of using the money in the interim and getting the compounding effect on that, making it worth less to you (as you aren't getting the compounding effect of the money). Discounted cash flow takes into account the fact that you will have the benefit of the investment and would be earning a return and gets the benefit of compounding in the interim so the amount you need to invest today to make a payment in the future is less than the payment amount.

The NPV is calculated by dividing 1 by (1 plus the interest rate)^N where "n" equals the number of years. For example if you had a value of money of 12%, and the agreement was to pay you $1.00 three years from now, the NPV calculation would be:

$$NPV = \frac{1}{(1+rate)^n} \text{ or } \frac{1}{(1+.12)^3} \text{ or } \frac{1}{1.12 \times 1.12 \times 1.12} \text{ or } \frac{1}{1.4049} = \$.7117$$

This means that a commitment to pay you $1.00 three years in the future is equivalent to you having $.71 today. From a discounted cash flow perspective it would mean that for you to have that $1.00 three years in the future, you would need to invest $.71 today at the same interest rate.

Net present value or discounted cash flow each deal with the concept of time value of money. That's important to procurement, as throughout a contract there are promises to make payments, hold inventories, and pay damages, all which may have a time value impact. For example, if you were purchasing a major piece of equipment there can be a significant difference in the NPV based upon the payment schedule. Sometimes the issue of time value of money exists in the subtleties of the language used or the changes suppliers try to negotiate. For example compare the same commitment, but with one word inserted:

"Supplier will pay all damages awarded."

Versus

"Supplier will pay all damages <u>finally</u> awarded."

What's the difference? The difference is when you will get paid. In the first, once damages are awarded the supplier must pay. In the second, payment will occur at some point in the distant future after the supplier has exhausted all appeals so the award is final. You will still get paid the amount awarded, but on a net present value basis you will get less. Using a 12% value of money, here's what they would be worth depending on timing:

Time to get paid	Current value of payment commitment
1 year	$.89
2 years	$.79
3 years	$.71
4 years	$.63
5 years	$.56
6 years	$.50
8 years	$.40
10 years	$.38

The simple reason for the difference is the compounding effect. The compounding effect means that over time you will make interest or a return on your previously earned interest or return, so that return compounds over time. If you keep money you get the benefit of the compounding. If the supplier keeps the money they get the benefit and that reduces the value to you.

If you look at time value of money from an inventory perspective, the impact is much greater because the cost of inventory will always be a much higher percentage because it's the combination of the cost of money and the costs associated with holding inventory.

2.6 Life Cycle Costs

In addition to total cost, purchases or relationships may be evaluated based on life cycle cost. Life cycle cost is the initial "total cost" - in current dollars *plus* the net present value for estimated future costs. The estimated future costs are calculated based upon the annual projected spending for on-going costs associated with the product for the estimated useful life of the item, calculated also on a net present value basis. An example of future costs for a piece of capital equipment would include: maintenance and service contracts, spare parts, repairs, enhancements and upgrades, consumable parts, consumable supplies, and follow on training. Life cycle costs could also include operating expenses and labor.

In addition to total cost and life cycle cost, many decisions need to be evaluated on a "total value" basis. The "total value concept" expands beyond traditional purchase factors and looks from the perspective of the value to the ultimate consumer of the product or service. The total value concept is the life cycle cost plus the assessment of:
- Direct transactional costs for the entire supply chain
- Supplier and relationship costs for the entire supply chain
- Logistics chain costs (to the ultimate consumer)
- Indirect financial costs (what it takes to manage and the financial impact)

For example, companies may go through the process of determining whether to make or buy an item or perform or subcontract a service. Direct transactional costs would look at the costs in a make scenario to purchase and manage all the necessary items for production, versus the transactional costs involved in procurement the finished item. The supplier relationship costs would look at the costs to manage the relationships with the multiple suppliers necessary to make the item versus the supplier relationship costs with the single supplier. The logistics chain costs would look at the cost of moving all the raw material to the place of manufacture and the movement of the manufactured item from there to the ultimate consumer, versus potential shipment of the finished item direct to the ultimate customer from the supplier. Indirect financial costs would look at things such as the amounts of inventories required to be held under the make model, versus the amount of inventory to be held at the buy model and the difference in timing for both. Immediate customer impacts would look at things such as how the different models would affect the ultimate customer needs / expectations.

When you look at relationships on a total value basis, buyer's may agree to pay a higher price to one supplier, if that supplier is able to reduce other costs involved in the entire fulfillment process so the value the buyer receives offsets any premium in the price.

Throughout every procurement contract there are terms that will impact cost directly, indirectly, or that represent risks, which if they materialize will create a cost. Cost exists in the contract terms by costs and risks that you either transfer or assume. For those that you transfer, cost exists in the degree and value of the remedies the supplier provides if they fail to perform or if the risk occurs.

Limitations of liability are cost limitations. They deal with the potential cost exposure for damages sustained, whether the costs are limited only to direct damages or may include other types of damages and the resulting costs such as consequential or special damages or other costs and they may include specific financial limitation on the amounts to be paid. Limitations of liability may limit a supplier's exposure, but many times the buyer's real financial losses can be far in excess of any limitation. Insurance and indemnity provisions deal with the issue of who will bear the risk and cost associated mostly with third party claims. If the supplier doesn't protect you, your company may wind up bearing the risk and the associated cost.

In negotiations the buyer's goal is to lower cost, lower risk, and make the supplier responsible. The supplier's goal is generally to avoid assuming costs or risks and make the buyer responsible as much as possible and still make the sale. Who wins this battle will be determined by the terms you negotiate.

John C. Tracy

CHAPTER 3 UNDERSTANDING COST IN CONTRACT TERMS

Let's take a look at some standard terms and link them back to cost.

Definition of the supplier. Who is defined as the supplier within the contract may impact enforcement costs and whether you would be able to recover damages under the contract. The supplier you contract with needs to have the assets and resources to stand behind the commitments. If they don't, their promises may be meaningless.

Pricing. In addition to establishing the price that will be paid initially, a pricing provision may also deal with the management of the future cost of your purchases by things like: how long it will be effective; how it will be established for future periods; any limitations changes to pricing, Etc.

Payments. Payment terms are really cost of money negotiations that decide how long you get the free use of the suppliers money and product before you need to pay for it.

Acceptance rights. Acceptance rights allow you to not pay for defective product and may allow you to charge the supplier for the return of the defective product back to them. Acceptance rights eliminate having to chase the supplier for a refund if they can't provide you with acceptable items and having the right to withhold payment is a cost of money issue.

Warranties. If a warranty is breached the buyer have certain remedies under law or equity. Those remedies may be limited by the limitation of liability but would normally allow the buyer to recover the direct damages (costs) they sustained from the breach.

Warranty redemption for warranty against defects in material and workmanship. In most situations this type of a warranty will do two things. First it should provide for a no cost repair or replacement of the defective item within the warranty period. If should also require the supplier to pay for the cost of shipping both ways so buyer avoids those additional costs. The buyer has already paid the cost to have the product delivered, they shouldn't have to pay again!

Epidemic Defects. An epidemic defects provision will normally provide for the recovery of costs that would ordinarily not be recoverable under warranty such as the cost to remove the defective item from the field, the cost to re-work any item on which it was assembled, or the costs to identify the problem. To be effective in recovering those costs, an epidemic defects provision needs to be carved out of the limitation on liability, otherwise only direct damages (those that are proximately caused by the defect) could be claimed and that would preclude recovery for things like rework or field costs.

Delivery. In delivery there are two things that need to be established, the specific delivery term and the delivery point. The delivery terms and delivery point establish whose responsibility it is for the cost of any transportation, insurance, duties, or fees from that point forward. For example if you purchased something ex-works the suppliers dock in Taipei, Taiwan by that term you would have assumed all costs and all risk of damage or loss from that point onward.

Remedies for failure to provide on-time delivery. Most on time delivery provisions will require the supplier to pay for any incremental shipping costs on late shipments. It may allow the buyer to cancel orders on products that are late without liability. More importantly it should provide the buyer with remedies they may have "at law or equity". As the late delivery term would be subject to the limitation of liability limiting buyer's recovery to only direct damages, it would allow the buyer to recover what called the cost of "cover" which is any excess costs of re-procurement from a third party. For example if the supplier didn't delivery and buyer needed to purchase it from a distributor the cost of cover would be the incremental difference between the price from the distributor versus the agreed purchase price. If delivery were critical a contract could also have a liquidated damages provision for late delivery where the parties agree in advance the amount that would be paid in the event of a late delivery.

General indemnification and intellectual property indemnification. In a liability claim or intellectual property infringement claim, the buyer could be liable for both having to pay for the legal costs of defending against the claim and any damages awarded. General indemnifications and intellectual property indemnifications transfer the cost of the defense to the supplier along with the cost of the damages if the suppler was at fault.

Limitation of liability. Limitations of liability do several basic things. First they limit the types of damages that can be claimed. Further they may include a limitation on the amount of damages that each of the parties will be liable for. Limitation of liability provisions are a double edge sword. The limitation of buyer's liability limits the types of damages a supplier may claim against the buyer and the amount of buyer's liability, so it limits buyer's potential cost exposure. The limitation of the supplier's liability limits the types of damages the buyer may claim against the supplier and the amounts the buyer may recover. As the obligations of the buyer and supplier are not equal, the limitations of liability should not be equal. In most purchase agreements the buyer's primary obligation is to pay for the goods and services delivered. Suppliers have a number of major obligations so the types of damage they could cause the amount could be substantially higher.

Termination rights and buyer's liability for termination costs. Termination rights provide the buyer with the ability to avoid having to make future purchases where the cost would be 100% of the cost of the product or service. Buyer's liability for termination costs will usually try limit those costs to what the supplier has already committed and which cannot be cancelled or rescheduled. A good termination provision will require the supplier to take actions to "mitigate" the buyer's costs reducing the potential exposure further.

Force majeure. For a buyer that suffers a force majeure, the force majeure clause prevents the buyer from having to receive and pay for something it cannot use because of the force majeure until such time as they have recovered from the force majeure. For a supplier, a force majeure will prevent the buyer from recovering costs or damages associated with the supplier's not delivering on time as the force majeure creates an excusable delay in their performance.

Supplier's responsibilities. In describing the supplier's responsibilities you would normally include the specific actions you want them to take and the deliverables. These fall into two categories, performance and tools needed to manage performance as the failure to perform may create a significant cost. As I say elsewhere, there are four basic ways to manage performance: relationship, structural, contractual and financial. In describing the supplier's responsibilities you may include structural tools such as milestone schedules, deliverables, escalation processes, etc. You may also include contractual responsibilities such as describing specific remedies for non-performance. The financial tool is the damages you would collect for their non-performance.

Quality terms. In every contract to manage the cost of quality there should be a number of quality management tools. For example, acceptance criteria allow you to reject and not pay for defective product. Control over modifications helps prevent the supplier from making changes that could increase your quality costs. Many times providing the same form, fit and function simply isn't good enough. Restrictions on assignment are to ensure that you are dealing with the same quality level supplier that you contracted with. They are there to ensure that from an enforceability standpoint the contract doesn't get assigned to someone that wouldn't have the assets or resources to stand behind the contract commitments. Restrictions on subcontracting are to ensure that you get the work performed by high quality suppliers and subcontractors. Product specifications define what the supplier must provide and the basis for acceptance or rejection and also are the basis for determining whether a product is defective under warranty.

Inventory. In every contract there will be things that drive inventory. For example if a supplier has the right to end of life a product, it could require the buyer to qualify an alternative one and if no alternative was acceptable it would force the buyer to invest in an end of life purchase to cover future needs. The length of the supplier's lead-time can drive you to carry more inventories for flexibility. Requirements such as minimum order quantities or vendor multiples may force you to purchase a greater quantity than you need. Restrictions on ordering flexibility such as limitations on increases, limitations on cancellations or limitations or restrictions on reschedules can all force you to purchase inventory that you don't want or need.

Warranty cost drivers. In every contract there will be warranty cost drivers such as the length of the warranty period and what starts the warranty terms will determine how long the protection is in place and will determine when the replacement or correction of the problem becomes the responsibility of the buyer. The shorter the warranty period, the sooner the supplier can sell you maintenance services, repairs of replacement products. Exclusions or limitations on what's covered in the warranty transfer risk and cost from the supplier to the buyer. Any terms within the warranty where the buyer is asked to assume any costs associated with the warranty or redemption adds to buyer's costs. If you already paid for a good one to be delivered, why should you have to pay again?

Contract language can add to your cost. There are a number of factors in every contract where the degree of the supplier's commitments will either add to or reduce your costs. The standard of commitment the supplier makes can add to or reduce your potential costs. Softening or qualifying language in commitments or rights will add to your cost. Every exclusion or limitation takes cost and risk away from the supplier and leaves it with the buyer.

Chapter 4 Understanding Procurement risks

4.1 Understanding procurement risks

In our daily life we all deal with and manage risks. We buy automobile insurance to protect against the risk of loss or damage to our vehicle and potential claims by others for damages to persons or property we cause. We buy homeowner's or renters insurance to protect against the risk of damage to our home and contents from theft or damage by named perils and for claims by third parties for injuries sustained at our house or apartment. If we hire a contractor to perform work on our house or apartment, we have the risks that:

- They don't perform,
- Their performance isn't acceptable,
- They damage your or third parties property,
- They injure another party,
- One of their workers becomes injured on your property, or
- The contractor doesn't pay a subcontractor who then can place a mechanics or materialman's lien placed on your property.

If we buy a house we may buy title insurance to protect against the risk of other claims on the property. When we buy a product or appliance we may check the warranties or buy an extended service plan to protect against the risk of it breaking and needing to pay for the repair or replacement of the product. When we purchase services we may want some form of service protection plan so if there is a problem, we're protected against the risk and cost of another service call.

There are a number of risks and when you represent either yourself or your company in a negotiation, you need to understand them and try to manage them through your contract terms. To do a good job negotiating the specific terms, you need to understand those risks. The scope or magnitude of a buyer's risk may vary substantially depending upon the commodity being purchased and how critical those purchases are to your company. For example, you will have one set of risks if you are buying a computer printer for internal use and you would have a much broader set of risks if you were buying that same printer to resell to customers under your own brand. There may be unique risks for a specific business or commodity. Most of the time the risks are the same and the difference between commodities is the magnitude, degree, or frequency of the risk.

In most procurement activities the following general types of risks are ones that you would try to manage through your contract terms:
- Performance risks with contract deliverables, quality, schedules, on-time delivery
- Risks from third party claims
- Risks of supplier claims
- Enforcement risks
- Defining and getting what you want

- Risks with change to the product, the relationship, your demand, the circumstances.
- Risks in pricing and payment
- Risks in long term support
- Risks in continuity of supply
- Legal risks associated with the product or service complying with laws
- Risks with defective products and warranty redemption, warranty support
- Risks with delivery performance and the need for flexibility
- Risks dealt with in the insurance coverage
- Risks with the import / export
- Risks with the supplier performance or interruptions to performance
- Risks in recovery should something go wrong

Within each of the above general categories there are a number of different risks that may be involved. For example, risks from third party claims may involve:
- Product liability, personal injury, property damage
- Auto liability (under potential claim of agency) for personal injury or property damage
- Premises liability (for guests and business invitees), for personal injury
- Financial claims to the product such as security interests in the product or liens against the product.
- Claims of infringement of intellectual property contained in product such as copyright, patent, mask works, trademark, misappropriation of a trade secret claims, and the cost to correct the problem.
- Claims from other suppliers for things like unfair trade practices, defamation, libel, slander
- Claims relating to supplier employees for personal injury (as guests or business invitees) and as workers under workers compensation, employers liability, claims for employment rights, and government claims for withholding taxes
- Claims by governmental agencies for complying with laws, regulations, ordinances and licensing or permit requirements.
- Claims that impact the potential ability to import product

Risks from supplier claims can be for:
- Breach of contract
- Breach of confidentiality obligations
- Damages to supplier's property on buyer's site
- Loss of anticipated profits
- Claims for delays, extra costs
- Claims for misappropriation of the supplier's trade secrets
- Claims associated with the supplier's actions under "agency" risks
- Claims involving buyer's requirements or instructions.

Risks with contracting Parties can involve:
- Enforcement or recovery issues associated with the contracting parties.
- Impact on recoveries or the ability to meet contracted obligations
- Risks in defining and getting what you want involve managing the rights of acceptance or rejection and the responsibility for costs associated with non-conforming product or services.

Quality Management Risks associated with changes include:
- Right of the buyer or supplier to make changes
- Effective date of changes
- Impact of supplier unauthorized changes
- Termination rights
- Order cancellation rights
- Ability to reschedule orders based on changes in demand

Risks with Pricing and Payment include managing
- Price firmness, and competitiveness
- Agreed currency
- Payment terms as it relates to acceptance or withholding payments
- Responsibility for taxes and duties

Risks with long-term support include managing
- Availability of spare parts, consumables, repairs, technical support to support products during their useful life
- Competitive pricing for spare parts, consumables, repairs,
- Access to technical support.

Continuity of Supply Risks includes managing:
- Product availability during the term of the contract
- Supplier product withdrawal - end-of-life issues
- Impact of the contract term
- Obligation to accept orders
- Responsibilities of the parties in the event of a force majeure

Standard warranties cover a number of legal and performance risks
- Legal right for supplier to enter into the contract (authority)
- Performance complies with laws (governmental claims)
- Avoidance of claims, liens, (third party claims)
- Products are free from defects in material, and workmanship
- Products are safe (third party claims)
- Products don't contain prohibited materials (third party claims / governmental claims)
- Products are new (third party / customer claims)
- Products don't infringe third party intellectual property right (third party claims)

Insurance provisions are included to help manage against certain risks and provide financial back up to the supplier's hold harmless or indemnity commitments.
- Comprehensive General Liability Insurance covers 3rd party claims for personal injury or property damage).
- Workers' Compensation Or Employer's Liability Insurance cover supplier employee claims for personal injury.
- Automobile Liability Insurance covers 3rd party auto related claims.

Terms within insurance provisions can also create risks.

- Buyer being a named party on the insurance is to protect against issues where the supplier has no insurance because they were fraudulent in their application.
- Waiver of subrogation rights against the buyer is to protect against the insurance company from coming after the buyer to recover the loss they paid out.
- Financial requirements for insurers such as an AM Best rating is to ensure that the insurance company has the assets standing behind the insurance.

To manage enforceability risks requires that the contract be written in a manner to ensure that all the terms are clear and enforceable. Problems with contract terms can negate the transfer of risk or costs and they can impact the ability to recover costs and damages for a breach or even being able to claim a breach.

Why should you be so concerned with managing risk in your contracts? Assuming a risk means you are also assuming a potential cost and assuming liability means you are assuming costs. Since risks represent significant potential costs if they materialize, a large portion of every negotiation is who is responsible for assuming the risk. Suppliers that have the most to lose are very cautious in terms of the risks they'll accept. Suppliers that have little to lose may quickly agree to accept all the risks to get the business. It reminds me of a Bob Dylan lyric "when you got nothing, you got nothing to lose". It should also be a signal that if it comes down to enforcement, the assets and resources to stand behind the commitments may not be there.

The difference between different types of procurement such as production versus administrative commodities is the probability or extent of the risk. For example, you can have some purchase activities such as the purchase of construction services that by their nature are significantly higher risk for things like personal injury or property damage, but would be low risk for other types of risks that you might have in buying products for production or other key support services.

If you are going to negotiate contract terms dealing with risk you need to begin to understand them so here's a summary of many of the most common, listed from A to Z that will identify what the risk is and explain why its important to manage,

Explaining Risks

Acceptance, Acceptance Criteria. Once the buyer has accepted a product, unless there was fraud or a misrepresentation, the buyer's sole recourse is the replacement of defective product or service is under the warranty. In many instances, especially with custom items, since supplier has no other customer for the item, the supplier will want to limit buyer's options under the warranty provisions to repair or replacement or correction of the problem. For critical, high value items the buyer should establish specific acceptance and test criteria that, if the purchase fails to meet those tests, that allows the buyer to reject it as non-conforming. This right eliminates buyer's obligation to pay until the supplier has provided the acceptable product or service. Acceptance also can impact warranty. If your warranty starts at shipment and you have no right to reject, all of the time to get correction under the warranty would reduce the effective period of your warranty as you warranty period is being consumed with the product is being repaired or replaced. The cost of failing to manage this risk is you may wind up with a product or service that's a problem and your sole recourse is under warranty. If that doesn't get you what you need, you may have wasted the purchase price only to have to chase the supplier for a refund.

Acceptance of Purchase Orders: Unless the supplier is obligated under a contract to accept buyer's purchase orders, even though the buyer may have executed a contract with supplier to make purchases, the supplier can decline to accept buyer's purchase orders. The buyer should insert a provision into the contract that obligates supplier to accept buyer's purchase orders that materially conform to the terms and conditions of the contract. The cost for failing to manage acceptance of orders is you could have an interruption in your supply and have costs such as lost revenue, and lost profit.

Amendments. Under contract law, a later writing between the parties will have priority. Amendments to a contract can create potential conflicts arising from differences between the requirements that were set forth in the contract and those set forth in the amendment. An improperly drafted amendment could change an entire contract even though the intent may have been to only change one section, or have it apply to one item.

Assignment. The decision to source and purchase a product or service from a supplier is based upon many factors, including specifications, manufacturing or service capabilities and controls, pricing, quality and reliability and technical support. If a supplier could "transfer" its contract obligations to a 3rd party without buyer's approval, the buyer wouldn't have the "benefit of its bargain" with supplier, and could face a number of potential risks including continuity of supply, quality, technical support, or having the party with sufficient assets and resources continue to be under contract with buyer, etc.

Authority of signing party to execute the contract. A supplier may refuse to honor a contract if the individual executing the contract didn't have the authority to commit to the contract. If a person did not have the authority to sign the contract, and there was no way to show that the person had the "apparent" authority to execute the contract because of their position, or there wasn't any on-going behavior that ratified similar acts in the past, the contract may not be enforceable. If the contract is a significant the buyer could require the supplier to produce a "Secretary's Certificate or "Incumbency Certificate" signed by the secretary of the corporation that specifically shows that the individual executing the contract does in fact have the authority. contracts usually contain language that the party signing the contract represents that they are an "authorized representative" of supplier. If a party without authority signed the agreement making that representation they could be personally liable.

Buyer instructions. The buyer may have technical resources that are extremely knowledgeable about the product, services design and/or process. If buyer's personnel make suggestions, provide specific requirements or instructions and those subsequently cause a problem, the supplier can argue that they no longer have responsibility as a result of the actions of buyer's personnel. For example, if buyer's instructions caused the supplier's product to infringe a patent of a third party, the supplier may take the position that it no longer has to indemnify the buyer for the infringement. Failing to manage buyer instructions can make the buyer 100% responsible for all problems associated with those instructions. If the product doesn't work, it may be buyer's problem. If the product infringes another party's IP, it may be the buyer's problem. A common way of protecting against this is to allow the buyer to make suggestions that the supplier is not required to implement, but if they do, they agree to accept them as their own and be fully responsible in the implementation.

Cancellation Rights. If you do not have the right to cancel open orders you could be forced to purchase the product or service even though you no longer need or want it. The contract should provide buyer with the right to have supplier stop all work in process. After imposing an obligation on supplier to mitigate its expenses and costs, the buyer normally will be obligated to pay the supplier for the reasonable value of the work in process and their costs of canceling any unique material or subcontracts. If you fail to manage cancellation rights your cost will be the full purchase price. If the supplier doesn't give you grounds to terminate for cause, you must let the work continue until its completion and pay for all of it, or you must breach the contract and pay for any damages incurred.

Changes. Once you have negotiated a contract, it's very important to understand who may change that and how it may be changed. A "changes" provision would require that the parties signing the amendment have the requisite authority to do so, to eliminate any claims or defenses that the party did not have the authority to bind the company make the commitment void. There would be a writing to document the change to the contract as proof of what had been agreed to,

Choice of Law and Forum. Choice of the applicable law defines what jurisdiction's law will be used by the courts to interpret the term and conditions of contract. Laws can vary greatly from state to state or country-to-country, so the buyer's goal is to select a an applicable of law that will be favorable to its interests. Jurisdiction is the general location where the case will be heard. The forum applies to the specific court location where the case will be tried. For example a buyer and supplier could agree to have the state of Delaware be the applicable law. The jurisdiction could be specified as the State of New York. The forum could be specified as the federal court in the Southern District of New York in Manhattan. The risk in selecting applicable law, is different location may be more of less favorable to business. The risk in selecting the jurisdiction is one of the parties may have significant influence in that locations or forum. The goal is to have the applicable law an jurisdiction and forum be one where you won't have a disadvantage. Include requirements in your contract. If these were not specified in a contract the suit could be make in any location that had a connection with the contract and the applicable law of that location would be used.

Conflict Between Documents. Contracts are frequently made up of multiple documents that are incorporate by reference into the contract or into other documents that are incorporated by reference into the contract. As contracts are modified over time, there may be changes to related documents referenced by the contract. When dealing with multiple documents and versions thereof, there will likely be inconsistencies between various terms that may impact the parties' rights under the contract. The only way to protect against this risk is to review the documents for consistency and accuracy. Further, the buyer should include an "order or precedence" provision that establishes the order in which various documents will be given priority in the event of a conflict.

Contracting Parties. Many companies operate through a number of different independent companies for tax, liability and marketing reasons, so it's important that the party buyer contracts with, and defines as the supplier, is the party that has the capabilities, resources and assets to make, fulfill and stand behind the obligations of the contract. If the buyer contracts with the wrong supplier (merely a sales subsidiary or division in its own name), the subsidiary or division may not have the ability to correct non-performance issues, or the subsidiary may not have the resources and assets (technical expertise, financial assets, or other types of assets) to perform the obligations of the contract, leaving buyer without recourse to recover its costs and any related damages. It's important to remember that parent companies can always avoid liability and expense by bankrupting or closing down their subsidiary, so if the risk may be large, always either contract with the parent directly or insist on a parent or company guarantee.

Currency. Any time buyer conducts business internationally with suppliers and their affiliates, there can be confusion and risk regarding what amounts are to be paid due to which currency applies and any changes in currency exchange rates can be significant. The buyer must define what currency is being used for establishing pricing and related financial obligations (tooling, non-recurring engineering charges "NRE", etc.) of the contract. For example, the term dollar is used in the United States, Canada, Hong Kong, Singapore, Taiwan, New Zealand and Australia, and the difference in value between these currencies is substantial. Specifically define in the contract what currency applies by either defining the currency or listing the currency adjacent to the affected item (e.g. US$, S$, NT$, C$). If the price is established based upon a currency exchange rate and may be adjusted based on changes to that rate you need to define what base exchange rate will be used for computation, and how, and when prices may be adjusted to account for exchange rate changes during the term of the contract. All currency risks are a direct price risk and the cost associated is changes to your price.

Damage claims There are many different types of damages, and the size and scope of damages a party may incur can be substantial   The greater the types of damages parties are allowed to claim under the contract, the greater the potential size of the claims.   Typical claims will cover damages related to lost revenues, profits, incidental, indirect, consequential, and special or punitive damages. The buyer should include a limitation of liability provision where the parties agree to exclude various types of damages so that the liability is limited, except for those specific provisions that are critical to buyer or where direct damages would not provide an adequate recovery.

Dates & date numbering conventions. Different countries use different date numbering conventions that could create confusion or cause problems with performance or enforceability. The United States numbering convention is month/date/year. Other countries have numbering conventions of day/month/year. So if the date were listed as 02/07/10, Americans would read the date as February 7, 2010, but to many Europeans, the date would read the 8th of July 2010. When writing dates, spell out the date as February 7, 2010 and do not use abbreviations such as 2/23/02 or 2.23.02.

Days. There is a significant difference in time depending on whether the parties classify days as work or calendar days. Workdays will vary company-to-company, location-to-location, and may or may not include weekends or holidays. There may also be confusion regarding whether work days means buyer's or supplier's work days. The default rule is to use calendar days. Decide which of the terms the parties want to use and be careful to document whose calendar (work days, holidays, etc.) shall control. Note that in some cultures, major holidays may vary (such as Chinese New Year) as well as the number of holidays celebrated yearly will vary widely. Make sure the defined term is consistent with the intent of the issue being addressed in a given clause (lead-time, cancellation notice period, etc.) so if you use workdays instead of calendar days you will want a shorter period of time. For example twenty-eight calendar days is 4 weeks. Twenty-eight workdays is 5 weeks and 3 days assuming a five-day week with no holidays.

Defects in design, material, and workmanship. Defects in design may cause the product to not work properly. Defects in material or workmanship may cause products to pre-maturely fail requiring the product to be replaced in the field and/or product reworked all at a very high cost. The heart of any warranty is that the product must be defective and if it is, the warranty redemption provisions apply so that supplier is responsible for some or all of the costs. If the problem is significant, such as an "epidemic defect" (where the cause of the defect has reached epidemic proportions), the contract should require that the supplier be responsible for all of buyer's costs, subject to any agreed to limitation of liability. The buyer should, as a part of the warranty clause, require an express warranty that "products are free from defects in design, material and workmanship" so that it would be interpreted as a statement of fact that is made about the product which forms a basis of the bargain agreed to between the parties. Since survival clauses make warranties survive the expiration or termination of the contract, this places an enforceable responsibility on the supplier to correct the problem, regardless when the non-conformance is discovered.

Deliverables. When buyer is responsible for providing specified deliverables as part of the contract (material, specifications, first article approvals, etc.), buyer may become liable to supplier for its costs incurred if buyer failed to provide the required deliverables on time. If supplier's performance is contingent upon buyer providing certain deliverables such as material, designs and/or approvals, the buyer should review those deliverables to ensure the specified dates can be achieved. If there is substantial risk in buyer being able to perform as specified, the buyer may want to establish a more conservative schedule. The buyer should avoid any commitment that it will be liable to supplier for supplier's costs should buyer fail to meet its deliverables. If the buyer is unable to negotiate this term, the buyer should add language to the contract that if buyer's performance is delinquent, the time for performance will be extended, and that supplier will use reasonable efforts to mitigate any costs associated with buyer's delay. The costs associated with failing to manage buyer or customer deliverables is claims from the supplier for additional costs associated with delays as a minimum and could include costs associated with their termination of the contract and your need to re-procure the work elsewhere double paying for the work.

Delivery term / location There are many different shipping terms that can be used by buyer and supplier all of which are subject to negotiations between the parties. The International Chamber of Commerce periodically publishes a set of these trade terms (Incoterms 2000) to help facilitate international trade. Delivery terms (e.g. FOB, EXW, DDP, etc.) determine who bears certain costs and risks related to the movement of the product from the supplier's delivery location to the buyer location. If the buyer buys product EXW (ex-works the supplier's location), the entire risk and cost of delivery is borne by buyer. In addition to determining the responsibility for costs and risk of loss, the delivery term will normally establish when the payment clock starts, and when the warranty begins which aren't a risk but can become a cost

Disruption of activities. Frequently contracts may provide a window for contract performance and what you wouldn't want is to have the supplier start the work, walk away from the work and then only come back at they very end of the term to finish it leaving you with an expanded period of disruption. You can manage this by either having a term within a term (where the supplier has a period during which the work has to be performed, but a much shorter term that requires that after they do certain acts they must be completed within X days so the interruption in minimal), or you can require continuous work once commenced and specify the minimum number of personnel that must be working at any time so the work flows promptly

Effective date of the contract. When determining the rights and responsibilities of the parties, the parties need to determine when the contract became effective and whether the event or claim occurred during the term of the contract. For problems that occur prior to the effective date of the contract, the contract will not apply. If the event or problem occurred after the date the contract expired or was terminated, the contract terms will apply only if the contract responsibility "survived" the expiration or termination of the contract as defined by the survival provision of the contract.

Effective date of changes. The effective date of a change will determine when the changed product is available and when any cost differences will apply. The effective date of any price changes will have a dramatic impact on buyer's costs depending on whether it is an increase or decrease. In the case of cost reduction changes, the benefit of the cost reduction will diminish as product is purchased in the interim. Hypothetically, a price change could become effective on July 1st, but only apply to orders received by supplier on or after July 1st. So, if buyer was purchasing a part with a sixteen (16) week lead-time, the earliest buyer could benefit from the new price would be November 1st.

End-of-life. Suppliers that sell commodity products to a number of customers may want to cease production of older versions of those products from time to time and replace them with new products which use new or different processes. Contract terms that allow a supplier to withdraw a product for purchase should require both an extended notice period before the product can be withdrawn (to allow buyer sufficient time to evaluate new or alternative products), and an end-of-life product buy option where the buyer can purchase product in sufficient quantities to have available for your production needs. You might also want sufficient time so you can switch to an alternative product, or until such time as you no longer will be producing your product that requires it.

Epidemic defects. Normally, warranty provisions only provide for the repair, replacement or credit for defective product. Unfortunately, at times these warranty provisions are inadequate to compensate buyer for extraordinary expenses incurred when an epidemic defect occurs. Normally, the supplier is not responsible for reimbursing buyer for the following expenses: buyer's costs for defect identification; Re-work of higher level assemblies to replace defective product, and; the cost of any field related service expenses required to remove defective product at end user sites. Most of these costs are considered consequential damages and therefore are usually excluded by the limitation of liability provision in the contract. Consequential damages can be enormous (i.e. 2001 Ford / Firestone defective tire case), so it is important that the buyer make every effort to persuade supplier to agree to accept liability for such expenses.

Errors and omissions. In procurement of some services the buyer may sustain substantial damages if the work product provided the buyer contains errors or omissions. For example, an error by an Architect could cause major structure damage or create a situation where a building wasn't usable. An error by an engineer on something like electrical or structural load could cause significant damage. If you purchase these types of services you need to have both terms that make the supplier responsible for the design error or omission and you should also have Error and Omissions (Professional Liability) Insurance to provide protection against such risks.

Force Majeure A force majeure event (war, natural disaster, labor strike, etc.), as defined by the parties, represents an excusable delay for the party that suffered the force majeure event. The risk that the buyer must address in the contract is liability for material previously ordered prior to the force majeure event, which could not be delivered when requested due to the force majeure event. supplier will likely want buyer to be obligated to purchase product from supplier after supplier has recovered from the force majeure event. The buyer's response should be based on the unique circumstances of the situation. Before agreeing to be liable for any unique costs un-recovered due to a force majeure event, the buyer must recognize that supplier's ability to recover from a force majeure event may take an extended period of time, forcing buyer to take alternative actions to protect its business interests. Also, most companies carry business interruption insurances that would cover supplier's losses sustained as a result of most force majeure events, so supplier may not need buyer's business to make them whole.

Financial resources to support contract obligations. Throughout the contract, the supplier is required to make certain commitments where, in the event a problem occurs, they will assume responsibility for correcting the problem. Unfortunately, those promises only provide value where there are financial resources to stand behind those commitments. If supplier's financial resources are limited, buyer may not be able to collect damages it is awarded by the court, or buyer may be forced to pay for any 3rd party claims that may exceed supplier's available resources. This risk is managed in several ways. contracts, when possible, should only be awarded to companies that have the resources to stand behind the obligations. When dealing with a supplier that has multiple subsidiaries, the contract should be executed in one of three (3) ways: 1) Signed with the supplier parent; 2) signed a subsidiary that has sufficient assets on its own; or 3) signed with the subsidiary but with a company / parent guarantee where the company / parent agrees to be responsible for the obligations of their subsidiary or affiliates.

Forecasts and responsibility / liability for forecasts: If buyer provides a supplier with forecasts of intended purchases, and then later failed to purchase the volume of products forecasted, the supplier could claim that they relied upon buyer's forecasts to make capital and inventory investments, and built product in support of such forecasts. supplier could make a claim or file suit claiming "expectancy" damages, meaning they want to be placed in the position they would otherwise have been in (earned profits) if buyer had purchased its forecasted requirements. Most contracts should contain a disclaimer that forecasts do not create any obligation on the part of buyer to purchase the amounts contained in the forecast, and that buyer's liability shall only commence with the issuance of a purchase order, and be subject to the reschedule and cancellation terms of the contract.

General indemnification (or hold harmless and indemnity) As third party claims for personal injury or property damage may be substantial and could be caused by the supplier's employees, products or services, the buyer will want to be protected from such claims. A typical indemnification provision requires three things. 1) The supplier must defend against the claim. 2) The supplier must indemnify the buyer against the claim (meaning pay all costs and damages awarded) 3) the supplier must agree to hold the buyer harmless or not responsible for the claim. Failing to manage this could have situations where the buyer will be liable for those 3rd party claims.

Incorporating by reference. The parties will often intend to incorporate documents (specifications, drawings, etc.) as part the contract. Unless the documents are properly incorporated by reference, they may not become part of the contract or there may be confusion as to which version of the document controls, and /or whether any changes to them apply. When multiple documents make up a contract, contract documents will be read together and considered complimentary. So if buyer's contract said A, B, and C were applicable, and the incorporated document said D, E, and F were applicable, the contract would be interpreted as meaning that A through F are applicable. Confusion as to which documents control, and what changes apply often result in disputes between the parties over what the specific contract requirements are and what product specifications control. As you will learn in the contracts section, the courts will only look at what's included within the four corners of the document to determine the intent of the parties so any document that's not properly incorporated in to the contract may not apply.

Incorporating by reference – supplier documents. When the buyer incorporates specific supplier managed documents by reference there is the additional risk that those documents will contain language or terms that either conflicts with or reduce supplier's commitments. Contract "Order of Precedence" provisions only apply when there is a direct conflict between the requirements and do not cover situations where the additional language could be read as complimentary. The other risk the buyer faces when incorporating supplier managed documents is the on-going need to monitor changes to such documents, and/or to freeze the contract specification by referencing the specific revision and date of the controlling document. When possible, avoid incorporating supplier documents. If the buyer must include supplier documents by reference, the buyer needs to conduct a thorough review of the documents to make sure that they don't contain any language that conflicts with or diminishes supplier's obligations under the contract. If the documents do contain conflicts or limiting terms, and the buyer still needs to use the documents, the buyer should specifically exclude those sections or language of the document that would conflict with or reduce the supplier's contract obligations. The contract should also have an order of precedence provision that always gives priority to the contract over any supplier documents.

Infringement. If a 3rd party claimed that a supplier's product used by buyer infringed upon their intellectual property right, and the 3rd party claim proved successful, the third party could seek a court injunction preventing buyer's use of the infringing product. buyer would be required to recall and replace the infringing product or refund the purchase price in accordance with the terms of its sales contract. The impact on buyer's customers and buyer's reputation would be substantial. This risk is managed through an intellectual property indemnification provision that requires the supplier to bear the responsibility and expense of defending such 3rd party claims.

Insurance

Insurance - Comprehensive General Liability Insurance. Comprehensive general liability insurance is designed to protect against the risks associated with 3rd party claims for personal injury (including death) and property damage that are based upon supplier's products or supplier's performance of their duties under the contract. If the supplier doesn't have insurance and doesn't have the assets to settle these claims, buyer could be responsible for paying these claims directly. Require the supplier to have comprehensive general liability insurance as part of the contract. If buyer is dealing with a supplier without the resources to indemnify buyer for these types of claims, require supplier to name buyer as an additional insured and be provided copies thereof, so that the buyer can verify that the insurance is in place. Require supplier to provide annual copies of certificates of insurance.

Insurance - Workers' Compensation or Employer's Liability Insurance. If an employee of a supplier is injured on your site, buyer could be sued for the injuries they sustained. While the supplier may have indemnified buyer for such claims, supplier should have insurance to stand behind that indemnification. Require the supplier to carry both workers compensation, and employer's liability insurance. Employers Liability Insurance provides coverage for an employer's common law liability for bodily injury to employees arising out of and in the course of their employment. It is intended to cover the gaps between Worker's Compensation and Comprehensive General Liability insurance. Workers Compensation Insurance is designed as the sole remedy for workers who suffer bodily injury in the course and scope of their duties.

Insurance - subrogation rights against buyer. Having an insurance policy from the supplier to protect buyer doesn't do any good if the supplier's insurance company could turn around and sue buyer for negligence and collect damages from buyer. If the buyer inserts a waiver of subrogation rights against buyer in the insurance portion of the contract, and includes a contract liability provision that specifically makes the rights subject to the terms of the contract, buyer will effectively block the Insurance Company's right to proceed against buyer under subrogation rights the Insurance Company would have in their policy with the supplier.

Insurance - Automobile Liability Insurance. This type of insurance is designed to protect against all 3rd party injury and property damage claims resulting from automobile accidents. Since auto policies are written extremely broad and cover almost all drivers, it provides the greatest amount of protection. Require automobile liability insurance provisions be included in the contract so that supplier's automobile liability insurance will provide the substance behind supplier's indemnification of buyer against third party claims.

Insurance - buyer as an additional insured. Suppliers could fraudulently contract for insurance where the insurance company could refuse to honor the policy to them. Inserting buyer as an additional insured on the policy will do several things. First, for any changes to the policy or policy cancellations, buyer as an additional insured will receive notice from the insurance company and be able to take appropriate action with supplier. Second, if there was an action such as fraud by the supplier in applying for the insurance, being a named insured on the policy will prevent the insurance company from using supplier's fraudulent acts to deny coverage to buyer. Lastly, as an additional insured, and similar to the waiver of subrogation provision, an insurance company cannot sue its own insured. For example, if a third party is injured on buyer's site, as part of the subrogation process, the insurance company could sue buyer to recover some of the damages based on buyer's negligence. By being named as an additional insured would prevent the insurance company from making a claim against the buyer unless it could prove that buyer committed fraud or misrepresentation in applying for coverage as an additional insured.

Insurance - definition of buyer's insurable interest. Situations may exist when buyer and supplier are jointly held liable for a third party claim. When this happens, there may be multiple insurances that could cover the loss. If supplier's insurance is not defined as primary, which would make supplier's insurance policy responsible for payment of the claim from the first dollar up to the limit of the insurance, then buyer's insurance could be responsible. Alternatively, the claim could be treated as contributory requiring both insurance policies to pay the claim in equal amounts up to the policy limits. Claims against buyer's insurance will impact the rates buyer will pay for future coverage, so the buyer should always have supplier's insurance be the primary insurance. Insert language into the insurance provision of the contract that establishes supplier's insurance as primary or non-contributory. This provision will make supplier's insurance the sole source for recovery up to the limits of the policy.

Insurance - requirements for insurers. Buyer looks to suppliers to carry insurance as a means of providing financial protection against insurable risks. The risk buyer faces is that the insurance company may not have the financial resources to support their commitments. Minimally, buyer needs to make sure that the insurance company has the financial resources to stand behind the insurances. This risk is managed by requiring the insurance company to maintain a certain financial rating according to an industry standard rating service called "Best's Reports" in which insurers' financial ratings and performance are rated similar to bond ratings (with an AAA rating being the best).

Key Personnel. If certain personnel from supplier's team are the reason why you selected them to perform the work, or any change to personnel could negatively impact the performance or quality of the work product you should be protected against the risk of the supplier performing a form of bait and switch where one team is promised to get the contract and another team is actually used to perform the work. You can manage this by specifying who is required to perform the work and including a requirement that any changes must have your approval. The real cost associated with key personnel is in several areas. If they do a "Bait and switch" the price you paid may not be consistent with the people assigned. Further the performance by a 2nd tier team can have a significant impact in the value of the product they delivery which can impact the ROI from that investment. For example, if you hire a specific consulting or advertising team and they disappear, will the work product have the same value?

Lead-time. buyer needs predictable lead times otherwise it will be unable to manage efficient production methods, maintain cost effective inventory levels, and ultimately adversely impact customer satisfaction. Changes to lead-times can have the same impact as a late delivery. If the supplier is unwilling to establish a standard lead-time, require that any changes from the current lead-time not impact open orders, and agree that the new lead-time will not become effective until after the mutually agreed to notice period has expired. The notice period should be a minimum of the increase in the lead-time plus a reasonable period for the buyer to respond to such lead-time changes so there is no disruption in the continuity of supply.

Liens, claims or action that would interfere with buyer's use or sale of products. Any time you purchase material, equipment or services that include material or equipment, the material or equipment may be subject to the ownership interests or claims of a third party. For example, parties may have security interests because they provided financing, or may have a right to make claims such as mechanic's or materialman's lien against the work that includes the materials. If there is a valid third party claim against the material involved, buyer could be prevented from using the material or be prevented from selling the material or product that contains the material. When purchasing materials for production, the buyer should require a positive representation in the warranty provision that no such liens exist which would impact supplier's ability to supply product, and so that compliance is held to the higher standard of a warranty. Since survival clauses make warranties survive the expiration or termination of the contract, this places an enforceable responsibility on the supplier to correct the problem, regardless when the non-conformance is discovered. For some types of procurement, such as building construction, where much of the work is performed by subcontractors, the buyer might implement a "waiver and release of lien" program where each time a payment is made, the supplier must provide waivers and releases of liens from subcontractors indicating they have been paid, and that they release any liens that they would have up to that payment. This is an affirmative warranty.

Limitation of liability. A limitation of liability will normally limits the types of damages that may be claimed to only direct damages except for certain 3rd party claims or claims for exceptional costs or damages such as epidemic defects. Buyer does want to include limitations to protect against supplier claims for things like lost revenue, lost profits. suppliers want limits of liability to protect against potential claims for incidental, consequential or special damages for a breach of their performance obligations. Without a limitation of liability provision, each party's potential liability is unlimited in terms of both the amounts and types of damages that may be claimed.

Long term support - parts, repairs, technical support. For all products that are sold to end customers, buyer may assume the responsibility to provide customers warranty support. Buyers may also want to sell to its customer's on-going maintenance and support for the products after the expiration of the product warranty or to supplement the product warranty. If an item fails after a supplier's warranty period has expired, it becomes the buyer's responsibility to purchase parts for repair or replacement of the defective product. If the buyer does not have the ability to purchase replacement parts, the buyer may have to spend the time, effort and expense of developing alternative sources. If the buyer doesn't control the cost of replacement parts, suppliers can charge premium or exorbitant prices when buyer has few, if any, alternative choices. This can make any commitment of availability useless. Contracts should include provisions that provide long-term access to repair services, replacement parts and technical support at competitive pricing. Minimally, the period of time should be no less than what supplier offers for similar / like products to its other customers. The buyer should also include provisions for end-of-life product purchases to cover situations where the supplier will phase-out the manufacture of the product but buyer has requirements extending beyond the final purchase period. No restrictions should be placed in the contract on buyer's ability to purchase what is needed to support its end of life support requirements.

Lot rejection. If you don't have the right to accept or reject lots, you are then forced to bear the expense of screening the product to determine which product conforms and which is defective. Include in the contract buyer's right to accept or reject product by lot, in whole or in part. If needed, the product can be individually screened.

Merger of prior agreements / understandings. Manages risks similar to an order of precedence where there may have been prior contracts, writings between the parties and excludes all of those so the only commitments are those included in the contract. For buyer's this means that any prior promises need to be included in the contract or they aren't enforceable.

Misappropriation of trade secrets. In some industries, buyer may be competing with supplier. If supplier provides information to buyer and buyer subsequently uses that information in the creation of its own product, the supplier could sue buyer for the wrongful taking of supplier's idea or misappropriation of supplier's trade secrets. When buyer and supplier work closely together on various programs, there is a significant risk that misappropriation of trade secrets may occur. This is sometimes referred to as cross-pollenization, when an idea from one source winds up being used in unrelated products. The ways you manage against this type of risk are 1) control the flow of information you receive to only that needed and requested. 2) Have residual knowledge rights included in any confidentiality contract so the information the individual retained in their mind may be used. 3) If that can't be done, you need to isolate and control the flow of information and people so any team members working on a competing set of technologies are not subject to contamination by receiving the trade secret information.

Mitigate Costs. While suppliers have a "common law" responsibility to mitigate damages, you also want them to mitigate possible damages they could claim in equity. Suppliers do not have the same responsibility to mitigate costs for what would be a voluntary cancellation of an order by buyer. Insert a duty on the supplier that, for certain situations such as cancellations of orders, supplier must use reasonable efforts to keep the costs of the order cancellation to a minimum by taking actions such as: ceasing product manufacturing immediately; returning raw material to its suppliers; attempting to sell finished product to its other customers; and /or re-working product for sale to other customers. As suppliers are in the business of selling their products to other customers, they can do that much more efficiently than buyer.

No defect found. suppliers may attempt to negotiate "no defect found charges" or ("NDFs"). When product is returned to a supplier under warranty and, after testing the product, supplier is unable to find a defect with the product; supplier may ask the buyer for compensation for such testing and returns. The easiest way to deflect supplier requests for NDF charges is to agree that buyer will pay supplier's costs for these quality problems related with buyer's return of good products if supplier agrees to pay all of buyer's costs it incurs every time supplier ships defective product. When the buyer is unable to deflect a supplier's request for compensation for NDF charges, the buyer should set a threshold that must be exceeded before any charges may apply, e.g. when the NDF rate exceeds __% of the previous month's volume. The threshold should be as high as possible since buyer will be at a disadvantage in verifying the accuracy of supplier's claims. Be certain to establish what the charge rate per unit will be when negotiating the contract; the charge should be based on specific and reasonable expenses.

Non-conforming product. Each time a supplier ships non-conforming product buyer incurs additional costs. Such cost may include additional inspection, sorting, and shipping and handling when returning non-conforming product. In addition to these costs, buyer may incur additional expenses (freight) for delivery of replacement product from the supplier. products are expected to meet specifications. Upon delivery, buyer becomes liable for inbound freight costs (assuming origin based terms), so buyer's costs associated with supplier's inability to deliver conforming product should be borne by supplier. The contract should include terms that hold supplier liable for reimbursing buyer for these expenses. Some companies may be less reputable and claim non-conformance as a means of managing inventory levels. To prevent abuse, suppliers will normally request the right to verify the defect as a way of managing this risk. While reasonable, a time limit should be set for defect verification to prevent supplier abuse. Further, many suppliers will request buyer to pay the freight costs for returning defective material. The buyer should not accept this liability. The buyer has already paid for delivery of conforming product, so additional costs related to return and replacement of defective product should be borne by supplier.

Notices. There are many reasons for a party to a contract to want to serve 'notice" to the other party. contract breach, termination, contract extension, change of address, etc. are examples why a party to a contract needs to provide notice to the other party. As an example, when wanting to terminate a contract for cause, the supplier would need to receive notice of the breach and have a period of time during to cure the breach. If the supplier fails to cure the breach, then the contract can be terminated. If the buyer fails to provide notice per the terms of the contract, buyer's right to terminate could be affected. If the parties list the names and addresses in the contract to whom communications or notices must be sent, and a party sends a notice or communication to the address listed using the means agreed to by the parties, then the obligation to provide notice is satisfied.

Numbers. It is easy to make an error in writing an amount in the contract. Whatever is listed in the contract is what the parties will be obligated to honor, even if it is in error. This occurs because most contracts have integration provisions where all prior contracts are "merged" into the new contract, becoming the sole source for interpreting the contract between the parties. When a number must be included in the contract, to avoid confusion, include both the numerical number and its written description. In the event of a conflict between the two (2) values, the written word will have priority. Example: The non-recurring charges shall be one thousand dollars (US$ 1,000.00). supplier shall provide the replacement part within five (5) calendar days. When it impractical to use both and you use only the numerical number, double check to ensure that the number used is correct.

Offset rights. Many times companies do business with each other as both buyer and Supplier and there may be occasions where a company you are buying from or selling to owes buyer and may not be paying the bill in a timely manner. To be able to collect on those debts, you may include the right of "Set-off". Set Off allows the netting of receivables against payables to reduce the amount of receivables. So if buyer were selling to your supplier and they were not paying buyer, the exercising the right of set off would be used to reduce any payments you would off the supplier or off set any payments which they own buyer. If the Right of Set-Off were mutual, it would allow the supplier to net their payables to your company against any receivables they have with you as the buyer. The primary advantage of the right of set-off is in credit management in managing receivables as it allows another way to collect receivables. The right of set-off, if given to the supplier can be a disadvantage to the buyer, as if the supplier were to use the right of set off on payables the buyer owes, as it takes away the leverage the buyer has to resolve certain issues by withholding payment.

On-time delivery. The impact of a supplier not delivering on time can be substantial. First, if there is any history of delivery problems, buyer will carry extra inventory what has a cost and risks associated with it. If the supplier is unable to deliver, the buyer may be forced to pay more for the product to purchase it elsewhere to meet their needs. Late deliveries can also problems like production line shut downs and the costs associated with those, and additional manufacturing costs to work around the shortage. They could also impact buyer's shipment of products to their customers (impacting sales and revenue) and could also make buyer subject to damages for their failure to ship to their customers on time as required by their contract. The impact of a supplier not delivering the required number of products because of quality problems has all the same risks and costs associated with that. The buyer should determine which of the following business terms apply:
- Supplier liability for incremental freight costs when delivery Is Late
- Liquidated damages to recover certain costs when delivery is late
- Right to cancel orders without liability when delivery is late
- Right to "over" – purchase product from an alternative source and charge supplier Any incremental costs
- The right to pursue other remedies under law or equity

Packing and Packaging. Except for Delivered Duty Paid (DDP). buyer assumes the risk and cost of any damage to products that occur during transit. Since the supplier doesn't bear these risks, they are not incented to use packaging and packing materials designed to reduce the risk of loss and damage. In fact, if a product is damaged in transit, may have to purchase a replacement product. Insert provisions in the contract that supplier must comply with buyer's packaging and packing specifications to reduce potential damage to products during transit.

Payment Terms. Unless otherwise agreed, accordance with the Uniform Commercial Code, payment is due at the time and place at which buyer is to receive the goods even though the place of shipment may be the place of delivery. So, if the buyer fails to establish a different contract payment term, the payment term becomes the equivalent of net zero. buyer should not be liable for payment for non-conforming material or invoices that do not conform to the terms and conditions of the contract or contain inaccurate information such as price or quantity errors. Insert the agreed upon payment term in the contract. The buyer should also insert a provision that states that buyer is not responsible for payment unless supplier's invoices are accurate, and conform to the terms and conditions of the contract.

Price protection. One of the primary advantages of having a contract is buyer's ability to fix the product price that buyer will pay. A supplier will have significant leverage over buyer if buyer has designed supplier's in to their product, but doesn't have control over the price and alternative sources aren't readily available. Once the supplier is designed in, the supplier may increase its price if they believe buyer has limited options to source its requirements with another supplier due to cost or technology impediments. Price protection is a continuity of supply issue / risk as without it, any time a supplier wants to stop selling a product all they would need to do is price it so the purchase is cost prohibitive.

Privity. The law of contracts requires that there be "privity" or a connection to the contract to allow you to enforce the contract. You get "privity" by either being the party that signed the contract or by having the parties to the contract specifically agree in the contract that you, as a third party, have enforceable rights. Someone that is not a party to the contract, but is given enforceable rights, is called a "third party beneficiary". Why is "privity" a risk that's important to manage? Supply chains have become increasingly more complex with multiple different parties performing tasks at many levels. Companies are becoming more international with buying and selling through subsidiaries and affiliates. Both of these situations can cause privity problems. If the buyer has a contract with a supplier, but wants to have a 3rd party make purchases against that contract, there is no privity of contract between the 3rd Party and the supplier that would allow the 3rd Party to enforce the contract. The result is the buyer could lose its rights under its terms and be dependent upon what, if any; terms the 3rd party negotiates with the supplier. When companies operate through subsidiaries or affiliates around the world, each is a different legal entity. A contract with one of those entities does not create privity of contract with any of the other subsidiaries or affiliates, nor does it create privity of contract with the parent company. If you write a contract with a subsidiary, the parent company and other subsidiaries or affiliates are not obligated to honor it. This presents significant enforcement risks, especially if the subsidiary doesn't have the assets or resources to stand behind the commitments or cannot make good on the promises.

Price competitiveness. Negotiations occur at a point in time and pricing is set based upon the market conditions and leverage that the buyer has when the pricing is negotiated. Once a product is designed in, leverage is lost unless there are multiple sources qualified for the same product where competition can be used as leverage to keep pricing over the term competitive. Where a part is single sourced the supplier knows that you don't have the competitive leverage and that you have to make an investment to either re-design your product for an alternative source or qualify an alternative source. This loss of leverage has an impact on your ability to get long term competitive pricing on the product as the market may change. Before you give up the competitive leverage you have with a supplier by locking them into a design, require them to agree to insert language into the contract where you can negotiate market competitive pricing based upon certain changes in the market, competitive benchmarking, or tying it to price changes you are seeing for comparable products in which you have competitive leverage.

Product compliance. Suppliers could ship you product that doesn't meet your specific needs and has no value to you. You need clear specifications that define the product or service requirements. If you are concerned about potential disputes between you and the supplier on whether a product or service does in fact meet the specified requirements, you should include specific test and acceptance criteria that you can use to verify compliance. If the product or service fails to meet those test and acceptance criteria, it would then be deemed a defective.

Product modifications. A buyer may invest substantial time and resources to qualify supplier's product. Any modification to supplier's product may negate buyer's qualification or force buyer to re-qualify the product. Some modifications may make supplier's product unusable in buyer's application, and could force buyer to have to re-design its product to use an alternative source or product. If modifications are made without buyer's approval and without sufficient time to evaluate the impact of the proposed change, buyer may be unable to ship its products because buyer doesn't have sufficient inventory of the old product and hasn't been unable to design-in, qualify and purchase substitute material. Contracts should contain provisions that prevent the supplier from making any modifications to the product or service without buyer's written approval. This provision will force the supplier to continue to supply the product or service until such time as buyer agrees, or supplier can withdraw the product or service from sale in accordance with the end of life terms of the contract.

Product non-infringement. If a product is found to be infringing the intellectual property right of a third party, a court may grant an injunction against the use of the infringing product. Such action would force buyer to either purchase a license to use these third party rights, or require the use of a substitute non-infringing product. Further, buyer could be required to remove the infringing product from the field, resulting in buyer having to refund some, if not all, of the product price paid by its customers. The contract should contain an "intellectual property indemnification" provision, which would not be limited by the "limitation of liability" provision of the contract. This provision would make supplier responsible for paying for any license needed by buyer to continue using supplier's product or, if this wasn't possible due to the unwillingness of the third party to grant such a license, to provide buyer with a non-infringing replacement product. If these two remedies were unavailable, then supplier would be required to refund the price paid for product. Including an intellectual property indemnification "that products don't infringe any intellectual property rights of a third party" in the warranty provision as a promissory warranty will provide buyer recourse against the supplier for any past and future claims after the contract has expired or been terminated.

Product Safety. If the buyer is a reseller of products and services, buyer is subject to liability lawsuits for any injuries and damages caused by buyer's products or Services to its customers and third parties. In product liability lawsuits, plaintiffs will normally sue all possible parties involved (buyer, the manufacturer, the supplier, etc.) with the goal of recovering damages from someone with "deep pockets". As a buyer, when there is a safety problem with a product, there are two risks. One is being a defendant in a suit for claims for personal injury, death, or property damage caused by the safety problem. The other risk is the cost associated with correcting the defect, and removing and replacing the affected product with product that is safe. The personal injury, death or property damage risk is dealt with in contracts by first having a general indemnification provision that makes the supplier responsible to buyer to cover any damages buyer incurs as a result of third party claims caused by suppliers' negligence or omissions. To add substance to that promise, the buyer should require "Comprehensive General Liability" insurance to provide additional financial coverage against that risk. The cost of correcting the safety problem may be partially borne under the warranty, or it could be covered under epidemic defects if a safety defect was classified as an epidemic defect allowing the buyer to recover more of those costs of correction.

Products are new. When paying for a new product, buyer wants to be assured that what it receives is "new". It the buyer were to include used or reconditioned parts, the buyer is prevented from calling its own product "new" which would adversely impact the price a customer would be willing to pay for buyer's product. buyer would also be obligated to provide notice to its customers that buyer's product contains used or reconditioned parts.

Purchases from resellers. A reseller is a different legal entity from a supplier. suppliers are not responsible for contracts made by resellers, and any promises made by resellers will only be enforceable against the reseller. If the reseller doesn't have the resources to correct a contract performance problem, or assets to stand behind its obligations contained in the contract, the contract becomes meaningless, and buyer will be responsible to deal with any problems and costs related to reseller's inability to meet its obligations to buyer. When possible, buyer should purchase directly from the OEM supplier (this also makes sense from a cost perspective as every layer in the supply chain adds cost).

Quality management The potential risks and costs caused by quality problems is tremendous. Quality problems can shut down manufacturing operations. They can cause missed customer shipments losing revenue, sales and potentially subject the buyer to customer damage claims for failure to meet delivery dates. This will drive increased levels of inventory, increase buyer's costs of inspection and re-inspection of replacement product and add the administrative cost of managing the returns. They can cause re-work or scrap. If the product were to make it to the field, poor quality also impacts customer satisfaction and may require expensive service calls and product replacements. Since buyer will assume many of the risks and costs associated with supplier quality problems, suppliers must be pre-qualified from a quality perspective to ensure that they have the processes, tools, training and systems in place to ensure they can produce a high quality product in volume. The buyer should be able to set specific quality control process requirements that supplier must satisfy. The purpose in being able to establish these quality control requirements is to ensure that the supplier has a controlled process designed to reduce and/or eliminate defects since the buyer is assuming much of the cost of any quality problems if all they are able to recover is repair or replacement. suppliers need to be incented to improve product quality. contracts should have terms that increase a supplier's cost exposure as an incentive to correct product quality problems. If the supplier feels no pain from the quality problems they create, they have little incentive to correct the problem.

Reschedules. Product demand requirements constantly change. If buyer doesn't have the ability under the terms of the contract to reschedule both the quantity and delivery schedule of product, buyer will constantly be dealing with inventory supply imbalances and related costs (product shortages and excess inventory.) These imbalances may have a compounding effect, causing other material to go unused, waiting for complete sets of material to be available for subsequent manufacturing. Since the buyer doesn't want to receive product it doesn't need, and especially product that the supplier may be able to use to fulfill other customer orders, contracts should always identify the amount of product that may be rescheduled without charge as well as the timeframe during which such changes can be made. The goal should be to keep inventory at the lowest manufacturing level where it is least expensive to hold. When possible, the buyer should avoid being held liable to eventually take delivery of rescheduled product. It is very difficult to track and reconcile order information over a period of time, so it is best to avoid any obligation to eventually take delivery of previously rescheduled product. For commodity products, a supplier's risk and cost is minimal since the product can be used to fulfill another customer's requirements. For custom product, a supplier's risks and costs are greater since the supplier doesn't have the ability to sell the custom product to other customers. Most suppliers will agree to hold inventory for a limited period of time but afterward, a supplier would expect buyer to either pay a carrying charge or treat the reschedule of the product as a cancellation, with the cancellation terms defining the party's obligations.

Right for supplier to enter into the contract. The formation of a contract must be by a party who is authorized to legally conduct business. In many locations, the requirement to be able to legally conduct business requires that the company be registered with the secretary of state in the individual state, or other appropriate governmental body. Language is usually inserted into the warranty section where the supplier is asked to warrant that they have the right to enter into the contract. If the contract doesn't include this warranty, buyer would still have the ability to make a claim against the supplier for "fraud in the inducement to contract". This would be an affirmative warranty.

Right of buyer to make changes to specifications. If the buyer is purchasing a custom product, there will be times when it needs to make changes to the product. If buyer doesn't have the right to make such changes, and does not have control over what the cost of the product should be after the changes are made, buyer might be left with the unenviable choice of accepting supplier's the new price or forced to develop and qualify an alternative source. If changes may be necessary during the term of the contract, include a provision that allows you to require the supplier to make changes to the design, and establish a formula or methodology for establishing the price of the changed product.

Severability of terms. If a contract included a term that was determined by the courts to be unenforceable, the entire contract could be voided (cancelled) and the responsibilities of the parties determined according to the Uniform Commercial Code. Include a severability provision in the contract where the parties agree in advance, that if one term is found to be unenforceable, the enforceability of the remaining terms is unaffected. Inserting this provision will limit the court's review to the constructive interpretation of this one unenforceable provision, without impacting the other provisions of the contract.

Shipping responsibilities and use of buyer's directed carriers. Except when the buyer uses Delivered Duty Paid (DDP) or FOB Destination delivery terms, buyer assumes the shipping costs, as well as the risk and cost of any damage to products that occur while they are in-transit. Not all carriers offer the same cost and quality of service. Buyer frequently negotiate terms and conditions with various carriers who assume responsibility for certain risks or costs in the event of loss or damage in transit. If buyer's supplier doesn't use buyer's designated carriers when shipping product, buyer will lose any benefits buyer negotiated in its carrier contracts, and face potential higher transportation costs, as well as potentially greater risks of damage or loss or reduced recoveries. Insert a provision into the contract that requires supplier to use buyer's specified carriers when buyer is responsible for transportation costs and risk of loss or damage to product.

Spare parts or repairs availability and pricing. The buyer may purchase many types of products that may require spare parts, or that can be repaired once the warranty has expired. If the buyer fails to include a contract provision that requires supplier to provide buyer access to such spare parts and/or repairs, the buyer may not be able to have the product serviced and/or repaired and be forced to replace it at greater expense. Also, if the buyer fails to establish pricing for spares and/or repair services, the supplier may make the cost of such spares and/or repairs prohibitive, effectively negating supplier's commitment to provide spares and/or repair services. When products use spare parts or may be repaired, the buyer should include a contract provision that obligates supplier to provide buyer with spare parts and/or repairs. The period during which supplier should be obligated to provide such parts and/or services should cover buyer's projected customer service requirements, typically no less than a term of five (5) years after the last purchase of product. Also, it is essential that pricing for spares and/or repair services be established during the contract's formation; otherwise buyer may lose its leverage. Such pricing can be set using supplier's current product / spares, services pricing. Also, there may be times when the parties agree to include a price adjustment process for future years, and base such adjustments using cost indices such as Producer Price Index ("PPI") or Consumer Price Index ("CPI").

Subcontractors. Just as buyer wouldn't want a supplier to be able assign its contract responsibilities to a third party without its approval, the supplier should also not have the right to make changes to subcontractors if doing so is material to the contract. product quality, reliability and supply performance could be adversely impacted. The buyer should insert a provision into the contract reserving a right of approval over any changes a supplier may wish to make to its subcontractors when buyer deems approval of such subcontractors, as material for supplier to meet is contract obligations. If supplier wants to use multiple subcontractors, the buyer should reserve the right to approve any new subcontractors.

Supplier changes. Many times contracts allow the supplier to make a number of changes without requiring the buyer's approval as long as the product meets specifications, and there are no changes to the "form, fit or function" of the product. If products are well defined in the specifications, the risk may be minimal. However, if the definition and specifications of the product are not well defined, the supplier may make changes to the product that, while not affecting the form, fit or function, may still deviate from what buyer was expecting to purchase. supplier's product may also be no longer compatible with buyer's application, or the change may impact the quality or reliability of the product. Before allowing blanket authorization of changes to be included in the contract, buyer should have the right to consider and reject the potential types of changes that could impact the cost to buyer (such as manufacturing location if you are buying with anything but delivered terms), the product performance, and/or the quality or reliability of the product. The buyer must ensure that if the contract gives the buyer control over those changes to supplier, it forces the supplier to assume any incremental costs incurred by buyer as a result of those changes. For example, if a buyer is purchasing under Ex-works terms, the movement of the production location from one country to another can increase their freight or duties cost. If the supplier wants to move production to another location, the price should be adjusted to offset any increased costs.

Supplier personnel acceptability. Supplier personnel that may work on buyer's site may be the cause of disruptions and/or claims by supplier or buyer's personnel (such as sexual harassment). Further, some supplier personnel could represent a safety or security risk. Insert language in the contract giving buyer the absolute right to have supplier employees removed from buyer's site and/or excluded from participating in supplier's performance of its contract obligations.

Supplier personnel liability for on-site actions. If supplier's employees or subcontractors are injured on buyer's premises, buyer could be held liable for any damages they sustain. These types of claims can be costly and could adversely impact buyer's insurance costs, so the buyer should shift liability to the supplier for payment of these types of claims under their own insurances. This risk would be managed through the use of a general indemnification provision that makes the supplier responsible for claims by their employees and subcontractors, and the specific insurance requirements for comprehensive general liability, automobile liability, and employer's liability / workmen's compensation insurances.

Supplier personnel claims. If buyer exerts substantial supervision and control over supplier personnel, supplier personnel could claim that they are really employees of buyer, and as such should be entitled to all the same rights and benefits as buyer's employees. The buyer must make it explicitly clear that buyer does not have responsibility for the supervision, control, compensation, withholdings, health and safety of supplier personnel. If buyer assumes responsibility for the health and safety of supplier personnel, buyer could be held liable to those personnel, and this fact could be used against buyer in any claim for indemnification from third party claims. The statement regarding compensation and withholding is to show that the arrangement is an independent relationship between buyer and supplier and in the event the supplier either failed to pay the employers or failed to properly withhold or pay taxes on those wages, buyer would not be held responsible for those actions. Insert an "Independent contractor" provision in the contract that re-affirms supplier's responsibility to manage all of these activities and, if there is a reason for specific direction to be provided to supplier personnel, that direction should occur through their management who can then provide the required direction to the supplier personnel.

Supplier unauthorized changes. Suppliers may make changes that have not been authorized by buyer, or there may be situations where the supplier has failed to provide buyer with the proper advance notice of the change. These changes may cause performance problems with the product itself, and/or adversely impact quality and reliability. If a supplier makes a change or modification to its product without buyer's written approval, it can cause a number of problems such as having to re-work or scrap its product to replace the changed product. Require the supplier to reimburse any costs associated with unauthorized changes.

Survival - enforceability of certain terms after contract expiration or termination. Once a contract has terminated or expired, most contract rights are extinguished, but certain contract obligations clearly need to continue after the expiration or termination. For example, the supplier will always want buyer's obligation to pay any monies owed supplier to continue. In turn, the buyer will also want terms such warranty, compliance with laws, general and intellectual property indemnity to continue so they may be enforced later enforced. Absent a term in the contract (survival of certain terms) neither party will have the ability to claim these rights. This risk is managed through inclusion of a "survival" provision in the contract where the parties review the contract and specifically identify all the clauses that they want to survive the expiration or termination of the contract. The objective is to protect rights that either party may want to enforce after expiration or termination of the contract. Alternatively, the parties could insert a more general survival provision where terms by their nature that should survive will survive the expiration or termination of the contract.

Taxes and duties. buyer negotiates price and makes sourcing decisions based upon certain assumptions. It is essential that the buyer define who is responsible for any taxes and duties that are due before buyer takes title to product, otherwise its sourcing and pricing decisions may be flawed. Most contracts hold supplier responsible for payment of all duties and taxes that may apply prior to the transfer of title. Further, buyer may be required to provide proof that taxes have been paid before buyer can move or export products. If buyer takes title to product from the supplier without recourse against supplier for these costs, buyer could be forced to make these payments to allow the product to be exported. Insert a provision in the contract that makes supplier responsible for payment of all taxes and duties prior to transfer of title. This provision will give buyer recourse against supplier if buyer is required to make such payments.

Term of contract. There are three (3) issues to be concerned with when considering the term. First - recovery of investment. The term must be long enough so that you are able to recover the value of any investments that you may have made to develop or qualify the product. Second - leverage. You never want a contract to expire when you need it the most, such as during the last month of a quarter. The contract term should also be long enough so that you have the time to negotiate renewals, and be able to implement alternative plans if you are unable to come to a new contract. Third - administrative burden. The term of the contract should consider the practical needs of the organization in having to re-negotiate and amend contracts. For any product that requires a substantial investment by the buyer, you should require a minimum term of availability of at least two (2) years or longer depending upon the investment or, as a minimum, have the ability to purchase that product for two (2) years, even if the rest of the contract was to expire. Second, you should have the term be long enough to allow negotiation of new terms or pricing far enough in advance of the expiration of the term so you have real options; so that you won't be locked into a situation where your alternative is to either purchase significant inventory to cover transition to a new supplier or be left with having to deal on the supplier's terms. If there is no obvious benefit in having a shorter term, enter into contracts that self-renew. Terms dealing with pricing, delivery, etc. can always be negotiated separately from the term of the contract (prices may be negotiated monthly, but the terms and conditions under which they are purchased in the "contract" may have a term for as long a five (5) or ten (10) years.

Termination Rights. Giving suppliers termination rights in a contract can impact buyer's continuity of supply. Depending upon the type of contract the buyer has with the supplier, the buyer may need termination rights for both cause (supplier did something that puts them in breach of their obligations in the contract (fails to deliver)) and without cause (the buyer decides to discontinue the contract but all parties have met their obligations under the contract). If buyer terminates without cause, buyer may lose certain rights such as: out of warranty repair services; technical support; end of life purchase rights; etc.) And, depending upon what is included in the contract, buyer may also be obligated to purchase of certain materials or be obligated to compensate the supplier for certain costs. suppliers' right to terminate should be limited to a "material breach" by buyer that buyer fails to cure. The normal "material breach" for the buyer would be the failure to pay the supplier. buyer's right to terminate for "material breaches" should include all performance related issues. For contracts that do not have firm purchase requirements, buyer may effectively terminate a contract without cause by simply not ordering. In turn, if the contract doesn't obligate supplier to accept buyer's conforming purchase orders under the terms of the contract, a supplier would also able to effectively terminate a contract simply by refusing to accept buyer's purchase orders. To eliminate supplier's ability to terminate a contract this way, insert a term in the contract obligating supplier to accept purchase orders that conform to the terms and conditions of the contract.

Third party claims. There are many different types of third party claims. Claims can be filed for negligent or intentional acts or omissions of supplier or supplier personnel, or breach by supplier of any term of the contract. Third parties may bring lawsuits against buyer for damages they sustain from a buyer product that was in fact caused by supplier's product. These claims may be for personal injury, death, or property damage. Third parties can also bring lawsuits against buyer based on the actions or omissions (failure to take necessary precautions on a work site) of the supplier or supplier's personnel, that occurred at buyer's work site, for damages related to automobile accidents, personal injuries, assaults, negligence, etc. While buyer may not have caused the injury, under law the supplier may be viewed as an agent of buyer. Under the laws of agency, a principal (buyer in this case) can be held liable for the acts or omissions of their agents (supplier in this case). This legal theory makes buyer liable for the actions of supplier and supplier's personnel. This risk is managed by a combination of using a general indemnification provision (where the supplier agrees to indemnify buyer against these types of 3rd party claims) and inclusion of specific contract requirements for insurances supplier must carry so that the proceeds from the insurance plus supplier's assets would cover the potential amount of any 3rd party recovery against buyer. Specific requirements on insurances are discussed elsewhere. This risk is also needs to be managed in the limitation of liability provision where indemnifications are excluded from the limitation of liability. This is so the supplier will have unlimited liability for those areas such as General Indemnification or Intellectual Property Indemnification. Even with requiring insurance and placing unlimited liability on the part of the supplier, buyer may still be exposed if the amount of the claim exceeds both the amount of the insurance and any assets the supplier may have. This is another reason for ensuring that the supplier's company you are contracting with has the necessary assets.

Waiver of rights. Under law, if a party fails to enforce certain rights available to it under the terms of the contract, they may be subsequently prevented from enforcing those rights for future similar / like situations. The law assumes that, by a party's action, they have "waived" or "given up" those rights. There may be many instances when a party may breach the terms of the contract, such as late delivery of product or late payment, but the other party does not terminate the contract. Practically speaking, a party wouldn't want its inaction to constitute a waiver of rights it might want to exercise in the future. This risk is managed by inserting a waiver provision in the contract where the parties agree that the failure to exercise any rights under the contract does not constitute a waiver of rights.

Warranty Exclusions. Suppliers use warranty exclusions to reduce their potential warranty costs and liability. If the buyer agrees to include warranty exclusions in the contract, these exclusions will prevent buyer from be unable to recover under the warranty provision that will then cost buyer to correct the problem on its own. Any proposed warranty exclusions should be carefully reviewed to ensure that they are reasonable and do not have a significant adverse impact on buyer's warranty coverage. Most supplier warranty exclusions are written in very broad terms, so when including exclusions in the contract, the buyer should carefully define exactly what is being excluded to avoid future debate and possible litigation. The buyer should also be extremely careful when incorporating supplier documents into the contract by reference, since many supplier product descriptions will contain exclusions to the their warranty. If you include that language by reference, you may be amending your own warranty terms to include those exclusions. In some contracts, The buyer may be asked to make certain representations and warranties to supplier. Normally we would want to make no representations, and provide the information or material on an "as is" basis, making it the supplier's responsibility to ensure that they will be able to provide their warranties on the impacted material. In situations where buyer cannot avoid providing a warranty to the supplier (such as buyer selling them the material), the warranty should be a pass through of what buyer receives from its supplier.

4.2 Modifying Templates to Manage Risk

Most companies have a library of standard contract templates for procurement people to use. **Standard templates are designed to deal with average risk purchases from average risk suppliers.** While the best protection is to deal with reputable, financially sound, experienced suppliers, you may simply not have that luxury every time.

When you deal with higher risk purchases or higher risk suppliers, those templates may not provide the degree of protection needed. Most templates are also structured based on the supplier accepting all of the terms and risks. This means that if one term gets negotiated or changed where the supplier is unwilling to accept certain costs or risks, those changes may require changing other terms or adding additional or different terms so the buyer can manage the cost or risk they accepted. A simple recipe for disaster is to have known or potential risks where the supplier isn't responsible and the buyer doesn't have the necessary tools and controls to manage against the cost or risks.

Here's a description of a number of different types of clauses that might be added to help manage against risks that may exist with the supplier, or the item being purchased. Below that are examples of changes you may want to make based on risks that you could assume in the negotiation:

Financial risk of supplier.

There are a number of things you could include in a contract to manage against potential financial risk or the supplier:

- You could require Performance Bonds in the event they fail to complete the work where the amount of the Bond goes toward your cost of completing the work
- You could require payment Bonds to prevent against subcontractor liens on the work.
- You could require the waiver and release of liens as a condition of payment to ensure the supplier is paying their subcontractors.
- If they are a Subsidiary of a larger company you could require a parent or company guarantee.
- As they may be susceptible to being acquired, you might want change of control terms so you can control who you may be forced to deal with in the future.

- If you will be consigning or loaning the supplier items, you would need protection of your ownership rights in that material and you may want offset rights so you could deduct anything that they owe you from your payments to them.
- You could require information be held in escrow and be released to you in the event of certain events or triggers such as a change in their credit ratings.
- You could require licenses in the event of certain triggers, such as licenses to make or have the item made, or license to any software along with the right to make any necessary changes or improvements.
- If you have an assignment provision you want to make sure that it prohibits things such as assignment of receivables.
- You also might want different termination without cause rights that trigger if certain conditions exist with reduced or no liability,

Control over charges
If your standard template doesn't already have them you would want:
- Audit or Examination of Books and Records rights to verify costs charged.
- A formal Change Management Process that includes pricing formulas for changes, additions, and deletion of work.
- Purchase options - Rights to purchase additional quantities, options.

"Bait and switch" risks.
To avoid problems with suppliers that have the tendency to promise one thing and provide another you would want:
- Rights to approve subcontractors. material suppliers and any changes to them.
- Approval of personnel assigned and any changes to personnel.

Performance risks
In managing performance there are tools you may want:
- Inventory stocking and Alternative Logistics Model requirements if certain problems occur:
- Escalation Procedures so their management is aware of the problem
- Licenses and Manufacturing rights if there are significant performance problems.
- Downtime management tools - Acceptable levels of downtime. Downtime credits.
- Disaster recovery requirements
- Rights to inspect Facilities
- Termination rights.
- Service Level contracts – Periods, Response times, Service level credits
- Performance / Risk Management Tools - additional controls, reviews, approvals, and any other requirements you need to manage them.
- Alternative Payment Terms to help provide incentive to perform such as progress or milestone payments, rights to retain payments, rights to withhold Payment if work is behind schedule.
- Warranty of a Specific purpose.
- Additional types of damages that may be claimed, such as liquidated damages

Loss or theft risks could require:
- Background Investigations
- Fidelity bonds.

- Employee Dishonesty and Computer Fraud Insurance

Concerns over character or actions that could negatively impact the buyer's image could require:
- Restrictions for any on-premise operations.
- Control over supplier, supplier personnel or supplier subcontractors performing other work or activities at buyer's site.

Competitive risk concerns may be managed by:
- Restrictions on work that would be a "conflict of interest"
- Key employee restrictions
- Ownership / exclusivity rights in developed materials
- Limitations on sales to others for a specified period.
- Prohibitions against recruiting / hiring of employees

Continuity of supply risks could require :
- Guaranteed availability of products, service
- End of life requirements
- Requirements for multiple production locations.
- Requirements for dual source

During the negotiation any change to what the supplier is willing to accept from a performance, cost or risk perspective needs to be evaluated before you agree. Ask yourself the following questions:
1. What is the potential impact of the change?
2. Does it impact other sections that relate to it?
3. What's the potential performance impact?
4. What's the potential cost impact or risk?
5. Do you have the tools to manage the cost or risk either the contract or internally?

Here are a few examples.

The supplier wants to sell the item Ex-works their dock. As that makes you responsible for any loss or damage in transit, do you have the tools in place to do that?
    a. Do you have the right to specify how the item will be packed and packaged?
    b. Do you have the right to select the carrier?

The supplier wants to have limited liability for defective items. Do you have control over things that can impact the quality such as:
    i. Who makes it,
    ii. Where it is made,
    iii. How it is made, and
    iv. What changes can they make to the product?

The supplier wants the buyer to mitigate the costs of recall. Do you have anything in your contract that says that they will pay you all reasonable costs associated with mitigating the cost?

The supplier wants to be free to change their product without your approval. Does your contract require them to provide you notice and a sample to determine whether the changed product will work in your application?

Suppliers want to be free to do whatever they want. When they propose changes to terms where they want the buyer to assume some or all of the risk, the buyer needs control over what they can do as a way of managing the risk. My position has always been it needs to be one or the other, but never both. If they want the buyer to assume the risk, the buyer must have control. If they are willing to assume the risk, the less control you need. As a concession the supplier may want to propose that changes won't affect the form, fit or function. "Form, fit or function" is only a minor limit on the types of changes that can be made. For example "form fit and function" would allow the supplier to make changes in the materials used and significantly cheapen the product. It would allow changes to the process used that could impact the quality of the product. If the required reliability weren't spelled out in the Specification, "form fit or function" would allow the supplier to make changes that impact the reliability of the product and that impacts your life cycle cost. If the item you are purchasing needs to work with another item, form, fit or function doesn't protect you against the item not working in your application unless the specific application is spelled out in the specification.

CHAPTER 5 UNDERSTANDING CONTRACTS

This chapter consists of several subsections to help build your understanding of contracts, contract law, how the contract should be drafted, and what to look out for in negotiating contract terms.

5.1 Basic elements of a contract

Most of you may already know that the requirements to create a contract are you need to show that there has been a meeting of the minds / mutual assent to a bargain between the parties to the form the contract. This occurs by an "offer" for which there is "acceptance" and in which there is promised "consideration". For some types of contracts, and in different countries for a contract to be formed it must also meet the certain legal requirements such as the Statute of Frauds that requires that some specific types of contracts must be in writing to be enforceable.

Offer and acceptance. The simplest form of a contract is a purchase order that is accepted by the suppler. A purchase order represents an offer by the buyer to the supplier to make a purchase in accordance with its terms. On its own, the supplier is not obligated to accept the offer, nor would they be liable for failing to perform under an offer it has not accepted. The buyer may withdraw that offer at any time prior to acceptance by the supplier. Acceptance needs to be communicated. The supplier may accept buyer's offer by executing the acknowledgement of the order or by performing. If the supplier does that, a contract is created based on the terms on the face, reverse, and any terms incorporated by reference in the P.O. or incorporated as an attachment to the purchase order. If the supplier made a pen and ink change or sent their own order acknowledgement with different terms back to the buyer, either of those actions would make that a counter-offer and not an acceptance. That counter offer must then be accepted or rejected by the buyer. If the buyer hasn't accepted it and delivery is made and accepted what's called the "battle of the forms" occurs. The battle of the forms refers to the resulting legal dispute of these circumstances, wherein both parties recognize that an enforceable contract exists, however they are disagree as to whose terms govern that contract as neither party accepted the offer of the other party as made.

Consideration. Consideration is defined as a bargained for exchange which can be to either your benefit or detriment. For example agreeing not to do something in return for the other party's promise to do something would be consideration. Consideration may also exist in situations where there is what's called "promissory estoppel". Promissory estoppel may occur where a party relied on the promise of the other party to their detriment, in which case the party making the promise would be prevented or "estopped" from withdrawing their offer. In most contracts the buyer promises to pay for the goods or services that the supplier provides and the supplier makes a number of promises with respect to those goods or services completing the element of consideration.

5.2 Statute of Frauds

The "Statute of Frauds" is a legal principle that started in English common law and has been made part of statutory law in a number of jurisdictions. It requires writing between the parties in certain situations such as the sale of goods over US$500, the sales of real estate, and any contract that can't be completed within a year. For much of what you would do in procurement, a writing is required. That can take the form of an actual writing, or it could take another form **that was agreed by the** parties such as you may do with electronic data interchange (EDI) agreements that authorize electronic transmissions to serve as writing between the parties.

5.3 Description of Types of contracts
There are a number of different ways contracts are described

1. **Express contracts** are stated in words – written or oral.
2. **Implied contracts** may be either implied in fact where the contract is formed by conduct of the parties, or Implied by law where one party has provided a benefit to another where there would be unjust enrichment to not compensate the party that provided the benefit.
3. **Unilateral contract** is a promise by one party and an act by the other. I promise to pay you $35 to mow my lawn and you mow it.
4. **Bilateral contract** is an exchange of promises
5. **Valid contract** meets legal requirements and may be enforced by either party.
6. **Unenforceable contract** does not meet legal requirements and cannot be enforced.
7. **Void contract** meets all the legal requirements but cannot be enforced by either party. contracts made under duress or to do something illegal are void and would not be enforced by the courts.
8. **Voidable contract**s are binding on only one of the parties. Most voidable contracts result from having the lack of authority to sign the contract. In negotiating contracts with suppliers its always important that the party signing the contract have the authority or the supplier could argue that its is voidable because they lacked of authority to bind the company.

In contract negotiations what you are negotiating is usually an express contract that is bilateral in nature that you want to be valid so you may enforce your contract in the event of a dispute between the parties, such as the failure of the other party to perform.

5.4 Laws Covering contracts
Contract issues such as disputes and breaches between the parties may be addressed under several different legal principles:
- **Common law** which is established based on previous case precedent, or
- **Statutory law** such as the uniform commercial code.
- **Equity.** Equity principles are based on the concept of fairness. In equity the court may order actions like injunctive relief, specific performance or contract modification to prevent unjust enrichment of one of the parties.

For example if a contract says that "buyer shall have all remedies available under the contract, at law or in equity" it means that the buyer wants all rights that can be found in the contract, in case or statutory law, plus any rights that may be available under equity principles.

In a contracts there may be contractual conditions that that are required for there be a contract. For example a **condition precedent** is an act that must occur before the contract will become binding on the parties. A **condition subsequent** may discharge an existing contractual duty if that condition occurs. For example assume you were a Chicago Cubs fan and wanted to hire a caterer for a party if the Cubs made the 2015 World Series so if your contract with the caterer said that I will hire you as my caterer for game seven of the World Series, if the Cubs make the World Series in 2015. The language "if the Cubs make the World Series" is a condition precedent. If the Cubs don't make it into the World Series there is no agreement, as that condition has not been met. The language "for Game Seven of the World Series is a condition subsequent where there would need to be a seventh game in the world series involving the Cubs for the subsequent condition to be met. If there is no seventh game the condition subsequent was not met and that would discharge the obligation of the parties under the contract.

5.5 Understanding Breach

A breach is the non-performance of a contract or a provision in the contract. There are two types of breaches, minor and material.
- A minor breach is usually cause for the collection of nominal damages.
- A material breach is a failure to perform that goes to the very heart of the contract.

Material breaches give rise to damages and under most contract termination provisions a material breach gives the non-breaching party the right to terminate the contract for cause if the breach is not cured within the allowable time to cure the breach. For example if your contract had language that said that the time for performance of the contract is of the essence of the contract, what you are saying is that the failure to meet the time for performance would be a material breach.

5.6 Remedies

In contract law typical remedies that may be available to the parties are:

Expectation damages (benefit of the bargain)
Reliance damages (recovery of costs reasonably incurred in reasonable reliance of a contract that was breached).
Restitution (recovery of the value provided by the non-breaching party)
Stipulated or Liquidated damages – This is fixed sum or formula to be paid in the event of a material breach. For example it could include an amount per day for each day a project is late.
Interest
Special or Punitive damages (Damages that are designed to punish the party. For example, willful Intellectual Property infringement in the US is subject to treble damages that would be considered to be punitive damages.
Contract agreed remedies, (If the supplier is late in making delivery, and the delivery term requires them to ship it by express freight with the supplier paying the incremental cost that is an example of a contract agreed remedy.
Specific enforcement/ specific performance (Ordering the party to perform)
Cover (Being able to charge the reasonable cost of excess re-procurement)
Incidental and consequential damages (recovery of costs that are not the direct result of the breach, but would be incidental to or a consequence of the breach.
For all remedies the non-breaching party has the responsibility to mitigate damages with reasonable effort and without undue risk.

In the contract you may also include specific remedies in many of the clauses that would be in addition to the remedies you have retained. For example, if a supplier fails to deliver a product on time, your contract could provide the right to cancel the order without charge for products or services not yet delivered; it could require supplier to deliver products using priority freight with any difference in cost at supplier's expense. If there were on-going performance problems you may have remedies that require the supplier to take additional actions to mitigate the potential impact to you. These can be used to improve performance, reduce your costs associated their performance problems or provide additional remedies for the breach. For example, a source code licenses or manufacturing rights license may be additional remedies you need if the supplier breached the contract and you needed to continue to get use and support the product or software. Most contracts will also provide catch all language where if there is a breach in addition to any contract remedies that you may have spelled out, you would have the ability to exercise all other remedies provided at law, or equity. Most of those remedies would allow you to collect certain damages you incurred. Equitable remedies go beyond just collecting damages.

5.7 Damages
As one of the main remedies for breach of a contract is damages, you should understand the different types of damages that could possible be claimed:
Direct damages are caused immediately and directly from the breach of the contract. An example of a direct damage would be the cost of "cover" which is the excess cost of re-procuring the item from another supplier.
Incidental damages are damages that are paid to reimburse the cost of mitigating the damages sustained.
Consequential damages are damages that may include lost profits and other indirect injuries caused by the breach of the contract provided the such damages were foreseeable and can be determined with certainty
Special damages are damages that are peculiar to the situation or circumstance
Liquidated damages are damages that are specified in the contract and agreed to by the parties that will be upheld if they are reasonable.

The damages you may claim may be limited in the contract either in a specific section of the contract or by a **limitation of liability** provision. The limitation of liability provision is a key term as it can limit both the types of damages that you may claim or the amount of damages you may claim. For example if you had the following limitation of liability provision: "In no event will either party be liable to the other for any lost revenues, lost profits, incidental, indirect, consequential, and special or punitive damages." By agreeing to that, you would be limited to recover only direct damages that occur as a result of the breach. For some breaches direct damages may not adequately cover the types of damages you may sustain. So the key in negotiating any limitation of liability is to understand the nature of the damages that you would sustain in the event there was a breach of that specific provision. For example, direct damages for a defective part is the cost of "cover" which is what it would cost you to re-procure a replacement. That may be acceptable if you had a limited number of failures, but what if the number of failures reached epidemic proportions? If you wanted to claim costs of having to pull the product that contains the defect from the field or the cost to re-work the product to replace the defective item, those costs would be considered to be incidental or consequential in nature, not direct. Even if you listed those types of costs in a clause on defects, if you didn't specifically exclude them from the limitation of liability section, the limitation of liability provision could limit your recover of costs to only direct damages.

Another example of this is third party claims that would be covered under a general indemnification or intellectual property indemnification. If you sustained these costs they are not a direct damages so to fully recover any costs you sustain as a result of those, you would want to exclude those sections from the limitation of liability. For example, to do that you would add the following to the above limitation: "This mutual limitation of liability does not limit the obligations and liability of supplier provided in the section entitled "Indemnification". This would exclude the section from that limitation, which means that if you sustained damages from the breach of either of that section, you would be able to claim all types of damages. Here's an example of why this is important. Under certain statutes, a party that has been wronged may sue for punitive damages. In the U.S. if there was a willful infringement of another party's intellectual property rights, the wronged party may sue for treble (3X) damages that would be considered as special damages. If you didn't exclude the IP indemnification from the limitation of liability you might have to pay the plaintiff the treble damages but only be able to collect 1 X damages from the supplier. Another alternative to carving indemnifications out of the limitation of liability would be to classify all damages awarded, and attorney's fees as direct damages so that all damages awarded including special damages would be paid. For any changes to a standard limitation of liability provision you should always work with your lawyer.

With the exception of "liquidated damages", there is a requirement of certainty with respect to damages. Damages are not what you anticipate, damages are what you actually sustain, so you would need to be able to prove those damages. Liquidated damages are pre-agreed by the parties, so there is not a requirement of certainty, liquidated damages only are required to be reasonable. The most common type of liquidated damages involve the failure to delivery a product or service on time where the buyer will sustain extra costs or damages as a result and in that case liquidated damages could be a rate per a unit of measurement (such as per hour, per day, per week) for each unit of measurement that the supplier is late. In some countries the law may allow for a party to collect a penalty. In those locations all that is usually required is that the penalty amount be pre-agree.

5.8 Equitable remedies

Equity principles are based on the concept of fairness. If you reserve equitable remedies in your contract, the non-breaching party could seek the equitable remedies of **injunctive relief**, **specific performance** or **contract modification** to prevent unjust enrichment of the other parties or if money damages were inadequate to the harm that could be sustained. Injunctive relief is a court ordering the party to not do something. For example, if a supplier breached a Non-Disclosure agreement, the collection of damages may be inadequate so the non-breaching party may seek an injunction preventing further breach, disclosure, or use of the information. In Specific Performance a court could order the breaching party to perform and meet their obligations. A common example of specific performance could be you have a purchase and sale agreement to purchase a new house and the builder or owner refuses to sell the house. If a court ordered specific performance they would be obligated to sell the house or be in contempt of court until they do.

5.9 Rules of contract construction
In the event of a dispute between the parties that needs to be resolved in court, the courts would interpret the meaning and intent of the contract according to the rules of contract construction. If you are going to draft or negotiate contracts you should be aware of the rules of contract construction.

Interpretation of a contract is to determine the intent of the parties. Court's determine what the parties intended by what they said in the contract. There are two major rules that negotiators should be aware of: The determination of intent is made from the "four corners" of the document by construing all provisions together and in harmony with each other. All terms will have equal priority unless the parties establish a separate priority such as in the order of precedence. This means that all promises, representations made by the supplier that are important to the purchase of the product or service should be made part of the contract. If you don't want a document to have equal priority you need to address that in the order of precedence provision of your contract. Where a contract is unambiguous, intent is determined from the contract alone. A court will not supply additional terms. It applies the contract as written. To a negotiator this means it's important to make sure that your contracts contain all the needed terms!

A court will only consider parol evidence (evidence that is outside the 4 corners of the contract) to explain uncertain or ambiguous terms. When there is ambiguity, the intent may also be determined by evidence of things such as the relationship, the subject matter of the contract, facts and circumstances surrounding execution of the contract.
When parties sign a contract or amendment that includes language that expresses that the terms represent the "complete agreement between the parties" ,which is a fairly common term in contracts and which is referred to as a merger clause, all prior conversations and writings are merged into the contract and evidence cannot be given for the purpose of changing the contract or showing an intention or understanding that is different unless a court determines it is ambiguous. For example if your standard contract has a merger clause such as this:

"Prior Communications. This contract replaces any prior oral or written agreements or other communication between the parties with respect to the subject matter of this contract."

All prior writing and conversations would be deemed to have been merged into the contract and you would not be able to present parol evidence to the contrary. This is probably the fifth time I'm saying this but the key is if the supplier made a key representation, proposal etc., that you are relying upon for agreeing, you need to make sure it, or the commitments included in it make it into the four corners of contract!

Another thing to understand in drafting contracts is that any ambiguity in a contract will be construed against the party that drafted the ambiguous language. If the contract was based upon the buyer's standard form, and it is ambiguous, it will be construed against the buyer. If a contract was heavily negotiated you might consider a clause such as:

> **"Joint Efforts:** The contract has been drafted jointly by the parties and the principle that a contract is to be construed against the party who drafted it shall not apply to this contract."

To put the contract Construction rules into the perspective of negotiating a contract here are several recommendations you should follow:

1. To make sure that the parties attach the same meaning to an item, contracts create defined terms and each time that term is used that has that special meaning. The defined term is capitalized to show that it is a defined term.
2. If you have a "merger clause" it means that if you are relying on any prior communications or commitments between the parties, you need to make them part of the contract, or incorporated them by reference into the contract, otherwise the "merger" language will preclude them from being introduced.
3. To deal with issues where a term may be found by the courts to be unenforceable, most contracts will also contain a severability provision which says that if the unenforceability of the one term doesn't materially affect the party's rights under the contract, the contract without that term will remain in effect.
4. Another key term in interpreting a contract is making sure that there is a clear understanding between the parties on exactly which terms will survive the termination or expiration of the contract. That is done using what is called a "survival" provision. If you need the supplier to honor duties after the termination or expiration of the contract those specific sections that need to survive need to be included in the Survival provision. A common example of this is warranty duties, indemnities, etc.
5. Another issue in interpretation of a contract can be the specific actions of the party during the contract. For example if you have a specific term within your contract that you continually do not enforce, in interpreting the contract a court could determine that by your actions you have "waived" your rights to enforce it. To prevent that, most contracts will normally include a "waiver" provision that requires that any waivers must be in writing and that the failure to enforce the term in one instance (a waiver) will not be deemed to be a waiver of future instances.
6. As contracts frequently consist of a number of documents that are either attached to or are incorporated by reference into the contract, every good contract will have an "order of precedence" provision that establishes the priorities in the event of a conflict between the documents. In situations where the parties have agreed to an order of precedence, that will be used to interpret the parties obligations. If there is no order of precedence, or if multiple documents that make up the contract have the same precedence, they will be interpreted to be complimentary. So if one document called for A to M and another called for N to Z, it would be interpreted to require A to Z. Even when there is an order of precedence, the order of precedence only establishes the priority between conflicting provisions. So if you have A to M required in a document that has priority and you have N to Z required by a document of lesser priority, you could still have A to Z required. If something in Section C (which has priority) were in conflict with something in Section P (which has a lower priority), the contract would be interpreted such that the conflicting language in P would not apply. It is important to establish the right order of precedence not just between contract documents like a contract and a statement of work, but also between things like the specifications that are made part of the contract. For example, you may want a Statement of Work to have precedence over the terms of a master contract, but do

you also want all the documents that are incorporated into that statement of work to also have priority over the contract?

In dealing with documents that are executed at different times, unless there is an order of precedence established between those documents, the latest writing in time will always have priority. For example an amendment could potentially change both the contract it is amending and it could change a prior amendment if it is written at a later date. In writing amendments it's important that they be drafted in a way where the scope of the change is clear and it identifies whether it applies to only a limited scope or the entire contract. Remember, as the drafter of the document any ambiguity will be held against you.

Negotiators should read every document that will be made part of their contract to ensure that there are no terms included in any of those documents that could conflict with or change the obligations of the parties. This is especially important when dealing with documents that are provided by the supplier including their specifications or proposals. Either remove the problematic language or if it merely would conflict with the contract, establish a precedence for those documents that places their priority below the buyer's documents.

5.10 Understanding the Sources of Liability

The potential liability a supplier may have can be broken down into a number of areas:
- **Contractual** - what the supplier is obligated to do under the terms of the contract.
- **Negligence** – Liability that is created by the failure of the supplier or supplier's employees or agents to act reasonably, which injures the buyer's property, buyer's employees or the property of person of third parties
- **Reliance** - buyer's reliance on the supplier's expertise to provide conforming goods or to satisfy a duty owed to buyer. Reliance is usually in the form of the fact that the product is of "merchantable quality", or is "fit for a particular purpose". (Note: In many instances suppliers will try to exclude any claim of reliance in the warranty section where warranty of fitness for specific purpose, or merchantability is disclaimed).
- **Warranty** - The assurance by one party to the other of the existence of a fact upon which other party may rely without having to verify the fact, e.g. that the parts sold to buyer will meet stated specifications. If parts fail to meet specification, supplier is liable for buyer's damages related to supplier's failure to comply with the part specifications.
- **Misrepresentation** - The amount and degree of representations made and whether they represent solutions that will work in practice.
- **Strict Liability** – this is a liability where the nature of the act itself would represent negligence such as the design of an inherently dangerous product.

Since the negotiation of cost and risk is a primary part of most contract negotiations, negotiators need to first understand how each of the parties attempt to manage their risk and potential liability.

5.11 Legal defenses that make a contract voidable

The following are legal defenses that could make a contract voidable if they were to exist:
- Mistake (such as a mistake in their Bid upon which the contract is based).
- Misrepresentation by the other party.
- Fraud in the inducement by the other party.
- Illegality of purpose, or subsequently illegality of purpose where a new law makes certain performance illegal.
- Lack of capacity such as the contract being signed by a minor, someone with mental problems, under the influence or not having the **authority** to make the commitment on behalf of the party.
- Failure to comply with requirements of the statute of frauds, (see below).
- Unconscionable (contains terms that would not be enforceable as a matter of public policy).

To make sure that your contract isn't voidable you should make sure that there were no mistakes in the supplier's bidding. That can be done by having them verify correctness of their bid or quote and by making sure that the party signing the contract for the supplier is authorized to sign the contract on behalf of the supplier.

5.12 Authority

There are two types of authority express or implied. **Express authority** means that the corporation has granted the party the authority. **Implied authority** may exist by the position of the signer or by previous dealings. If an officer of the company is signing the contract they will have implied authority to bind the company. If a non-officer is signing the contract, one way to show authority is by including the words "duly authorized" as part of the signature block. To make sure a party is authorized you may also ask for what is called a "Secretary's Certificate" where the Secretary of the corporation provides a certificate that an individual is authorized or provides a copy of a resolution from the Board of Directors granting their authority. If you have a contract that isn't voidable, the only thing left to making sure that you have an enforceable contract is making sure that performance isn't excused.

5.13 Excuse of Performance

If a contract isn't void or voidable, once it is signed and takes effect, the parties must discharge their duties to perform. This requires either performance, or they must be excused from performance by certain conditions such as:
- Subsequently illegality such as a change in the law that makes the performance illegal,
- Impossibility, where the work cannot be done.
- Impracticability, where it is not capable of being done
- Frustration, such as one party failing to meet their obligations can frustrate the other party allowing them not to perform

- Rescission, where the parties have agreed to stop it.
- Novation, where the parties agree that another party will complete the work and the original party is excused from performance, and
- Lapse; such as where the contract term may have lapsed without the work being completed.

An **assignment** of a contract does not excuse the assigning party from their obligation to perform. The assigning party will remain secondarily liable for performance unless there is also a "**novation**" where the other party to the contract excuses the assigning party from performance and agrees to only look to the new party for performance under the contract.

Having a **force majeure** event is also not an excuse to performing the contract. A force majeure, will excuse performance during the term of the force majeure event. For example if a supplier claimed a force majeure event because of a fire at a factory where they were unable to ship products as a result, the supplier would be excused from the obligation to ship products, but the buyer would not be excused from its responsibility to pay for prior shipments. Once the supplier recovers, they would be obligated to perform and the buyer would be obligated to perform unless the force majeure provision included certain restrictions. For example, you could negotiate language into a force majeure clause where buyer may have the option of terminating the contract, and be released from purchase obligations or have the ability to cancel open orders without liability in the event of a Force Majeure where the supplier is unable to recover within a specified period of time.

5.14 Privity of contract

The Privity doctrine means that for a person or entity to have a legal right to contract benefits, they must be a party to the contract. An exception to this is when a contract is assigned to another party or a party is made what's called a "third party beneficiary" to the contract. For example, if the buyer negotiates a contract with a supplier and then wants a third party to be able to purchase at buyer's terms, on its own the third party has no right to do so as they do not have Privity of contract with the supplier. If the third party purchases the products under their own contract, the buyer does not have privity of contract on those purchases and could not enforce the terms it has with the supplier directly with the supplier on those purchases as the buyer does not have Privity of contract on those purchases. With outsourcing you may need to have third parties make purchases on your behalf and to deal with this there are several approaches. One approach is to have the supplier agree to extend the buyer's terms to the third party and agree that the buyer will be a "third party beneficiary" to those purchases so the buyer has privity of contract with the supplier and can enforce its terms on those third party purchases. If was obligated to extend the terms to the third party and the supplier failed to extend those terms, they may have breached the contract with the buyer and could be subject to damages. If they have extended them, then the buyer has the right to enforce them as they have privity of contract as a third party beneficiary to those purchases. Another approach has the supplier agree that the buyer may enforce the terms and conditions of its contract directly with the supplier on those third party purchases, making the buyer a form of third party beneficiary to those purchases. If a third party will be involved in the transactions where they will be buying the product or service, you need to have one of these approaches so that you retain "privity of contract" with the supplier and can enforce your terms or you need to have a contract with the third party where they are fully responsible for the supplier.

5.15 Why the buyer's need protection against the supplier's actions.

A buyer / supplier relationship can be interpreted under the law as a form of agency. Under the law of Agency, the principal may be held liable for the acts of their agent. If the buyer / supplier relationship is viewed by the courts as a form of agency, the buyer would be the principal in the relationship and the supplier would be the agent, making the buyer potentially liable for the supplier's acts. As a result most contracts will include a general indemnification or hold harmless and indemnification provision that require the supplier to "defend, indemnify, and hold the buyer harmless against any third party claims for personal injury or property damage caused by the supplier to a third party. To ensure that there is substance behind the supplier's promise most contracts also include requirements for insurance that would be used to protect against the financial losses of such claims. If the buyer is purchasing the supplier's product with the intent to resell that as part of the buyer's product, that puts the buyer into the liability chain where the buyer could be sued for product liability injuries incurred from the product. The same indemnifications and insurance requirements are intended to protect against these potential claims. If the supplier sold a product or service to the buyer and that product or service infringed upon the intellectual property rights of third party, the buyer could be sued for damages resulting from the infringement and the third party could seek an injunction preventing further use of the product by the buyer. To protect against these types of claims, contracts will generally include an intellectual property indemnification. Such an indemnification requires the supplier to "defend, indemnify and hold harmless" the buyer from such claims. The intellectual property indemnification will also include certain additional remedies that the supplier must provide such as get a license to use the IP, or redesign their product or service so that it non-infringing, etc.

CHAPTER 6 LIMITS OF LIABILITY

Limits of liability are so important in negotiation that I felt an entire chapter was warranted. The key is limits on liability aren't found only in a limitation of liability section. Limits on liability come in many different forms and can be found throughout a contract. There can be:

- Limits on the type of damages that may be recovered. "Neither party shall be liable for incidental, consequential, special damages, lost revenue or lost profits".
- Limits on the amount of damages that may be recovered. This can be dollar cap, multiple of sales or percent of business.
- Limits on various types of claims For example exclusion of warranties for merchantability or fitness for a particular purpose is a form of avoiding liability for those.
- Limits on total liability for the contract term. "Suppliers total liability for all causes during the term of this contract shall not exceed $ _____
- Limits on liability for a defined period such as annual limits. "Supplier shall not be liable for any more than $_____ per calendar year
- Limits on liability per occurrence. "Supplier's liability shall not exceed $___ per occurrence".
- Limits on the types of costs that may be recovered. "Supplier shall reimburse buyer's reasonable out of pocket costs. That type of limitation would preclude any internal buyer expenses.
- Limits on other remedies. "This shall be suppliers sole liability and buyers sole and exclusive remedy.
- Limits on individual costs. "Supplier shall not be liable for more than x times the Price for any cost or re-procurement".
- Limits on periods when claims may be made. "Any legal or other action related to a breach of this contract must be commenced no later than two (2) years from the date on which the cause of action arose"
- Limits on individual charges. "Supplier shall reimburse buyer for its reasonable costs incurred". This places a reasonableness standard on the costs that may be claimed.
- Liquidated damages. Liquidated damage provisions are a form of limitation of liability for the specific provision that allow collection of the liquidated damage.
- Thresholds that must be met before it triggers the right to claim a remedy is a form of limitation. "If one percent of the products are defective then ...." That would have the buyer be assuming most if not all of the cost until that threshold is met.
- The standard of commitment used limits what the supplier is responsible for. For example "Supplier shall use reasonable commercial efforts" can mean that if its costs any more to do it, it doesn't need to be done. Best efforts can mean a requirement to use all resources available to complete it.
- Refusing to accept certain terms and responsibilities also helps limit the supplier's exposure should they not be able to meet those commitments.

In the negotiation of anything that will limit liability, there are many things to take into consideration. The most important consideration is who has the greatest ability to manage against the risk and cost. Assuming risks or costs that you can't control or manage is not a great idea. The more flexibility a supplier wants that can create or impact risk, the more you need them to be responsible. If neither party can manage the risk, asking the supplier to assume all the risk will only burden your cost with contingencies they need to protect against the risk, so it may be wiser to share some of the risk. For limits on the type of damages that may be recovered you need to think about the types of damages that could reasonably be sustained, and whether the limitation will provide an adequate remedy for the losses you will sustain. If the nature of your losses would be incidental or consequential costs, you may want to exclude certain sections from the limitation of liability. For limits on the amount of damages that may be recovered you need to think about both the type and amount of loss you can sustain and what the financial impact would be to the supplier. Few suppliers will agree to limits that would be equivalent to betting their business on the one contract and those that would you probably don't want to deal with. Think of the lyric from a Bob Dylan song "When you got nothing, you got nothing to lose."

In reviewing a request to exclude warranties for merchantability or fitness for a particular purpose you need to think about whether you intend to sell the product as is (in which case you would want the merchantability warranty) and if you are clearly relying upon the supplier's expertise to sell you a product that meets a specific need they are aware of, you would want the warranty of fitness for the particular purpose.

In negotiating limits on total liability for the contract term you need to be concerned about the length of the term of the contract and take into account that all claims that occur during that period will reduce the amount available for future claims. It would be better to have annual limits that reset each year otherwise it forces you to write contracts with shorter terms.

In negotiating limits on liability for a defined period such as annual limits you need to think about both the type and amount of losses you can sustain and what the financial impact would be to the supplier and compare that against your ability to manage the risk or cost.

Insurance policies are frequently written on a per occurrence basis. Other uses for per occurrence limits are when a supplier does not want to have individual claim costs be open ended. For example they may have a total dollar cap, but also want to limit individual claim amounts. The key in negotiating you need to consider how closely the cap amount would be to the normal damages you would sustain.

In negotiating limits on the types of costs that may be recovered such as "reasonable out of pocket costs" you need to consider what the nature or your costs will be. If your costs would be mostly internal labor you wouldn't want to accept out of pocket costs limits as out of pocket would provide no recovery for internal costs.

In considering whether to agree to a sole and exclusive remedy you need to determine if the sole remedy proposed is adequate.

For limits on individual costs you need to determine whether that individual cost is adequate for the damages you sustain.

For limits on periods when claims may be made you need to consider what the likelihood is that all claims will be made within the period. Remember that third party claims are only going to be limited by the applicable statute of limitations for that type of claim. If you agree to a shorter period than the statute, the supplier may be excused from liability leaving you solely responsible to pay the claim.

For limits on individual charges such as reasonable costs you need to be concerned about the fact that each party may have a different standard of what is reasonable and you may need to provide examples of what is reasonable. I once had a supplier that wanted to make it clear that paying premium freight for a late delivery did not include chartering an aircraft to have it delivered and wanted to include the example that doing so was not reasonable. Obviously they had a problem in the past!

For thresholds that must be met before it triggers the right to claim a remedy you need to consider how the threshold is measured. For example if the measurement was 1% defects in a thirty-day period, if you change either part of that formula it will impact the measure. For example moving it from 1% and 30 days to 1% and ninety days would triple the number of problems that could occur before the trigger is me. Always do a numerical example to calculate the impact or any difference.

Standards of commitment that would limit what the supplier is responsible need to be reviewed to determine if the standard provides the appropriate action and investment of supplier resources to perform or correct the problem.

When suppliers refuse to accept certain terms and responsibilities, that limits the supplier's liability but it may not limit the buyer's exposure. What you need to consider when this occurs is whether you have the adequate control over what the supplier can do that increase your risk and whether you have the ability to manage against the risk. My opinion is that if a supplier wants to have the freedom to operate however they want, they need to accept the responsibility. If they won't accept the responsibility you need to limit and have control over what they can do as part of managing the risk or you need a different supplier.

In the end "it is what it is". The damage the buyer will sustain won't be any different. The only difference is with any form of limitation of liability it transfers the risk and cost to the buyer at some point. With financial limits after the financial limit has been exceeded all costs above that become buyer's costs. With other limits such as a limit on the types of damages that may be claimed, it transfers all costs for those types of damages to the buyer.

CHAPTER 7 STRUCTURING CONTRACTS TO DRIVE BEHAVIOR AND PERFORMANCE

7.1 Driving Behavior

Most buyer standard contract templates contain a number of potential terms that can create cost or liability for the supplier. There are several ways you can look at those terms. One is that they are there to provide the buyer with the ability to recover costs and damages they may sustain by supplier's failing to perform. Another way to look at it is those terms are there for the purpose of driving the right behavior on the part of the supplier.

To correct problems usually involves the supplier having to make an investment. As an investment, the decision to invest to correct problems will be weighed against all the other investments that a supplier needs or wants to make to increase sales and profitability or reduce costs. If the supplier has no pain from the problems they cause you, there would never be a return on investment to correct the problems. So the terms need to be there to provide the incentive for the supplier to make any needed investments to correct the problems they are causing you or that are costing you. The vast majority of buyers don't want to be collecting damages or pursue remedies, what they want is performance and contracts need to be structured to drive that performance. The simple fact is that if you want a certain behavior, you need to structure both the relationship and the contract in a way that helps drive the behavior you want. This may sound like motherhood and apple pie, but it's a mistake I've seen made time after time.

Let's start with the issue of cost. In hiring an Architect to design a building, the standard practice of their industry is to charge a fee that is based as a percentage of the cost of construction. While this seems simple enough, what type of behavior does it drive? First, it creates a major negative incentive for the Architect to reduce the cost of construction, because when they reduce the cost of construction, they also reduce their fee. It also creates a major challenge to owners in managing the Architect's design, as that design will impact your cost. Architects may argue that they will always do what is best for their client, but I've seen a large number of buildings that have been over designed, over specified, and loaded with high cost materials, where it's apparent that tying their fee to end cost of the work created the wrong behavior. The same scenario probably exists in almost every other type of purchased service where the supplier's compensation is based a percentage of the spending.

These problems aren't unique to services. In hiring a contract manufacturer to produce a product, frequently the cost formula for their compensation has their overhead and profit calculated as a percentage of the direct materials cost or direct cost of the product. If the contract manufacturer helps reduce the cost of the product, they will earn less of a contribution to overhead and profit. This creates a negative incentive for them to reduce cost. In addition, if they can reduce the price of what they buy and not pass that on to the buyer, they have an even greater incentive that's against the buyer's interests. In those situations instead of getting compensated less because the direct cost is less, they keep their overhead and profit up and all of the savings they generate they keep and the buyer gets nothing. If the contribution to overhead and profit is 10%, for every dollar they report of savings they will lose $.10 contribution. If they don't report it, for every dollar in savings they achieve, they keep the $.10 they would have lost, and they also keep the dollar they saved. This type of structure drives a behavior that creates a need to continually manage and monitor the supplier costs if you want to reduce cost under this type of structure and that monitoring adds to your cost.

If a supplier is paid a percentage mark-up on changes that involve subcontracted work, what is their incentive to negotiate reductions in the cost of that sub-contracted work, as all it will do is reduce the amount of the payment they receive. In situations where you look to the supplier to manage certain subcontractor negotiations, how aggressive will they be if they wind up getting compensated less if they are successful? Not many.

I was once asked to evaluate an outsourcing relationship where our external customer was unhappy with the level of savings being generated through a procurement group on the outsourced service we were performing for them. The savings generated was less than prior year and their management thought it was a procurement problem. What I found was that the customer's contract compensated our company a flat percentage of the spending. When our procurement team was successful in significantly reducing their cost initially, the resulting effect was to reduce our compensation. Since that compensation provided the funding for the procurement people who were reducing the cost, the reduced compensation required us to cut the staffing of the group. With the cut in staffing, the remaining staff generated fewer savings making the customer unhappy. Their contract compensation structure created a form of downward spiral that guaranteed they would get less and less over time. It simply drove the wrong behavior. These are a few examples of terms or approaches that can drive the wrong behavior. While they may have seemed like a good approach when they were negotiated, they drove the wrong incentives, or they created negative incentives to the right behavior.

Here's an example of driving the right behavior. As part of managing the procurement start-up of a plant in India, I picked up the additional duty of having to manage the contracting for the construction and fit up of the plant. One of the things I discovered was that, except for major projects, general contractors or construction managers were not used in India at the time. The system was that all trades were contracted and managed by the owner. Working with our team and management we structured a unique approach to speed up the performance and reduce the amount of our involvement as we had a number of other things to manage. After negotiating all the contractors down to their lowest price we called them all together and offered to pay each of them a bonus of several percent if the work was finished by a specific date. The hook in the offer was that for each of them to collect their bonus, not only did they but all the other suppliers had to finish on time. This was to prevent the potential chaos of each of them rushing to finish their own work without any coordination, and potentially damaging the work of others. Since the Mechanical and Electrical suppliers had the largest value contracts and the most financial stake in completing on time, they became the de-facto construction managers and began setting up the work schedule, and working coordination issues. With all suppliers being dependent on the others for their bonus, there was also substantial peer pressure applied to expedite the work. They finished early and were paid their bonus, and we were able to commence production months earlier than people expected. The cost of the bonus was more than covered by returns from the earlier start of production, plus it saved us from having to manage all the coordination and deal with all the claims that would result from coordination conflicts. We wanted behavior where they would cooperate and coordinate the work in a way that required minimal supervision on our part and that's what we got. We also wanted them to finish on time and the structure helped do that.

Most contracts do not have remedies structured for failing to meet individual commitments. Many times a contract has language that says what the supplier can or can't do, but many times it doesn't say what will happen if they didn't do what they were supposed to do or did what they weren't supposed to do. Most contracts are also structured in a way where there can be repeat failures without much of an impact to the supplier. If there is a breach, the supplier has a certain number of days to cure the breach before you could terminate and if they cure the breach you can't terminate. This doesn't protect against frequent breaches and cures that can be a nightmare to the buyer. The only time the supplier needs to be concerned is if the supplier fails to cure within the allowable period making termination possible and subjecting them to damages.

Many times the threat of termination doesn't really exist because the buyer wants or needs what the supplier is providing or they can't wait to get it from another source. The threat of termination may also not drive the desired behavior. If contracts allow suppliers to continually breach the contract as long as they cure the breach within the required cure period, what type of behavior does this drive? Problem suppliers will continue to be problem suppliers because the simple fact is that if they don't feel the pain of their actions, they won't change.

How do you drive the right behavior? Think about the behavior you want from your suppliers on all the key issues and make sure that your approach and terms drive that behavior. Make sure that the things that you want to use to drive behavior are real and can be employed to get the supplier's attention to drive them to change.

One of the best ways to get their attention is to have the amount of pain increase with either the frequency or magnitude of the problem. I call it letting the penalty fit the crime. Make it so it's more painful for repeat offenders and more painful for bigger problems. Another simple way of driving the right behavior is to require a management escalation process or periodic management reviews that elevate issues to management. This does two things, it brings issues that may have been caused by lower level managers of the supplier under scrutiny of their management and it also moves the discussion of resolution of the problem to a level that can see the bigger picture.

The remedies for performance problems can also be tailored to the impact and that may be different depending upon when it occurs. In working for a major bank I negotiated a processing contract for debit card transactions. One of the keys in the negotiation was down time, as when you are down, you either aren't performing transactions and are losing all the fees associated with that and have unhappy customers or, you may be allowing transactions below a certain dollar limit to be automatically authorized which increases the frequency of fraudulent or overdraft situations. The real impact of downtime really depended upon when the down time actually occurred. There were critical hours and even more critical periods in which downtime would have a huge impact and there were other times like between 3 and 5 am where there was minimal impact because there was minimal use. If the downtime occurred on a Saturday or Sunday during prime business hours during the holiday shopping season, the impact would be enormous as transactions were in the many millions. When it came time to negotiate liquidated damages for down time we took a slightly different approach. Rather that have a single amount across all time periods, we structured it where the amount was directly tied to the impact. The damages were substantial for periods when it could hurt us the most, but it was minimal or none for times when the impact to us would be minimal. In explaining it to the supplier in the negotiation I noted that our goal was not to collect liquidated damages, it was to drive their behavior. We knew that there would be periods where they would need to take the computers down, do maintenance or make changes and we simply wanted that done during periods where it would have the least potential impact to our operation. In giving them a window in which they had time periods where there was no damages it gave them time to do what they needed without being at risk, but they also knew that if they did something to impact us during prime time it would be very costly. We wanted to drive them to do all their work in those periods and also not attempt any major changes during the holiday season. The easiest way to do that was to structure the damages in a way that drove the behavior we wanted.

One of the more important behaviors you want to drive is cost. If you want the supplier to help manage or reduce cost, don't have a compensation structure that rewards them for not managing cost or penalizes them for reducing your cost. If the supplier provides you with a win, they shouldn't lose. If they cost you money, they shouldn't win. This applies to suppliers that can drive cost (like designers) and those who help you manage the cost of purchases. Using the two examples, with the Architect it would be better to fix their fee so they have protection against getting less if you require something that costs less, but which also provides you with protection against them benefiting from the adding to the cost to the work. For contract manufacturers, it might be better to provide them with a different formula for sharing of savings where they have a greater incentive to help you reduce your cost if they can improve their profit. If you have a huge disparity in rewards the only savings you'll get are ones that you force them to provide.

Driving the right behavior is especially important when there are problems. If you need the supplier to be around to help solve a major problem (such as a patent infringement claim) you also need to structure your contract to ensure the supplier doesn't have an easy or cheap way out. The behavior you want is for them to solve the problem, not find the easiest way to exit the relationship. The more dependent you are on a supplier for performance the more important it is to ensure they don't have easy way to walk away from problems. For example agreeing to a low limitation of liability amount could allow the supplier to make a simple business decision to breach the contract and pay the liability amount rather than pay all the costs it would take to resolve the problem. Is that the behavior you want? If you want the supplier to correct problems that are causing you pain (such as quality problems or problems with their internal processes), make sure that they feel the pain of the problems they cause. If a supplier is consistently late, having them pay for the cost of premium shipping doesn't cause enough pain for them to change, so you may need other remedies that step up the pain depending on the severity and frequency of the problem. For example, if they failed to ship on time x number of times, you might require them to stock inventory at your location at no cost.

I'm repeating myself but this is an important point to remember. The correction of most problems is an investment decision. What is usually needed to correct a problem is an investment of capital or resources. If the supplier doesn't feel the pain and cost of the problem they cause, they may never make the investment that's needed. Investment decisions are financial decisions. If it isn't costing the supplier enough for the problems they create, the decision to make investments to correct those problems will always lose out to their other investment decisions that will create savings for them, increase their revenue or generate more profit for them. If your terms create enough pain and cost for the supplier, it will drive a behavior where they will aggressively work to solve the problem.

If you want better performance, quality, etc. you also need to look at your side of the equation to see that you aren't the cause of the problem. Behavior is a two way street. For example, one of the things that cause quality problems is the design's ability to be manufactured in high volume at high quality and your design could make it almost impossible to produce a quality product. Your behavior could make it difficult for them to perform and it may not be a quality problem, it may be a design problem.

To get high quality levels, have the supplier pick up increasing levels of your quality costs the worse the quality you receive, or provide them with incentives to improve quality by offering increased portions of your business or sharing in your quality cost savings. That will drive the desired quality behavior.

To improve overall performance, when there is a competitive supply base you drive the right behavior by tying the volumes they will get to their performance versus the competition. Improvements = more business. No change or reduced performance = less or no business.

Tie the price paid to supplier to performance via total cost. To do this, assume that the price you agreed to pay will buy you the product or service and the desired performance. Then have deducts to the price you pay based upon their actual performance.

If you want greater flexibility and you have a competitive supply base, drive the behavior you want by adjusting volumes or price based on flexibility and inventory you must carry. The more inventory they force you to carry, the more inventory and possible obsolescence costs = a lesser price. For shorter lead times and less inventory, provide incentives in sharing any inventory reductions.

If you want predictable deliveries, the first step may be to threaten cancellation of the order if that is a real threat. If it's not, start with having them pay for premium freight. If the problem continues add requirements that if they fail to meet certain levels, they will stock at your site at no added cost of if meet certain levels of performance you will pay their price, if not, have the price be reduced.

If you want better total costs and lower life cycle costs, you need to structure your contracts and award of business based on total cost or life cycle cost not just price. If all you do is award based on price, what you may be doing is giving more business to companies that increase your total cost or life cycle costs negating the value of any difference in price.

Driving the right behavior means your contracts need to be structured in a manner that allows for a change in the supplier's commitments based upon their actual performance. For example, under warranty provisions you will always negotiate the turn around time the supplier has to provide you with a repaired or replacement product under the warranty. The response time you accept should be for normal situations in which there are few failures. If you experience actual performance that's different, shouldn't the terms drive a faster response? Otherwise, as the buyer you will be bearing the full impact of a problem you didn't create and the supplier won't see any additional costs for the problem they created. I believe in tying things to actual performance where the commitment you negotiate is based on an assumption of receiving the desired performance. The obligation of the supplier, in those instances, is that when you fail to receive the committed level performance, their responsibility changes to adjust for that failure so they begin to assume the burden their performance created. Using warranty repairs as an example, you could agree to a time frame for repair or replacement of 30 days for products. If you have failure rates that are less than an agreed level the 30 days applies. If you experience a larger number of failures, the time frame to respond is reduced accordingly. The greater the deviation you see, the greater the adjustment there needs to be to the commitment. What this does is reduce the impact on you of the increased failures, and increase the impact to the supplier for the problems with their performance where they may need to pay expedited and overtime costs.

Most standard contracts are structured in a way that a failure to perform is a breach and the failure to cure (correct) that breach within a specified time frame will allow you to terminate the contract and sue for damages. The threat of termination may not drive the behavior you want, as it may simply not be feasible or desirable. Look for other commitments or remedies as an alternative to termination. That will provide you with what you need and rely on termination as a last resort. You may also want to build in mechanisms to reduce the possibility of repetitive breaches and cures such as adjusting the cure period after a certain number of breaches have occurred to make the risk of termination more threatening.

When you structure the relationships and terms always ask: "Will this drive the behavior I want"?

7.2 Using contracts to manage performance

While it would be nice to nice to transfer all risks and costs to the supplier, even it the supplier would be willing to accept the risks, the potential cost to do that could be prohibitive. There will always be costs and risks that the buyer needs to accept and manage. The contract is where you provide some of the tools to manage those costs and risks. There are seven basic ways to manage a supplier's performance. Every contract should have five ways of managing performance.

The first is what I would call **relationship** management where you build a strong relationship with the supplier's account team so that they know and understand what you need, want and what will impact them getting future business awards if they don't perform. This does not need to be addressed in the contract.

The second method to manage the supplier's performance is **structural.** In the contract you would include all the structural tools you need to manage their performance. The larger or more complex the purchase, the more you need the structural tools as part of the contract requirements that the supplier must meet.

Examples of structural tools that would be used to manage performance are:
A. Having clear specifications or a statement of work that makes it clear what they must deliver.
B. Establishment of a team to manage performance and supplier contacts.
C. Identify tasks required.
D. Establish schedule, milestones and deliverables
E. Have a clear process by which the work will be tested and accepted
F. Establish a strong program review process
G. Establish meeting review schedule, frequency, attendees.
H. Implement action item lists
I. Identify content and frequency or required reports
J. Have rights to audit any on-site work being performed for quality and performance,
K. Establish Senior Management involvement and reviews
L. Establish formal escalation process
M. Include ability to back charge management costs for significant problems, delays or resources provided.

The third method of managing performance is **control.** If you have agreed to assume a cost or risk, you simply can't let the supplier do its own thing, so your contract terms need to provide you with the necessary control over what the supplier can do over the things that can impact your cost or risk. Control is a way of managing behavior or performance. Examples of control type of provisions would include:
1. Control over the supplier's team that performs the work and any changes to that team.
2. Control over where the work is performed
3. Control over subcontracting of the work
4. Restrictions against assignment of the work
5. Control over changes to the product or service
6. Control over changes to the process.

For example, lets assume that the supplier will only agree to sell to you on ex-works delivery terms. What this means is that from a cost and risk perspective you are responsible to pay for all the costs to get it from the supplier's dock to your point of use. If further means that you would also be responsible for any loss of damage that occurs while it is in transit. To manage this potential risk the controls you would use would be to require that they comply with packing and packaging specification you provide that are designed to reduce the amount of damage that may occur in transit. You could also specify that you must either select or approve the carrier and lane used, as the potential for loss or damage may vary by carrier and by shipping lane. You could also require the supplier to ship it with pre-paid insurance that would be reimbursed as a separate line item. If you didn't have the controls the supplier could take whatever actions were the cheapest for them which could increase your potential risk of loss or damage.

If you can't transfer the cost or risk of problems that the supplier has control over back to the supplier, then to manage the risk you should require strict control about what the supplier can or can't do with all the various factors that may impact risk. For example if the supplier was unwilling to assume the major risks and costs of quality problems they could create, you would want to require approval of subcontractors, material suppliers, restrict any assignment, and not allow them to make any changes to the product or service without your advance approval, as all of those would reduce your potential risks. The old axiom is that anything that is left unmanaged will cost more and if the supplier isn't going to bear the cost or risk of an item, in most cases they won't make the investment to manage those risks for you unless you force them to by the contract terms or specifications.

The fourth aspect of managing performance is **financial.** The four main financial ways that manage performance are:
- The remedies that you have in the event of a breach of the contract (the types and amount of damages you may recover).
- The costs of any remedies the supplier is required to provide for failing to meet the specific obligation.
- Any pre-agreed impact to price for non-performance such as liquidated damages or price adjustments for being late with deliveries.
- Impact to their payments and cash flow. For example, a terms that would allow the buyer to not make progress or interim payments if the work was behind schedule would be designed have the cash flow impact to try to drive the supplier take necessary actions to get back on schedule.

The fifth aspect of managing performance is **structure terms to drive the desired performance**. A classic example of this is many times a buyer will want the supplier to help you reduce the cost of the work. Which approach will work better in meeting that goal?
1. Fixing their overhead and profit amount and sharing in the savings, or
2. Paying them a fixed percentage for both overhead and profit based on the cost of the work?

To me the answer is clear. A provides the supplier with an incentive to perform, whereas B provides a negative incentive. How much help would you expect to get if helping you penalizes them by reducing the amount the supplier gets paid for their overhead and profit?

The sixth aspect of managing performance is making sure that you include and **negotiate express conditions for that performance.**
- Make it an express commitment in the contract.
- Use language that establishes it as a firm commitment.
- Avoid any softening or qualifying language that would reduce the commitment.

Any commitment that includes "efforts" as part of it whether its best efforts, reasonable efforts or commercially reasonable efforts doesn't guarantee performance. All it does is require the supplier to extend that level of effort in trying to perform.

A seventh and last way of managing the supplier's performance is **contract administration or contract management.** Any activity left unmanaged will always cost more. The amount of contract administration you need will be dependent upon the supplier and the risks. There are three main focus to contract administration. One is to manage the delivery of any buyer deliverables. That is to avoid claims by the supplier. The second is managing supplier performance with the goal of obtaining products, supplies or services, of requisite quality, on time, and within budget. For contract administration to be successful you need the structural management tools to be in place. A good contract file should consist of the following:

- A record copy of the contract, highlighted to show any amendments made and when those amendment were made.
- A record copy of the applicable statement or scope of work, annotated to show any changes agreed and the effective date of those changes.
- Copies of all amendments
- Copies of any change requests and their disposition.
- An action item log.
- Copies of all correspondence to and from the supplier
- Minutes from all meetings and calls with the supplier
- Copies of any inspection reports on the progress of the work, site visits, audits, etc.

Whether you win or lose on a claim or a law suit will be dependent upon being able to establish who did what and when and what the requirements were at a specific point in time. Below are two examples of what I mean.

When I worked in construction I once had a claim by a site work contractor for additional costs to bring in new soil to make the necessary elevation grades that were called for by the drawings and specifications. The first thing I did was to review our on site inspector's daily reports that included all on site activities including deliveries and things being removed from the site. There was a clear record of the contractor being delivered all the soil that he claimed. A further review of earlier reports disclosed two things. One was the contractor had previously removed substantially more soil and that was taken off the site. The second was the architect instructed supplier to not remove broad segments of topsoil and expose the remaining soil to the elements where if it got wet it would need to dry out before use. I was also able to see from the daily reports the weather and their progress and how the rain made some of the remaining soil unusable. Based on my findings I refused to pay any amount toward the claim based on the position that 1) there was an excess of soil on the site and had they not removed it, they would not have needed to bring in new soil. Their actions of uncovering too much soil they created the problem that required new soil.

In another situation we had a situation where a electronic circuit card that was supplied by a contract manufacturer had a specific component on it that was failing and costing significant field costs. The contract manufacturer argued that because it was a component that we had specified and they had purchased from our approved supplier they should have no liability. The component supplier was currently approved and the CM was authorized to purchase from them, but we did specific research on what the dates of the purchases were that were failing. We then went back to the contract to see at what point in time the specific part number was added to our contract. What we found was that these purchases were made by the contract manufacturer before they were ever added to our contract with the supplier. Under the terms of our contract with the contract manufacturer these would be considered as parts they directly sourced for which they assumed full responsibility.

The more you have changes in the personnel that will manage the contract on both sides the more important it is to document and maintain this type of information so it isn't lost. It also doesn't hurt to have a running summary of all the problems that the supplier caused that cost you extra money and have that documented and available for use at the end of the work. That's when suppliers may come in with a claim for extra work and extra costs. It's at that point when you would present your list of counter claims and use it to reduce or offset their claims and recover any excess costs.

CHAPTER 8 HOW COMPANIES OPERATE

To negotiate, you need to know how suppliers operate and how they sell. The key factors that will impact your negotiation are:
- How they are legally organized and who you are buying from, Their selling models and their sales decisions in managing their profitability and managing their risk.
- The point of sale, selling entity and taxes.

Sales channels may be designed to reach a broad range of potential customers, but they are also designed to manage the supplier's profitability, limit their liability and risk and manage their taxes. To start with understanding how suppliers operate let's first look at the development process.

8.1 Product and service development

Few products or services just happen. Most are thoroughly planned by development, product marketing and sales organizations to win in the market. Many times it starts with a "market requirements plan" usually managed by a "product manager". A typical market requirements plan will include things like: the market opportunity, market needs, and specific product requirements by: a) geography b) industry, c) service, and d) sales channel. This means that before a supplier ever considers offering a product to you for sale, they have done vast amounts of work determining the market, market clusters, the competition, their product positioning, the competitive advantages, their weaknesses, and each of their competition's advantages and weaknesses. They have also done a financial model based on the anticipated volumes from each selling channel, and established pricing for the product or services. Most will create list pricing and standard discounts for all channels and tiers, established allowances and terms, and determine through which channel or channels they will sell the product or services along with the applicable pricing and terms for each channel and tier. suppliers know more about their product and their competition's product than you ever will. That knowledge, when combined with their understanding of how any unique features they have meet your needs or desires and provide you with benefits, helps them sell but it also helps them understand the true competitive landscape they face.

In "product positioning" there are several keys. The first is finding a way to differentiate their product from the competition. They do that because they know that if they can differentiate their product, they may not need to directly compete with other products in head to head competition. Differentiation may allow them be to charge a price premium for the difference in value. If the differentiation is based on unique features that only they have, as long as the customer needs and wants those features, they'll know that they don't have any real competition. That provides them advantages not just in pricing but in negotiating the sale of the product and the contract terms. Product differentiation can be based on a number of factors. Features and their resulting benefits are the primary means of differentiation. Product quality, being first to the market, owning a specific product attribute that customers want, or being a market leader can also be a means to differentiate themselves. Differentiation may come from the reputation associated with their brand. If there is nothing that differentiates them from the competition, the only differentiator in the buying decision will be price. If the supplier can't differentiate the product itself, they may try to differentiate themselves in other ways such as warranties or service offerings, their overall track record, value added services, expertise, execution performance, or product availability commitments such as stocking or quick shipments. Suppliers try to avoid a point-by-point comparison against a competitor because in doing so, it would also highlight deficiencies in their offering that they would need to offset by offering more, charging less, or providing better contract terms.

The other aspect of positioning is understanding the customer value perception in comparison to the perceived value of the competitor's product. Do customers need and value their differentiators? If the customers don't need or value the differentiators, they aren't differentiators. Is the price charged for their product is consistent with its perceived value? Buying decisions are based primarily on their perceived value. customers will look at a product, its features and benefits and price and compare that to their preferences, needs, restrictions and the price and value of competing products. If something is of equal value to them but at a lower price, customers will usually purchase the lower priced item. If something provides them with more value, customers don't always want to pay more to get that increased value. Customers will compare the products and differentiators against the price to determine the relative value but in many cases things like available budgets or even approval levels required may be a determining factor. Suppliers have been known to take normal approval levels into account in establishing their price. A classic approval level may be $100,000 so a supplier may offer a product in a stripped down version at less than $100,000 so customers that want to buy their product don't have to go through that additional internal approval levels which could impact their sale.

8.2 How suppliers Sell

If you ever attended a sales training program you would find that customer needs are always the focal point of any selling activity and the sale process is the means by which the sales person tries to discover the customer's needs. Customers don't make buying decisions based on the supplier's product's features, they make buying decisions based on the combination of their needs and how the features provide them with the benefits they want. It's called "need satisfaction selling". Customer's needs come in many varieties. They may have an immediate problem they need to solve. They could have dissatisfaction with an existing product, service or supplier. They may simply want or desire the product or service. To sales people, procurement is frequently considered to be the gatekeeper and there are many strategies that are used to work around the gatekeeper. As part of any pre-sales effort there can be trade shows, samples of product for evaluation, demonstrations, road shows and design assistance. Every one of these activities is designed to open communication with the user or technical expert without the involvement of the gatekeeper. If they can open that line of communication, they can learn who makes the purchase decision, who will influence it, and who the decision makers are. Once they know that, they will focus their sales efforts on those individuals.

Selling requires them to show how the features provide the customer with benefits the customer will value. Selling is nothing more than:
- Uncovering the needs of all the interested parties of the buyer.
- Explaining how their features provide certain benefits.
- Show how those benefits meet the buyer's needs and provide value or solve their problem.

The most successful sales approach is problem solving where they get the buyer to allow them to do the analysis, provide the analysis, and prepare a sales presentation showing the analysis of how their product or service will help solve the problem. For an immediate purchase the buyer usually needs to be in pain, so the decision will need to reduce or eliminate the pain. Other motivators can be pleasure or recognition that makes it worth being the champion for the purchase by things like using the product or service to reduce cost or improve productivity.

When a supplier knows that you need and want their product many of the tactics you would normally use simply won't work. The one tactic that does work is to use the financial approver to make demands on the supplier that must be met to get their approval. The reason this works is that while the sales people may know the specific problem and how they would fit solving it, what they don't know is where this purchase stands in terms of all the other investments that may be required by the customer to solve all the other problems. That uncertainty can be the thing to drive concessions. In that instance the competition is not against other supplier's, it's against competing buyer investments for which they won't know the priority or return on investments.

Suppliers always want to take competitive leverage away from the buyer. The more freely they are able to communicate with the decision makers within your company, the more likely they'll win and you'll lose. There always needs to be communication but to win in negotiations that communication needs to be orchestrated as a team. Everyone on the buyer's team needs to cooperate in setting the right expectations with the supplier and maintaining or strengthening the competitive leverage. Even if you do everything right to maintain maximum competitive leverage, that may still be impacted by other factors such as where the product sits in the product's life cycle.

8.3 Product Life Cycles
Almost every product goes through a product Life Cycle that consisted of a number of phases: early introduction, early growth, late growth, mature market and declining market:

Over time, the net result creates a price curve that acts like this

- At initial entry there is little competition which means the highest price, and purchases will be made by market leaders and innovators

- As competitors enter the market, Price erosion occurs

- The lowest price will be when there is maximum supply and competition. That is usually also the point at which market leading supplier begin to exit market and introduce a new product.

- As companies exit the market and market leading buyers move to newer products, the price will increase because of reduced capacity combined with the demand from buyers that haven't migrated to the new products.

The slope of the price curve will depend on the balance of supply versus demand. Excess supply will cause a faster downward trend in pricing as competitors reduce pricing to capture demand. Excess demand will slow or even reverse the downward trend as suppliers take advantage of shortages and allocations. Technology leaders / innovators usually expect to make their profits in the early product stages and tend to move on to the next innovation and start a new product life cycle as the product begins to mature. Low cost suppliers tend to enter markets later and stay longer in the product life cycle because they can compete on cost and will see increased profits as competitors exit the market and create a supply / demand imbalance. This means that for negotiations you need to understand where you are in the product's price curve. If you are in the early stages, you wouldn't want to lock in extended pricing as that could have you pay more as competition erodes the price. If you are in the late stages of the price curve you probably want to lock in extended pricing, as the price will normally increase when companies begin exiting the market.

8.4 How companies are organized

A large multinational company will have numerous subsidiaries with different physical addresses. In addition they may also have a number of different "paper companies" that may exist in offshore tax havens. Those serve as holding companies of the different subsidiaries. For example, a multi-national company could consist of:
- The parent company will own the holding companies as wholly owned subsidiaries.
- The manufacturing holding company will usually be located in a tax haven and will own or have controlling interest in the individual manufacturing subsidiaries.
- Other holding companies or service companies will usually be located in a tax haven or other advantageous location (e.g. companies may have their own insurance company located in Bermuda). It they are a holding company they may either own or have controlling interest in corresponding local subsidiaries (e.g. there can be a service holding company that owns or controls a service subsidiary in a location), or there can be a service company sell services, leases assets, provide financing or insurances to the individual subsidiary.
- The sales holding company will usually be located in a tax haven and will own or have controlling interest in the individual sales subsidiaries.

- The manufacturing subsidiary will produce product and will sell that product to the manufacturing holding company. In the sale of the product they will include profit and overhead to cover only their operations. Any excess annual profit from their operations will usually be paid to the manufacturing holding company.
- The sales subsidiaries will be located in specific countries with each subsidiary organized under the laws of that country. The sales subsidiary will purchase the product from the manufacturing holding company at "transfer price" which includes a substantial portion of profit and overhead on the product. The sales subsidiary will then establish the local sales price, tiers; discount structure and terms for sale to both direct customers and local channels. The profits made by the sales subsidiary, will be paid to both other owners of the Subsidiary and the sales holding company based on their ownership share, less any profits the subsidiary needs to retain for on-going operations.
- The Sales Subsidiary will make direct sales of the product to large customers (named accounts), major original equipment manufacturers (OEM's) and value added resellers (VARs). All other sales will normally be pushed through another channel.
- The Sales Subsidiary may also use Manufacturer's representatives to cove geographical areas where they don have sufficient sales to warranty direct sales staff. Manufacturers' Reps are usually paid a percentage commission on the sale.
- Companies may have Internet based sales tools for direct sales to customers. In most cases the purchase terms and prices through this channel are fixed.
- Companies may operate with multiple channel models selling to Industrial Distributors who may sell to OEM's or VARs not covered by the company directly, or may also sell to other distributors or retailers. Distributors may sell direct to customer or to retailers.
- Companies may also sell to master resellers like chain stores. Smaller retailers will usually be forced to buy through distributors.
- Brokers traditionally are not part of an authorized channel for the supplier and wind up buying product through either excess inventories of users or channels, or may buy product from one of the authorized channels on a grey market basis. (An authorized channel buys more than what they need and sells the excess to the broker).

Subsidiaries may be wholly owned (where the parent company or holding company owns 100% of the stock in the subsidiary) or the parent company or holding company may own a controlling percentage of the stock (more than 50%). Ownership in subsidiaries may be controlled by requirements of the countries in which the subsidiaries are headquartered, where they may require a certain percentage of local ownership. Companies will also sell through Channels (Value Added Resellers, Distributors, Resellers, etc.)

Companies are organized this way primarily for tax reasons, but they are also organized this way to manage profitability, liability, and risk. For example, if a supplier has a high-risk operation, they may choose to establish that activity in a separate company. Then if something happens, the remainder of the supplier's companies will be insulated from the problem and risk. They may only sell through channels in certain locations for many of the same reasons.

Each subsidiary is an independent legal entity with it own Board of Directors who is responsible to manage that company's business. Since the parent corporation and all their subsidiaries are all legally independent companies, the parent corporation cannot bind the subsidiaries unless the subsidiaries legally agreed they have that authority. Subsidiaries cannot bind the parent unless the parent has provided that authorization. One subsidiary cannot bind other subsidiaries. For each to be a party to the other's contracts, they must legally agree to be bound to it. For a subsidiary to be bound to the contract, they must be either a signatory to the contract or they must have a separate contract saying that they agree to be bound to those terms. For a parent to be bound to a subsidiary's contract, they must be a signatory to that contract where they agree to be "jointly and severally liable", or they must provide what's called a company or parent guarantee. Simply having both the parent and the subsidiary sign the same contract will not make the parent responsible for the subsidiary.

A common mistake made by many buyers is thinking that there is no distinction between companies of the same basic name, when each subsidiary and possibly each location is a separate legal entity. In negotiations it is important to identify exactly which supplier company the contract is with by including the correct supplier legal name, place of business, and the location of incorporation. It also important to ensure that the company your contract is with has the resources and assets to stand behind the commitments of the contract because many subsidiaries may not.

As a buyer, another thing you need to be concerned about is that each time the product changes hands in the sales chain, additional overhead and profit is added and that impacts your price. It can also impact your terms and what's standing behind the suppliers promises. The other impact this has is since the structure may be based on what is best for the supplier from a tax standpoint, they will be reluctant to change the point of sale as that point of sale will impact the tax they have to pay.

The supplier manufacturing companies and the sales companies are frequently different legal entities. In fact, sales subsidiaries "purchase" products from the manufacturing subsidiary a manufacturing holding company or the parent company. The price they pay for those purchases is called the "transfer price".

8.5 The concept of Transfer Price.

When a product is made by the supplier or service is performed by the supplier are sold by a subsidiary, what happens is the supplier will sell that product or service to the subsidiary and then the subsidiary will sell it to you. The price at which the supplier sells the product or service to their subsidiary is the transfer price. In most cases the majority of the supplier's profit will be included in the transfer price. Subsidiaries then establish their own selling price for their sales. There is only one transfer price for sales to all supplier subsidiaries even if the product is made in multiple locations. The transfer price cannot change for different customers and suppliers must be able to substantiate the transfer price, to prove that the value added in the selling country is properly accounted for and taxed. Since there can be only one transfer price for a product, if a supplier reduced the transfer price so you could buy it at a lower cost from their local subsidiary, that transfer price would have to be applied to all their sales to all their other subsidiaries purchases. That impacts where their profits are made and the taxes they pay, so they probably wouldn't agree. If you have the leverage it is always best to negotiate with the supplier rather than their subsidiary.

In negotiating with a subsidiary they are always limited by the fact that the transfer price is a cost to them so they can't discount that. The only thing they could discount would be any locally added overhead and profit. You never get to go after all the profit that may be included in the transfer price. The sales subsidiary prices may also be set higher in certain countries because of costs, taxes, currency risks etc. associated with that Country. So you may also be starting at a high price to negotiate from. If you are buying large volumes of product around the world and the product is easily transferred and supported, if the supplier won't sell to you direct, buyers may search for the lowest cost subsidiary and purchase all their requirements there and ship them to their other locations.

Transfer price doesn't have the same impact on custom or unique products if only the one buyer purchases the product. In that case transfer price can be tailored to support the buyer. Whether a supplier will work with the buyer on that will depend upon several things. Most important is whether the subsidiary you will buy from is wholly owned or just controlled by the supplier having a majority interest in the ownership. Suppliers will still be concerned about where they are making their profits as that impacts the taxes they will pay.

The real effect transfer price has on negotiations is subsidiaries are limited in what they can discount, because they can't sell product for less than they paid under the transfer price. The margin they add to transfer price also the finances the operation of the subsidiary. Since much of the profit is made in the sale to the subsidiary, the profits subsidiaries make may be minimal, and subsidiaries may not have substantial assets or resources to cover any significant problems. Where this becomes important is if you only contract or purchase from a subsidiary, that subsidiary may not have the assets to correct the problem. Where suppliers make their profits has a direct impact on the taxes they pay. This is important to remember as it impacts the delivery terms the supplier will agree to or whether they will do programs such as local stocking or vendor managed inventory.

8.6 Taxes
To manage their taxes companies will manage the locations where they sell the product or service to avoid what is called "permanent establishment" in a country. For example, a supplier may be selling their product under FOB Origin or Ex-Works terms, so that the sale occurs in that country or location. If the buyer tries to force the sale to occur in a different country or location under other terms such as delivered duty paid

(DDP), the buyer adding the cost of freight, duties, and risk of loss or insurance to the price. Those are costs the supplier would pass through to the buyer in their sales price. What they can't pass on to the buyer is the tax impact a local sale would have. They would also be legally impacted. If the supplier sells a product or service in a different location they would be conducting business there. They would have "permanently established" themselves in that location. If you have the sale occur in a location it 1) requires the supplier to be legally registered to do business in that location, 2) The supplier become subject to that location's taxes on the profit from those sales, and 3) The supplier would also subject themselves to the laws of that location. If you've ever run into problems getting a supplier to agree to a different delivery term or set up a stocking program in a certain location, this is probably the reason why. Suppliers won't agree to sell in locations where it negatively impacts them because of a higher tax rate on their profits.

Suppliers could offer to accommodate you through a local sales channel that avoids the tax liability issue for them but that creates a different problem for the buyer as you would no longer be buying from the supplier. If you were going to purchase large quantities and needed to have a form of supplier stocking close to a point of use, the only approach that avoids the permanent establishment and income tax issues would be to have the stocking located in a "Free Trade Zone" in the country. Most countries allow for free trade zones. A free trade zone is simply an area set aside where items are held in "Bonded" locations prior to import clearance. In those situations the buyer takes delivery in the Free Trade Zone and is responsible for import, payment of any duties and transport to the using location. Since the sale is occurring before the item has been imported into the country, its technically and international sale and the supplier would not be taxed in the import country as the sales transaction didn't occur within the country.

8.7 Understanding Sales Channels

Most companies have a variety of different sales "channels" involving both direct and third party sales of their products. The supplier or its Subsidiaries make direct sales to the customer. Companies may have direct sales to Major customers (dedicated or named accounts). For example, a company may have customer accounts where there are teams focused on selling products on an OEM basis. Direct sales by supplier are usually made to large Original Equipment Manufacturers (OEM's), large Value Added Resellers (VARS) and may be made direct to major customers. More recently direct sales are also being made through cost effective models such as Internet sales. In locations where the supplier doesn't have sufficient business to warrant direct sales staff on their own, they may conduct a form of direct sales through manufacturer's representatives who will sell on their behalf for a commission. If you are buying and a manufacturer's rep is involved, they are adding cost to your purchases so if possible, its always better to deal direct. For any sales that the supplier doesn't want to focus it selling resources directly on, they will use Third Party Sales Channels such as Distributors or Value Added Resellers.

In terms of direct sales, the discounts companies routinely offer are frequently similar. Direct sales to large Original Equipment Manufacturers (OEM) are usually the highest discount levels offered by the supplier. This is because the volumes are high, the selling and support costs are usually low and the OEM will buy the product for use their product that will be resold, so it doesn't compete with their and their channels sales. Sales to Value Added Resellers (VAR's) are at the next highest discount levels and are focused at customers that will take the product and add certain customization or features to target a specific market(s) broadening the market for their product. Sales to distribution are at the next level of discount and are focused at companies that will sell the product to smaller companies (who may need less quantity, or where it may not be economically feasible to sell direct). Sales to master re-sellers (major retailers) are usually for finished product.

8.8 Distribution Sales Models

There are two basic models that OEMs use to sell to distribution, which can impact how those channels sell to you. One model is a form of price protection model where the discounts they get are closely tied to the selling price. The closer they sell to the target selling price the more of a discount they'll receive so it provides them with incentive to sell at the target prices. If they move away from the target price they may sell more, but they'll get less discount (and less profit) and in the future the OEM may decide to not have them as a sales channel. In the other model the OEM sells to the Distributor at a price or discount off list and then the distributor is free to establish its own selling price. There are variations to both of these as there are variations in the ways some companies use distribution. For example, some companies may use distribution to supplement their own sales force or to operate in locations where they may not want to sell direct and other companies may sell exclusively through distribution as a form of outsourcing much of their logistics. If you are forced to buy through a third party sales channel its important to understand what type of sales model the supplier is selling to them under. For suppliers that sell to their channels under a more price protected model you may be limited in what you can negotiate as they are effectively limited in what they can do by the way their compensation is structured.

8.9 Understanding Tiers

In addition to suppliers having multiple channels, many suppliers also have multiple tiers within the individual channels including the direct sales. For example, for the OEM customer channel, a supplier may have multiple tiers based on factors such as volumes and the importance of the customer. The top tier or Tier 1 customer would receive not only the supplier's best pricing, but would also receive the most favorable treatment on contract terms and other possible concessions. Tier 2 would receive less, and tier 3 may be only slightly better than buying the product through distribution. For the most part tiers may be invisible to buyers and may not pose a problem as long as you get what you need. Where tiers do become a problem is with Outsourcing. When you are involved in outsourcing and you are a Tier 1 customer, you probably don't want your benefits to be diminished because you introduced a third party into the equation, nor would you want to provide other customers of that outsource supplier (who may be your competition) with the same advantages you have. Even if you don't feel you have any special competitive advantages you need to protect, many suppliers have the same concern in reverse because of their tiering practices. When they plan the sales of a product both the assumptions on price and terms will usually be tier driven. That allows them to charge more or offer less to customers in lower tiers. Since the outsource supplier may serve customers of all tiers, it creates a problem for the supplier that could impact their tiering stratification. If they provide the outsource supplier with your tier 1 terms, the outsource supplier will try to use those for all their customers and it's difficult or impossible to prevent. If they do, that impacts the supplier's revenue (since the price they get will be less), it impacts the supplier's profit (because they are now selling at the lower tier 1 price to a larger number of customers) and it increases their risks and costs (because they would be extending the more favorable tier 1 terms to customers that would not have qualified for them on their own). It would upset their overall financial model.

Who you buy from will affect a number of things in the relationship and in your contract coverage. For example, if you buy from a supplier subsidiary or affiliate company, your relationship may only be with that subsidiary or the affiliate company and not the supplier. If there is a problem you may not be able to look to the supplier, as they aren't a party to the relationship as there is no privity of contract with them. If you buy from an authorized distributor, your relationship may only be with that distributor and not the supplier. If there is a problem you may not be able to look to the supplier, as they aren't a party to the relationship. You may get certain protections that the supplier gives to the distributor and allows to be passed on to their customers.

When a manufacturer's representative is involved what you get will depend upon on how orders are placed. If orders are placed on the supplier in care of the manufacturer's representative firm, once the supplier accepts them by performance they are the same as dealing direct with the supplier. If you place the orders on the manufacturer's representative firm, your relationship may only be with the supplier's representative firm and not the supplier. If there is a problem you may not be able to look to the supplier, as they aren't a party to the relationship.

When a broker is involved, they are selling materials they have procured from the supplier or a 3rd party and there is no direct involvement with the supplier so if there is a problem you can't to look to the supplier and may be dependent on the broker for any problems that occur.

If you buy another company's excess inventory all protections need to come from that company unless the supplier becomes involved as a means of preventing the dumping of the material into the market.

Suppliers will frequently sell through channels, and may even force you or a third party buying on your behalf to purchase from their channels. If you have significant leverage and they want or need your business, you can try to negotiate a solution that will work for both parties. As a buyer you will want several things: 1) The cost to you should be no more to buy it from the channel; 2) The terms get should be no less than what you would get if you were to buy direct; and 3) you want the supplier responsible for purchases through any of their "authorized channels" so you can look directly to the supplier in the event of a problem. If a third party may be purchasing on your behalf, it may also be important to also negotiate 3rd party beneficiary status on those purchases so you can continue to enforce your terms directly with the supplier on those purchases so you have privity of contract with the supplier on the purchases.

An important thought to remember: A contractual promise is no good unless the party making it can fulfill it. You can have a contract with all the right terms and conditions and still not be protected if the entity you contracted with doesn't have the resources and assets to stand behind the commitments. Many sales subsidiaries won't have those resources or assets because of the way companies are structured and work financially. Many third party channels also won't have what's needed. If you need the supplier's assets or resources to provide the protection, you need to have them provide you with the necessary commitments. For subsidiaries one way to get that protection is to have the parent company provide a parent guarantee for their subsidiary. The extend of the parent guarantee a supplier may be willing to provide will vary based upon whether it is a partially or wholly owned subsidiary. In buying through distribution one way to get the protection is to a separate agreement with the Supplier where they agree to be responsible for providing certain protections for purchases through their authorized distributors.

8.10 Final Comments on How Companies Sell

Virtually every company will have:
- Standard sales terms
- Standard sales policies
- Standard price lists and discount schedules
- All will be tailored by Channel and frequently there will be tiers within Channels

The lowest level sales person's job is to make the sale using those standard terms, following those standard sales policies and sell at a price that is appropriate within the list prices and standard discount schedules. For the most part they will not have authority to make any changes from those standards and will need to elevate it to their management. They will be armed with all types of documents showing the legitimacy of their position:
- The preprinted sales contract
- Written company policies
- Pre-printed standard pricing and discount schedules

All these documents are a negotiating tactic intended to show legitimacy for their position.

When you push for something greater than the standards, there are several dynamics that occur. First, if you are pushing for a lower price, the sales person may be measured based on not just the volume of the sales, but also the profit margins, so there will always be a reluctance to provide the reductions that may impact their metrics and compensation. They may not have the authority to agree to something better. They may need to get approval from their next level of sales management or higher depending upon the magnitude of the change. The next level of sales managements is also measured on both revenue and profit margins (or the amount of "allowances" they offer to make the sale). They may be given an amount of allowances they can make, but to exceed that they will need to get their management's approval. So there will always be a trade-off that occurs in the sales person's mind or the sales manager's mind as to whether the value and volume of the sale will offset the impact to their compensation and be worth involving their sales management to support those additional concessions. As there are usually multiple layers of sales management, the same decision process will be made every time before escalating it for approval of the next higher level of management. The one advantage that this escalation process has for the buyer, is the higher up you move within the sales organization, the more that level of sales management is able to look at the sale in relation to all their other sales, and that may lessen the impact. It's at those higher levels in sales management where key strategic account decisions may take precedence over the impact of the sale on metrics and compensation. If they feel that the sale is strategic or the customer has value that extends beyond the value of the sale itself, they may decide to agree to terms that are more favorable to the buyer to get that strategic customer and the value they bring.

A second dynamic in sales is the management of expectations. I've talked about it before and you'll probably hear it ten more times because of its importance. Sales people will frequently need to provide information to their sales management on what they have in the sales pipeline; what the probability of the sale is; and what it will take to win the business. That sets an expectation with their management and their management will use that information to set expectations with their management and so on. If you don't set the expectation from the beginning that they will need to make significant changes to their pricing and terms to win the business, all the expectations within the sales management chain will be formed. If you come in later to push for a significantly better deal, you have placed the sales person in the awkward spot of having to reset the expectation with their management, which is something they won't want to do. It gives the appearance that they weren't able to read the account, but it also creates the potential where the sales manager will have to go to their management to also re-set expectations. No one wants to go to their management to say that they hadn't read the situation properly, so in many cases the sales person will try to hold firm. If you want better terms and pricing, you need to set that as an expectation early and often so that the sales people you are dealing with will set it with their management and so on. If you don't and a sales person doesn't need the sale to meet their quotas they may rather hold firm and risk losing the sale rather than have to go back to their management to reset expectations and need their management to reset expectations further up the chain.

The third dynamic in sales is the "golden rule". "He who has the gold makes the rules". In sales this gets into the dynamic of who needs the sale more, the supplier or the buyer? At the sales person's level that dynamic will usually be decided by where they stand in meeting their sales quotas and what impact will that sale will have on their compensation. If they have already made their quota's they may not be willing to negotiate anything, as the return to them may not be worth what they will need to do to get approvals through their sales management. As you move further up within the sales organization it becomes less of a personal decision, as a single customer's purchases may not have a significant impact on that level of sales management's quota's or compensation, and they can look at the negotiation from a more strategic perspective:
- What's the value of having this volume on costs
- What's the value of having this volume on ability to focus sales efforts on higher margin opportunities?
- What type of an annuity stream will we get from this sale?
- What's the likelihood it will lead to follow-on sales?
- What is the value of the buyer as a customer
  - Will they provide credibility in the market
  - Will they provide marketing value
  - Will their being a customer help us sell to other customers
- What impact will this have on our total sales financial metrics?

Based on this, the buyer's goal should be to start the negotiation as far back in the sales chain as possible and as high within the supplier's sales organization as possible. This helps avoid the mark-ups added by each level and avoids the dynamics that occur in dealing with the lower level sales staff. The larger the volume you can offer and the more valued you will be perceived as a customer, the stronger your likelihood of being able to start at a higher level within their sales organization.

8.11 Customer service organizations

As customer service is closely related to sales and performance, and many times to get customer service will require its own negotiation, who should you negotiate with in customer Service organizations? For the most part "customer service" is really a misnomer as many of the "service" people you deal with aren't measured or goaled on you getting what you want, they're goaled and measured based on how they manage or contain cost. As a buyer, if you don't get what you want to hear from a supplier's customer Service organization, always ask to escalate it to their management. If you still don't get what you want, escalate it back to sales management on the basis of the impact to your supply relationship and your willingness to use them in the future. Get past the individuals whose job it is to say no.

8.12 General Tips for Negotiating With Sales People

- Set their expectations early on.
- Tell them what you want
- Remind them of the competitive nature of the activity
- Make sure the entire team protects the existence or perception of competition.
- When there is a value difference between what they offer and what the competition offers (where they provide something less), do a point-by-point comparison to highlight their diminished value that needs to be offset with price reductions or other commitments of value.
- If they offer more value, discount the value that differentiation provides to you.
- Provide them only with the information they need to know so they can't shift the sales approach or try to defend their price by other means.
- Counsel everyone to avoid sending buying signals during the negotiation as the more buying signals you send, the fewer concessions you'll get. What are buying signals?
  - Questions on details like payment, delivery, and quantity discounts etc.
  - Questions on availability
  - Questions on discounts or other incentives to make the purchase
  - Questions about long-term support.
  - Positive comments about their product.
  - More detailed request to test the product (unless you need to verify it performance or compatibility with you needs)
  - Talk about how the product is planned to be used.

Most of these points that would be considered buying signals in the negotiation can and should be asked as part of general qualification of their product or service or of the supplier in advance of the negotiation. For you to be successful in negotiations, you must have uncertainty. Uncertainty drives concessions. The sales person must believe that there is a real threat that they will lose the sale to the competition, to other decisions that will cause the buyer to not make the purchase, or their position will impact other business they have with the buyer. You can't send buying signals and at the same time be maintaining uncertainty.

John C. Tracy

CHAPTER 9 STANDARD TERMS - WHY ARE THEY THERE

I once had a commodity manager tell me that all the contract terms represented was a bunch of "legal mumble jumble". It was clear with that attitude he simply did not understand what the terms meant, why they were there, and the risk and costs they were intended to protect against.

Most purchase contracts will contain common terms that describe the following:

- The **parties** to the contract
- The **obligations** of the Parties
- The **term** of the contract and any rights to extensions
- How **changes** or modifications to the contract are made
- The **price** that will be paid
- The **payment** terms
- The **delivery** terms
- The **warranties** and **representations** of the supplier regarding their performance or their product or Service
- **Limitations on liability** on both the types of damages that may be claimed and/or limitations on the amounts of damages
- **Insurance**
- **Termination** rights of the parties of the contract (with or without cause)
- **Confidentiality** or lack of confidentiality of the information exchanged
- The events that constitute a **breach** / default of the contract, the breaching party's right to cure, and consequences / remedies for the breach
- How **disputes** will be managed and where there will be heard
- **General indemnifications** for personal injury or property damage
- **Intellectual property indemnifications** for claims of Intellectual Property Infringement
- **Governing law** for disputes, where actions may be commenced
- Provisions for recovery of **Attorney's fees** in the event of a dispute
- Requirement for **notices**
- Entire agreement or **merger** provisions that limit interpretation of the contract to its four corners
- **Severability of clauses** in the event the courts find one of the clauses to be unenforceable or illegal
- **Time of the essence** provisions for performance
- **Survival** provisions that describe what terms will survive the termination or expiration of the contract.
- **Order of precedence** provision in the event there is an inconsistency between various documents
- Requirements for a **waiver** of contract rights
- Catch-all provisions for **performance** of work or services
- Rights to **equitable remedies**
- Representation of **authority** by signing parties
- **Force Majeure** rights in the event of acts beyond the parties control
- **Assignment** rights, if any.

In addition, most contracts will also contain either specifications or a statement of work that fully describes the product or service that the buyer wants to purchase. Within those documents there may also reference other documents that further describe the responsibilities of the parties. Depending on what you are buying or licensing the terms you use may have certain variations or additions to cover the unique issues or risks associated with that type of purchase. For example some of the warranties that you would require for a supplier providing a service will be different than the warranties you would want if the supplier were providing you a product or piece of equipment.

Let's talk about each of these terms from the perspective of why you would have them in your contract and the legal issues, costs or risks are involved they should manage. Additional tips and thoughts on negotiating many of these terms are located on my blog at knowledgetonegotiate.blogspot.com

Parties to the contract. Many times a supplier is not one company, they are a number of legally independent companies that may share the same brand name and have interlocking ownership. The parties to the contract section will define the specific legal entities that are entering into the contract. From a legal perspective, since this identifies the company you are dealing with, you need to make sure that the specific party that is signing the contract has the authority to bind that company, and that the company name is correct, otherwise the other party could argue the contract is voidable If the contract were voidable, you have the risk of not being able to enforce the contract or being able to pursue any of the remedies. The second aspect of defining the parties to the contract is that it will highlight any time the supplier's entity is not the parent company. If the contract is with a supplier's subsidiary or affiliate, that's who your contract is with and you would be limited to only being able to seek recovery from that subsidiary or affiliate, unless the supplier parent company was made part of the contract by providing what is called a parent or company guarantee. If you contract only with the subsidiary or affiliate, depending upon their size and assets, this could substantially reduce the amounts you could recover in the event of a problem with their performance. It does you little good negotiating terms and conditions only to find out that the entity signing the contract doesn't have the assets or resources to meet those commitments, so if there is the potential for major cost or risks being involved in the relationship. Always try to get a supplier entity that has the assets and resources to stand behind the commitments to be a party to the contract. Either having the contract be with that entity, or have them provide a guarantee for their subsidiary can do that.

Intent of the parties entering the contract (recitals). As we discussed in the basics on contract law, in the event of a dispute the courts will use the rules of contract construction to interpret contracts to determine the parties' intent. As you are limited to what's within the "four corners of the contract" in that review a recitals section of the contract will basically explain what the intent and/or circumstances where that led up to the contract that helps establish the intent of the parties. From a cost or risk perspective the main risk is that without it, your intent may not be clear and the courts will determine the intent by the contract itself, only looking to parol evidence where it is unclear.

Obligations of the parties. The obligations of the individual parties may be spelled out either within the contract or may be established in the statement of work or specifications. As we found out about how courts will interpret a contract, you should realize that what you want the other party to do needs to be included within the four corners of the contract or it may not be enforceable. Everything that was important to you in making the decision to purchase the product or service from the supplier such as representations about what they would do, how the product would perform all need to be captured as part of their obligations or the risk is you may wind up purchasing something that doesn't work for you, meet your needs, require additional work or correction which can add substantially to your cost. Since specifications and statements of work need to become part of the contract to establish the obligations of the parties, they also need to be checked to ensure that all that has been promised is included in them. Just like terms of the contract they also need to be written using language that established the right standard of commitment for the supplier's performance. For example a quality specification that says that the supplier "should" do something doesn't obligate the supplier to do it. If it's critical you need language that established firm commitments by using "shall" or "will" take certain actions. In a later paragraph I'll highlight some of the keys in writing good specifications / statement of work.

Contract term. As we learned one of the excuses from performance under the contract is if the contract were to lapse. This means that the selection of the term of the contract is important if you have a long-term program that may require performance over an extended period of time. Another reason to be concerned about the term of the contract is that once the contract has lapsed, the supplier no longer is required to honor the terms of the contract except for those that were included in a "survival" provision and suppliers could use this along with your need for continuing performance to simply change your price or the terms they will agree to so the risk with the terms is primarily financial as you may wind up paying more and getting less if you don't manage the terms correctly. If you want to manage against this risk you either need to have a long enough term so you know all work is completed, or you need to have a way built into your contract where it either self extends in limited increments unless either party provides notice of their intention to not have it extend, have an option to extend it for a pre-agreed term, or have a method by which you have advance notice of what the supplier will do so you can plan accordingly.

Changes or modifications to the contract. In most companies you want to have control over who on your side may agree to changes and for the supplier, you also have the issue of whether the party agreeing to the change has the authority to makes the change which could potentially make the change unenforceable. So most contract will require that changes may only be made by certain authorize parties or the contract may delegate authority to certain individuals or authorize the use of certain processes or tools to make limited changes to the contract. The main risk associated with this is making sure that you get what you negotiated and that well-meaning individuals aren't making changes to the contract without getting the appropriate consideration for making those changes. The other risk is without the controls being in place, you could have individuals that have apparent authority be authorizing changes and additional work that adds to your cost.

Price. The pricing terms will establish the price that you will pay for the product or service and pricing should include the pricing terms should include pricing for any future items that you may need or want to buy from the supplier. If the contract contemplates repetitive purchases over time you would include the prices based on the various items and volumes both for current and future purchases. If you will need to purchase spare parts, repairs or maintenance services or upgrades, there is no time better than with the initial purchase to establish what the cost of those items will be so you can control the life cycle cost or the product or service. The biggest risk to manage in negotiating the pricing is being able to control the cost of those future purchases especially if you are not dealing with a commodity type of product where multiple sources of supply would be available. As part of the pricing section you would always state the currency of the purchase so there is no confusion. For example if you said dollars that could mean US dollars, Canadian dollars, Australian dollars, Hong Kong dollars, Taiwan dollars, Singapore dollars, etc., State the price in both words and numbers (in event of a conflict the written amount would have priority over the number). The major issue cost issue in the price that will be paid is any foreign exchange risk that may exist if you commit to make payments in another currency.

Payment Terms. Payment terms don't just establish the number of days in which to make a payment, they may also establish the requirements for a payment to be due, such as the work or product must be accepted and the supplier must submit a correct and "conforming" invoice. They must provide all of the detail that payment term requires be included on the invoice that would allow you accounts payable function to do things like match the supplier's invoice to your. The major cost issue in payment terms is simply cash flow, and the time value of money where the longer you can hold onto and get the benefit of the money involved the better it is for you. On vary small purchases this may not mean much, but across a large company the cumulative value of a difference between 30 and 45 or 45 and 60 day payment terms can be substantial.

Delivery Terms. From a legal perspective the delivery terms that you select will determine when the title and risk of loss transfer from the supplier to the buyer. Delivery terms should include both the specific delivery term, such as FOB, Ex-Works and the specific delivery location where delivery will occur. In a contract you always want both as the difference in costs may be different depending upon the specific delivery location, so you don't want to give the supplier flexibility to ship it from another location where it could cost you more unless you specifically agree to it. From a cost perspective the delivery term will determine when the responsibility for the cost of delivery such as freight, duties, freight forwarders, or custom's brokers will transfer from the supplier to the buyer. From a risk perspective the delivery term will determine who is responsible for any loss or damage that will occur to the items while they are in transit. The delivery terms may also impact cost and risk of any other activities that may be linked to when delivery occurs. Payment obligations, periods of time in which to accept or reject the product or when the warranty commences may be tied to delivery of the product or service and there could be a significant difference depending on whether delivery occurred at the supplier location or your location. For example if you purchased a piece of equipment in Asia that needed to be shipped to your location in the United States by surface shipment, it could take 30 days to do that. If you tied payment to delivery, and per your delivery term the delivery occurred at the suppliers dock, you could wind having to pay for it before you receive it losing any cash flow value the payment terms provide. If you had the same thirty days to accept it, you could wind up having your right to accept or reject lapse prior to its actual delivery at your location. If you have a warranty of 12 months and that was tied to delivery, you would be losing a full month of the warranty benefit while it is in transit. Depending upon the delivery term you may need to adjust your other terms to ensure you don't lose those benefits. For example instead of a 12-month warranty, you could go after a 13-month warranty so you get the full 12 months benefit of the warranty. For a good understanding of the specific delivery terms and what the responsibilities of the parties are under each, I would suggest that you buy a copy of the "Incoterms" that are published by the International Chamber of Commerce.

Warranties and Representations. As we learned earlier a warranty is a representation of a fact or a representation of performance. As a warranty, if the fact or performance were not true (meaning the fact isn't true or the performance isn't as committed) that would constitute a breach of the contract. Under a breach of the contract, if the breach is un-cured by the supplier the buyer could claim damages and may terminate the contract for cause. Lets look at several common warranties:

It has the right to enter into this contract	The purpose of this is primarily for enforcement to show that they had the right to enter into the contract so the contract isn't voidable.
Performance will comply with applicable laws	The purpose of this is to both set expectations on their performance but also to be able to recover the cost of any damages sustained by the buyer if the supplier failed to comply with such requirements. If would also give the buyer the right to terminate the contract if the supplier was not complying and failed to cure that after receiving notice from the buyer.
No claims or lien exist or is threatened	The purpose of this is to avoid having to pay any additional cost beyond the purchase price because a claim or lien clouds the title.
Products are free from defects in material and workmanship	This is the normal product warranty for which the supplier will be obligate to provide a repair, replacement of possibly refund or credit of the purchase price if a defect in the product occurs. If you wanted to recover more than just your direct costs sustained, in addition to the warranty you would need a separate provision such as an Epidemic Defect provision that would allow the recovery of incidental or consequential costs

Products are free of defects in design	This is included so if there was a defect in the design of the product that couldn't be cured, you could terminate the contract for cause without being liable for any commitments. Further it would allow for the ability to collect direct damages associate with the defect,
Products are safe for use	This is included for several purposes. If there was a safety problem that couldn't be cured, you could terminate with cause and without liability for any commitments made. It would also provide for the ability to recover any direct damages associated with the problem
Products are new and do not contain used or reconditioned parts	For you to sell your product as new, all parts of the product must be new, and selling you a used or recondition product would not only be of less value, it could cause you to sell your product for less value. To prevent that you ask for a warranty that the product is new
Services will be performed in a good workmanlike manner using reasonable care and skill and in accordance with the relevant specification	This is used to primarily set the standard of performance. If performance was problematic you could claim breach and if that breach was not cured, you could terminate the contract and sue for any damages sustained.

Limitation of liability. The traditional limitation of liability provision will have several main sections.

The first is the general limitation of liability that will preclude the parties rights to claim damages other than direct damages
 "Neither party shall be liable to the other party for indirect, consequential, special damages or for loss of profits or revenue".
This limits both what the buyer can recover but it also limits what the supplier can recover from the buyer to only direct damages

If there are certain sections or paragraphs where you would need something more than direct damages because of the nature of the problem or costs you would need a carve out from the limitation
 "The above limitation shall not apply to sections ___ and ___,

The third portion is supplier will want to limit their liability to a specific dollar amount. In general there are several types of liability that will exist under the contract. For example there will be contractual liability for things like the breach of the contract. There may be liability associate with third party claims for either personal injury or property damage caused by the supplier, their personnel, subcontractors or their product, There may also be third party liability for claims of intellectual property infringement, Lastly the contract may contain certain sections where you need to recover other than direct damages, The key here is if you negotiate a single limitation amount, that amount would apply to all claims so you either need to have that amount be high enough to cover all the potential costs and risks, or you need to separate it out and establish different limits for the different types of potential liabilities. The other key in negotiating caps that the amount is the basis or frequency of the cap. If you just establish a cap, it will apply to the entire contract, as long as that contract is in effect. Alternative to that can be to negotiate caps that are linked to sales where when the amount of sale increases the cap increases, make it an annual cap, so the full amount refreshes every year, or tie it to a per incident situation. As this is the biggest way the supplier may transfer cost and risk to the buyer, this is one of the most important clauses in any negotiation.

The last portion is the buyer limiting their liability. Unless you have specific firm purchase commitments you have made or have included confidentiality provision in the contract, the buyer's primary obligation is to pay for the products or services ordered and in most cases the buyer would limit their liability to the amount of the orders made, but not yet paid for.

From a cost or risk perspective, the limit of liability provision has a huge potential cost and risk impact on the buyer as:
- It creates limitations on the types of damages that the buyer may claim
- It can create limitations on the amount of damages the buyer may recover where the buyer would be assuming the risk and cost of any damages in excess of that amount.
- It is needed to limit the types of damages and the amount of damage the buyer may sustain if the buyer were to breach the contract. For example without it, if the buyer breached the contract the supplier could potentially seek damages for lost revenue, lost profits, special and incidental costs, etc.

Insurance. There are a number of different types of insurances that a buyer may want to require a supplier to maintain as part of the contract. The most common are Comprehensive General Liability that is intended to cover personal injury or property damage caused by the supplier, suppliers workers or subcontractors, Workers Compensation or Employers Liability Insurance is intended to cover any injury to supplier's own personnel. Automobile Liability covers personal injury and property damage cause by a vehicle driven by supplier or supplier's employees. In addition there could be other types of insurances that may be required depending on what you are purchasing such as Errors and Omissions for any design or consulting liability, insurance on stored materials and completed operations still under the supplier's control. In addition a contract may also require bonds that are usually issued by insurance companies such as performance (covers any increased cost of re-procurement if supplier fails to perform), payment (covers and costs should the supplier not pay its subcontractors and suppliers) and fidelity (to cover potential theft by the supplier's employees.) For the basic liability provisions (General, Auto and Workers compensation) what the insurance provisions do is provide protection that stands behind the general indemnification. A general indemnification does not do much good if the supplier has no assets to stand behind it or could easily move assets to another company to avoid the liability, so insurance provisions provide the guarantee that you will at least have the value of the insurance policy that could be collected if you can't collect from the supplier.

Termination without cause. Buyers use the termination without cause provision mostly in three situations. One is the relationship with the supplier is not working, and performance is not bad enough to terminate for cause. A second is the business needs or reasons for the contract may have changed and it requires the buyer to mover in an alternative direction. A third is the buyer has identified another source that can provide the product or service better or cheaper. The issues that you encounter in the negotiation of a termination for convenience clause will have remedies for the supplier that vary based on the nature of what you are buying. For example, if you are buying a custom product, they may want to be covered to all their costs associated with the cancellation such as materials on order, in inventory, the cost of any work in progress, etc., For example, in a service contract involving personnel, they may want to be reimbursed for reasonable down time until the personnel can be re-assigned. The most difficult negotiation of termination without cause provisions are usually with suppliers that made significant investment to win the business and will now have a major gap in their production schedule that they need to fill and they will normally want the cost to terminate to be substantial so that cost of termination will need to be taken into account in determining when it will be used. Many times you may be able to reduce the cost of termination simply by committing that if the work is started again within a certain period of time, they will be given the business subject to mutual agreement on any changes to the cost needed to complete the work.

Termination for cause. The main use of a termination for cause provisions is when the performance is continually failing to meet the commitments of the contract and is affecting the buyer and their costs in a number of ways. For example, if a supplier is having a consistent problem with quality, that will be creating both direct and indirect costs for the buyer in terms or higher inventory levels, more re-work, additional management, etc. etc. In the negotiation of a termination for cause provision, the main issues that you negotiate are:

1. The acts that give rise to termination for cause.
2. The period of time in which the party has the right to cure the breach.
3. The rights and obligations of the parties resulting from the termination.

While normally you may be able to simply agree that termination may occur for any material breach of the contract, there may be times when you need to spell out the specific provisions that can give rises to termination. Number 1 on the suppliers will always be payment by the buyer. For a buyer the key provisions would always include breach of any warranties or separate representations, the bankruptcy of the supplier and the failure to meet the various performance and delivery requirements in the contract. Part of that may be the negotiation of various performance standards that constitute a breach. For example how late must a delivery be for it to be a breach or be counted towards a breach? How many times must something occur before it becomes a breach?

As part of any negotiation, the issue of cure is important and it may require clarifying what is subject to a cure and what is not. For example, if you have confidentiality obligations in your contract that the supplier breached, that may not be subject to cure as there is no way to remedy that type of breach and the damage done. Also as part of the negotiation for the items that you will allow a cure period to correct, you may need different cure periods depending upon what is breached. One of the problems that I've always been concerned with is repetitive breaches and cures where the performance is a problem but they continue to cure within the cure period. To deal with that I've included language in contracts where there is a limit on the number of times they may cure the breach and once reached, the next breach would not have the ability to cure and that would constitute grounds for termination. In the negotiation of a termination for cause provisions I've seen some suppliers want to be compensated for their costs for any finished goods, work in process, and customer materials they have or can't cancel. To me this is like rewarding them for bad behavior since they were the ones that breach the contract and I've consistently avoided paying them anything. It was their problem of performance that caused the termination in the first place and the cost of that should be an expense to them and not the buyer who may not have any value or use for the products.

Confidentiality. The receipt of another party's confidential information creates both a duty to manage the information and confidential and a liability if you fail to properly manage the information. The receipt of another party's confidential information also creates a potential risk if the information is used by recipient in their product. It makes not difference whether the use was intentional or inadvertent. The unauthorized use creates an infringement of the disclosing party's intellectual property rights. As such most companies include confidentiality provisions to limit and control the receipt of another party's confidential information as a way of managing the risk. For example, they may include language that says that everything exchanged is non-confidential and if it is confidential it would need to be managed under a separate non-disclosure agreement.

Consequences / remedies for breach. In specific sections of the contract you may establish specific remedies that will apply for failure to meet the requirement of an individual term. Those remedies can be extremely broad such as would occur if you said "In addition to all remedies set forth in this contract, buyer shall have all remedies available at law or in equity". The remedies may be included in a single section such as for on-time deliveries, you may establish specific remedies or consequence if the supplier failed to meet the delivery date which could range from canceling the order without, liability, having the supplier pay for costs of expedited shipment, or requiring the supplier to take extra steps or investments to prevent future late deliveries such as establishing on site stocking at no charge. In warranty provisions you could have language that allows you to have warranty work performed by others with the supplier bearing the cost if they fail to meet their obligations, or you could require that they stock replacement material at their cost and risk. These additional remedies are intended to reduce the risk or cost of the non-performance by the supplier, prevent on-going occurrences, or transfer the cost and risk back to the supplier. Here's another example, you could agree to a specific response time for providing replacement of defective products or warranty returns based on average number of failures, but could have requirements that require shorter response time the more frequently the problem occurs as each problem adds additional cost of risk to the buyer. Quality or warranty problems require carrying additional inventory levels to deal with higher than normal levels of defective products and that adds to the buyer's costs. With some of the remedies or consequences the goal is to push the cost of the problem back to the supplier. A good example of this is having the right to do inspection or rejection of products by lot. That would allow you to send the entire lot back if you find a certain number of defects. This avoids the cost of the buyer having to inspect all to determine if they are good or bad and pushes that cost back to the supplier.

Disputes. There are several ways that disputes may be managed. They can be resolved between the parties through a problem escalation process, the parties can agree to use a third party such as an arbitrator to decide for them, or the dispute can be litigated in the courts. Each approach has its own advantages and disadvantages. Problem escalation may resolve a number of disputes simply because the matter is being heard by individual that may not be directly involved in the "heat of the battle" and can look at the issue from a broader perspective, but there is no guarantee there will be agreement. Most companies do not like to use arbitration, as they believe that it is too easy to commence a claim, and the decision of the arbitrator may be biased. For disputes that would be litigated in the courts, the contract should establish which law will govern and where the case must be brought (jurisdiction). For example if you were a buyer in New York and were dealing with a supplier in California and only specified that the applicable law be New York law, if your company had legal presence in California such as a sales office, the supplier could commence the action in the courts in California and serve your California office where you would then have to defend the action in California, but the California court would have to interpret the contract in accordance with the laws of New York. If you wanted to make sure that the action was heard in a New York court, you would need to specify that the jurisdiction for commencement of any actions is either the courts of the State of New York or the Federal Court in the State of New York. If you didn't want to have to defend it any place in New York, you could be specific on which court it would be heard in. Each party will want the applicable law and jurisdiction to be most favorable to them.

General Indemnification. Under the theory of agency, the buyer may be liable for the negligent or intentional acts of the supplier, the supplier's employees and the supplier's subcontractors. If buyer purchase a product from the supplier and resells that product, by being part of the sales chain, the buyer may also be liable to 3rd parties for personal injury or property damage that is caused by the supplier's product. To protect against the risks and costs of those potential 3rd party claims most buyer's contracts will require the supplier to "defend, indemnify, and hold harmless" the buyer from such claims. The requirement to "defend" makes it the supplier's responsibility to pay for all legal costs associated with the defense of the claim. The requirement to "indemnify" makes the supplier be responsible to pay all costs or damages awarded by the courts that the buyer may be required to pay. The requirement of "hold harmless" eliminates the supplier making a claim against the buyer for actions caused by the supplier's negligent or intentional acts. From a cost and risk perspective the goal is to transfer all cost and risk of actions by the supplier to the supplier to both avoid those costs and to avoid the impact any claim like that would have on the buyer's cost of insurance as rates vary with the incidence of claims.

Intellectual Property Indemnification. Third parties may make claims against the buyer for infringement of their intellectual property rights if the buyer or the supplier caused that infringement. If the claim is based on the product or service that was provided by the supplier, there could be an injunction against further use; there could be royalties that need to be paid for what has already been used or sold. It could require the replacement of infringing items with non-infringing items so the potential risk and cost to the buyer could be substantial. In a traditional Intellectual property indemnification provision you would have many of the same terms as the General Indemnification. It will require the supplier to "defend, indemnify, and hold harmless" the buyer from such claims. The requirement to "defend" makes it the supplier's responsibility to pay for all legal costs associated with the defense of the claim. The requirement to "indemnify" makes the supplier be responsible to pay all costs or damages awarded by the courts that the buyer may be ordered to pay. The requirement of "hold harmless" eliminates the supplier making a claim against the buyer for actions caused by the supplier's negligent or intentional acts. In addition to the indemnification, an IP indemnity provision will usually include specific remedies that the supplier is required to perform as a result of the infringement such as get a license from the Intellectual Property owner to use their IP, Provide a product that is not infringing. The more you need or are locked into using the specific product, the more important having these alternative remedies becomes. Traditionally the major point in this negotiation is who can decide which remedy is implemented. The supplier will want to have the option to take the remedy that is the least expensive for them. The buyer will want the remedy that is the least expensive and has the least impact on their business to manage the potential cost and revenue impact. The last part of any IP indemnity provision is exclusions that the supplier may have from providing the indemnity, such as claims resulting from their following a buyer provided design. As exclusions eliminate your ability to recover any costs, any exclusion needs to be clear and carefully drafted.

Recovery of Attorney's fees. If a claim goes to litigation the old saying that "only the lawyers will win" is probably true. The cost of litigation can be substantial and in claims made against the buyer by 3rd parties such as for personal injuries, property damage or infringement, if the plaintiff wins they will normally be awarded attorneys fees that can be substantial. So being able to collect for attorney's fees is being able to recover a potential cost. One of the tactics that I've seen in negotiation of attorney's fees with a supplier is their desire to include a reasonableness standard on attorney's fees. As between the buyer and supplier limiting the liability to reasonable attorney's fees may be acceptable as it protects both parties from excessive costs. It is not OK when dealing with 3rd party claims where legal fees are part of the courts award. That's what the buyer would need to pay the 3rd party and that's what the supplier needs to pay the buyer. If you included a reasonableness standard on legal fees including in a 3rd party award, it would do two things. It would allow the supplier to delay payment while the concept of the reasonableness gets agreed or litigated. It creates a situation where the buyer may get less from the supplier than what they were ordered to pay creating an additional cost to the buyer.

Notices. The requirement to provide a notice to the other party may exist in a number of clauses. For example if you were going to terminate for convenience or wanted the supplier to cure the breach of the contract, you would need to provide them notice. If the supplier is allowed to stop producing a product that you use, you may require and "end of life" notice. You could have a contract where the term self extends unless either party provides notice of their intent not to extend it. If the supplier is allowed to make periodic price adjustments you may want advance notice of any price changes so you can take appropriate actions. A notice section within a contract will usually define who the notices must be provided to for them to be effective, how notices must be provided, and when notices are effective. For example, if you sent a supplier a "Notice to Cure" a breach, its important to be able to establish that it was delivered to the required party, and when it was delivered as their obligation to cure and your clock for when you could proceed to terminate is normally tied to a certain period after their receipt of the notice. The risk of costs associated with the notices provision is if you fail to follow the specific requirements of the notices provision, the notice may not be effective, which would prevent you from taking certain desired actions until you do it correctly

Entire agreement or merger provisions. In the rules of contract construction we learned that courts would look only to the four corners of the contract to interpret the intent of the parties. An "entire agreement" or "merger" clause re-affirms that and basically says that the parties agree that the contract represents the final agreement of the parties on the subject matter and that any and all prior agreements discussions or document have been merged into the contract so the full intent of the parties is expressed there. There is nothing wrong with this type of provision, it just requires that you make sure that if there was discussions, promises, commitments and other document that were part of the motivation to get you to agree to sign the contract, they need to be addressed in or made part of the contract or they will not apply. The main risk is if you failed to capture everything within the contract you could wind up getting less that what you believe was committed or promised and correcting that could cost additional money.

Severability of clauses. All a severability clause does is tell the courts that the intent of the parties is not to have the contract voided or voidable if a specific clause becomes unenforceable or illegal. In agreeing to a severability clause the parties are saying that they will look to the courts to determine the intent of the parties or to insert a term in the interpretation of the contract based on prior dealings between the parties or common trade practice. This clause eliminates the risk that your entire contract could be unenforceable of a single clause became unenforceable of illegal.

Time of the essence provisions. When inserted into a specific section or the contract a "time is of the essence" standard would require that the specific date or times for performance must interpreted exactly. It can also help establish that the breach of a specific date or time for performance is a material breach. The risk that a "time of the essence" standard is used for is to prevent delays that may be legally acceptable, but would not be acceptable for you. For example, if you had a major event and ordered materials for that event, receiving them after the event would not be acceptable, so you would establish a delivery date prior to the event, make it clear that time is of the essence for that delivery, and if the supplier fails to delivery by that date you may terminate the contract for cause effective immediately and try to avoid any liability of cost if the supplier delivered it after the needed date. It clearly puts the supplier on notice that the date is fixed and must be met.

Survival. Upon the termination or expiration of a contract, all terms are no longer applicable between the parties. As the parties recognize that there are activities and actions that will need to extend beyond the term of the contract, they will include a "survival" provision where both parties mutually agree upon which of the contract terms will survive the termination or expiration of the contract and be applicable for that period after the contract has expired or been terminated. For example any provision dealing with potential future liability such as taxes, warranties, Indemnification will need to survive. Terms that would be used to interpret the contract and the liabilities under it such as limitations of liability, order of precedence, merger, and severability of clauses would need to survive. Terms addressing potential litigation between the parties on those surviving obligations such as the choice of law, forum or jurisdiction, limitation of actions, waivers of jury trials would also need to survive. There may be other obligations that, depending on the nature of the relationship will need to survive. If you ordered a product prior to the expiration of the contract and the product was delivered to you after the expiration, you would want all the terms of the contract to apply to that purchase, and I'm sure that the supplier would want the buyer's obligation to make payment to also survive.

Order of precedence. Frequently contracts are made up of a number of documents. There will be the contract itself and there will also be other documents that are incorporated by reference into the contract or are incorporated by reference into a document that is incorporated by reference into the contract. There is a general presumption that all the documents will be complimentary in creating the obligations of the parties. All this creates the potential for inconsistencies between all the various documents and what an order of precedence clause does is in the event of an inconsistency, it will determine what the intent of the parties was in establishing the order of priority given to the various documents in resolving the inconsistency. For example if one document said that the supplier must do A though M and another document said that the supplier must do N through z there would be no inconsistency and the supplier would be required to do A through Z. However if one document said that the supplier had to do A within thirty days and another document said that the supplier had to do A in forty five days, there would be an inconsistency and you would need to look at the order of precedence to determine which document had priority so you could decide if it was 30 or 45 days.

Waiver. A waiver is the intentional and voluntary giving up of a right that may be done either by express statement or by one of the parties conduct (such as the buyer not enforcing a right they have under the contract against the supplier). Waiver provisions are intended to prevent the giving up of a right by conduct, so that for waver to be effective for the remainder of the term of the contract it must be done by an express statement such as amending the contract. For example is the supplier breached the contract by failing to deliver on time and you took no action in that one case, by your failure to take action you would of waived the right to take action on that breach. If the supplier continued to fail to delivery on time and you continued to let them and take no action, without a waiver clause you could be prevented from taking future actions if they were late in delivering as by your actions you would waived your right. With a waiver clause, irrespective of the number of times that you failed to take action you would still retain the right and could take action on the next or subsequent occurrences. This eliminates the risk to a party of losing the ability to enforce a contract right simply because in the past they failed to enforce that right.

Catch-all provisions for performance of work or services. Within the body of the contract or sometimes within the scope of services, statement of work or specification most companies will include a "catch all" provision such as "supplier will provide all management, plant, labor, materials and equipment necessary to perform the work" or "supplier will provide and pay for all necessary permits and fees necessary to perform the work". The goal of catch all provisions is to simply ensure that the price being paid is all-inclusive and there are no additional or hidden costs or charges that must be paid by the buyer to complete the work.

Commencement of actions. What a commencement of actions provisions will do is place a finite time limit after the cause of action has occurred for one of the parties to bring an action against the other. What this does is prevent a pilling up of claims to the end of a long term contract and it forces the claim to be made while the information about the circumstances is still fresh in the memories of the parties and while most of the parties are still available to provide their information and/or recollection of events. A commencement of action provision does not force all claims to be made in a specific period; it simply forces claims for which the party has knowledge to be brought within the required period. For example if a Commencement of actions provision required that all actions must be brought within two (2) years from the date on which the cause of action was first discovered, if there was a product liability suit against the supplier for which the buyer could be liable, the supplier would have 2 years from that date to commence action against the buyer. If two years later there was a different suit against the supplier that would be a difference cause of action, and they supplier would have two (2) years from that suit date to commence an action. The biggest risk and cost that a commencement of action suit is intended to protect against is not being able to adequately defend against a claim because the information is no longer fresh or the knowledgeable people are not available or can't be found. They may also be used for managing ensuring that invoices are prompt so they are billed against budgeted years or against end customers who benefitted from them.

Jury trial waivers. If a dispute were to be brought to court there are two ways a case may be heard. A Judge will rule on the facts and provide the appropriate award, or it can be brought to a jury who will determine the facts and the award. Under law, a plaintiff or defendant can request a jury trial. To avoid having a jury trial the contract will seek agreement by the parties to waive the right to a jury trial.

Rights to equitable remedies. contractual remedies primarily provide you with the right to collect money damages. There can be situations where money damages would not be sufficient for the potential damages you could sustain, so you may want the right to equitable remedies which are primarily injunctive relief of specific performance. For example if you provided a supplier with confidential information under a confidentiality agreement and they breached their confidentiality obligation money damages may not be enough to cover the damages you may sustain, so if you had the right to equitable remedies, you could go to the courts and seek injunctive relief to force them to stop disclosing the information in addition to being able to sue them for damages. If you contracted to purchase something that was absolutely unique and could not be procured elsewhere and the supplier refused to later sell it to you, if you had the right of injunctive relief you could seek an order for "specific performance" where the courts would order the supplier to transfer it to you. One of the advantages of injunctive relief is if the court orders it and the other party fails to do it, it becomes contempt of the court's order which can result in criminal charges. The risk of not having equitable remedies provided for in your contract is simply limiting the types of remedies that may apply which may be inadequate for the type of damage that could be sustained.

Representation of authority by signing parties. As we learned, if a contract is signed by a party that does not have the authority to enter into the contract on behalf of their company, such a contract is voidable. As the goal is to create an enforceable contract, one way of reducing the risk of having the contract be voidable is to require the parties to the contract to represent that they are duly authorized to sign the contract and that may be done by a separate clause or simply noting within the Signature Block the words "Duly Authorized" or "Authorized Representative". If the individual that signed the contract wasn't authorized to sign, the company may still be able to void the contract, but the other party may be able to go after the signer of the contract personally for fraud as they represented that they were authorized.

Force Majeure. A force majeure event creates an excusable delay in performance for the period of the force majeure. The most commonly negotiated things within a force majeure provision are the events that constitute a force majeure. For example in addition to the normal natural disasters, wars or embargoes, a supplier may want labor actions such as strikes or lockouts to be a force majeure event. I've had some that wanted to have the failure of their subcontractors or suppliers to perform to constitute a force majeure. As a buyer you traditionally want to limit the events to things that are strictly beyond the supplier's control. A strike may be beyond their control, but a lockout isn't as it would be the supplier that is preventing the union members from working. Simply saying that you can't perform because your suppliers or subcontractors didn't perform shouldn't be acceptable as they should have tools in place to protect against such non-performance or it should be limited to when the subcontract is unable to perform because of acts of god. Another issue that may need to be addressed in creating a force majeure provision is what is the impact to you if you were to receive the performance at some time in the future when they have been able to recover? Do you still need or want the product? Should you have the right to terminate any orders without liability if they are unable to recover within a specific period? The key cost or risk points in a force majeure situation is what, if any, impact will there be if you receive performance as a much later date where you may no longer want or need it, or may have needed to procure your needs from another supplier in the interim?

Assignment, In an assignment, the party making the assignment is transferring rights and obligations to a third party. Many times the reason why you selected a supplier in the first place and agreed to pay the price was because the work was going to be done by them and not some third party. Likewise a supplier may have agreed to sell to you at certain terms and pricing based on their dealing with your company not some third party. So most contracts will either prohibit the assignment of the contract, or require approval of the other party where consent to the assignment would not be unreasonably withheld or delayed. For both parties the restriction against assignment can be a problem if there were to want to sell the business that is associated with the contract, so some assignment provisions may allow assignment without consent if the major portion of the Business associated with the contract is sold to a third party. There are two types of assignment. An assignment only would have the original party remain secondarily liable under the contract. An assignment and novation would excuse the original party from liability and the party whose contract was assigned would only be able to look to the new entity. The risks to the buyer under an assignment fall into either the potential loss of value or the ability to recover potential costs or damages from the new party. For example, if you contracted to have Michelangelo paint a picture, you wouldn't want that to be assigned to Joe Smith. For example, assume that you had a substantial amount of products that you purchased from the supplier in which you could have potential warranty, defect, or third party liability claims, you wouldn't want to have the contract be assigned and novated to a new company that didn't have the assets or resources to meet the contact commitments.

Depending on what you purchase or license, the marketplace you operate in, the risks associated with the purchase, or the risks associated in dealing with the specific supplier, there are a number of additional provisions that you may want or need to include in your contract, but making sure that you start with at least these will provide you with a good starting point.

CHAPTER 10 NEGOTIATION BASICS

Negotiation is the ability to convince the other party to change their position to provide you with increased value at lesser costs or risks. There are three primary ways to do this:

- You can demand they give you what you want if they want your business (take it or leave it)
- You can provide them with good reasons to agree to your position
- You can explain the problem(s) their position is creating, and work to solve the problem.

To drive significant concessions requires three things:
- The supplier must need or want your business.
- You must have competition or alternatives that can meet your needs and,
- The supplier must fear they will lose your business.

The combination of the three forms "competitive leverage".

Since the majority of procurement negotiations are also with the supplier's sales organization there is one additional dynamic they may take place in agreeing to significant concessions and that's how much of a commitment will it be and when will they see the revenue. If it isn't going to give them immediate returns, their need or wanting the business may be less. This means that a take it or leave it approach only works well when those four things are in place. The less leverage you have, the more you need to sell the supplier on why they need to provide the concessions. You can sell your position by either providing the supplier with reasons why your position is logical and reasonable, or you can explain the problem(s) their position is creating and provide them with the impact that will have on either the purchase or longer term relationship such as the total cost impact of doing business with them.

To reason with the supplier or explain the problem requires that you set their expectations of what you need and why you need it. This does two things. First, it creates a starting point for the negotiation (sometimes referred to an "anchor"). Second, it allows your counterpart at the supplier to also set expectations with their management of what it will take for them to win the business. It's important to have those supplier internal expectations set, as most of the time for you to get a significant concessions it will require higher-level approvals within the supplier's management.

Reasoning and explaining needs to be a strong part of your overall portfolio of tactics to get the desired result. If you use tactics alone, but don't create convincing arguments to reason with them or explain the problem, your tactics probably won't work. For example, everyone knows the price negotiation tactic "you have to do better". On its own the tactic may get limited success. When you use it and then can explain why they need to do better and what problems their current pricing is creating that will impact them, it provides a more convincing argument. suppliers need to be convinced that their position will impact them getting the business either today or in the future. If they think they'll get the business anyway, there is no incentive to change their position. It's uncertainty that creates the fear of losing the business and the incentive to change their position.

Much of negotiation is setting and managing expectations. Suppliers do that from the beginning with all their "legitimacy" tactics such as price lists, discount structures, standard agreements, etc. Let me give you an example of what I mean about setting expectations. If you send the supplier a copy of your contract without setting the right expectations in advance of what's important and what you are willing to negotiate, don't be surprised when it comes back to you with the supplier wanting to make many changes you won't like. To set expectations and sell what your need, you need to thoroughly understand everything you are negotiating, what it means, the impact, the risks, how each item impacts you from a cost, total cost, or life cycle cost perspective. You also need to understand the business problem or problems certain positions create. That's why we're focusing on building that knowledge!

10.1 Negotiation Strategies

Negotiation strategies can be zero sum, win-win or problem solving. **Zero Sum** is based on the assumption that there is a single universe to be carved up in which for you to get a piece of the pie, the supplier must give that up. For you to avoid a risk, the supplier must assume it. For you to reduce your price, the supplier must reduce their profit. In Zero Sum negotiations you:
- Find the supplier's minimum they will accept
- Negotiate toward their minimum
- Manage the perception of your acceptable position

The primary use of Zero Sum negotiations is basic buying or selling relationships.

Win-Win or Problem Solving. The assumption in win-win or problem solving strategy is that you are not limited to a zero sum, what you are looking for is something that is acceptable to both parties. It could include different factors than zero sum negotiations. In win-win or problem solving you:
- Try to separate people from problems and move from positions to needs.
- Establish objective criteria for discussion
- Try to Invent options for mutual gain
- Problem solve to produce positive result

The primary use is for these strategies are in relationship building, or where supplier's has more leverage in the relationship than the buyer.

Frequently the biggest obstacle to getting the best cost and terms is not the supplier or the negotiation approach. It's the actions that occur within buyer's company that impact negotiation leverage. This is like self-inflicted wounds, but instead of shooting yourself in the foot, someone else is pulling the trigger. Successfully negotiations require that the procurement process be managed from end to end in a manner where leverage is created and maintained by all individuals who are in contact with the supplier until the agreement is reached. You won't get the best cost and terms if :
- Development or User sourcing activities commence and the procurement is an afterthought.
- You invest substantial money in one supplier before concluding negotiations, which makes changing suppliers more costly than any price difference.
- You allow time to trap you into using one supplier, where changing suppliers will significantly impact your desired schedule or time leaves you with no other choice.

- Your focus is strictly on time to market, and the supplier knows that.
- The supplier knows they are the only one who can meet your schedule.
- The supplier knows that you need them more than they need you.
- Every person on the team doesn't stress the need for it to be competitive.
- You aren't prepared when you negotiate.
- You and your customers don't ask for or set the expectation that a better deal is needed to win the business.

10.2 Phases of Negotiation

For many suppliers the negotiation process really begins during the conceptual development of the product or service. The buyer's negotiator normally doesn't become involved in the negotiation process until their internal customer has identified a need or desire to make the purchase, which can be several steps after the supplier has already started steps toward the negotiation. The primary exception to this is when a custom product being developed so the buyer is involved from the conceptual phase onward.

The important thing to understand is that negotiation is not a single point in time activity. It occurs in one form or another throughout all phases of the relationship. Here are three important things you need to remember: How well you manage all the activities leading up to the formal negotiation will have a major impact on how successful you'll be in the negotiation and whether your tactics will work. How well you manage all the activities following the formal negotiation will determine how much of the value you negotiated you'll actually keep. Anything left un-managed will always cost more.

Based on these three simple concepts, my phases of negotiations consist of
- Conceptual planning
- Product or service development
- Marketing and prospecting
- Pre-qualification by buyer
- Bid. Quote, Proposal Stage
- Review and Planning / Preparation
- Negotiation and Agreement (multiple sessions)
- Mobilization
- Performance
- Changes
- Close out
- Warranty
- Claims

As the Conceptual Planning, product or Service Development, Marketing and prospecting phases are primarily managed by the supplier, we'll jump to the prequalification phase.

John C. Tracy

CHAPTER 11. USING PREQUALIFICATION TO PREPARE TO NEGOTIATE

When many buyers do pre-qualifications, the pre-qualification activity is focused on the ability of the Suppler to perform the work. Do they have the necessary finances, technology, capability, capacity, quality, and design and support structures? While pre-qualification is important to help manage against problems that occur if you select the wrong supplier, what buyers almost always miss is the fact that the pre-qualifications should be multi-dimensional. While it's important to make sure that the supplier is qualified to perform the work or provide the product, it's equally important to evaluate the supplier from a cost perspective and also evaluate the supplier and what the supplier does, and how they do it for future use in your negotiations.

In a traditional supplier pre-qualification activity you could do the following:

- Solicit and review preliminary Information as part of a screening out process
- Conduct an interview with the supplier
- Ask for a tour their facility
- Evaluate key supplier activities
- Have them present a representative product or project to show what they have done.
- Review staffing issues and concerns
- Check the supplier references
- Perform supplier financial evaluations
- Review subcontractors, material suppliers
- Evaluate the suppliers product or service on a technical basis for compliance with requirements

The more you know about what they do, how they do it, who they do it with, who they do it for, and what issues or problems they have, the better prepared you are for the negotiation. The more you can compare them against the competition and highlight risks or shortcomings, the more leverage you have to create hurdles they need to overcome to keep in the running. They either need to prove that the risk or shortcomings don't exist, or they need to provide concessions or price reductions to level the playing field. You should use the chance you have as part of pre-qualification to probe for as much information as they are willing to provide you to better evaluate them. suppliers will share much more information and provide you with greater access to people who will provide you with important information during the pre-qualification stage than you will ever receive once the negotiation starts.

Interviews are the time to probe to get information about all aspects of the supplier to understand the character of the supplier, the risks and the opportunities. Getting a sample part will tell you whether the part meets the requirements, but it doesn't tell you anything about the supplier. Any time you find a situation where there is a huge problem with a supplier or the suppliers performance, you'll probably find that if someone had taken the time to thoroughly interview the supplier and fully check them out, you probably wouldn't have done business with them. For any major Procurement, the cost of conducting a detailed interview and evaluation will pay for itself if you can eliminate potential problem suppliers, and the information gained will also help negotiate a better deal and better cost. One of the critical pieces of any interview is the tour of their facility. It's like you're a spy dropped behind enemy lines with the job to do as much reconnaissance as possible to win the war, except in this instance they've invited you in and have given you access to the critical information you need.

One of the things I always asked for was a tour of their facility, from receipt of raw materials to shipment of finished goods. A tour like that provides the opportunity to check for issues or problems.

- Receiving: Check who their suppliers are and the level of purchase (raw, sub-assembly, assembly, finished product). Understanding who their suppliers are will allow you to better assess the cost of the materials being purchased, their quality, reliability etc. Any shortcomings in their raw material supply base should be highlighted to either allow for them to be changed or provide the lead for negotiating a lower price based on perceived risks of using them.
- Warehousing: Check the amount of inventory and also look for supplier / vendor managed inventory presence or programs. The more they have been able to push the materials back in the supply chain, the lower their manufacturing overhead should be because they are not inventorying the goods at the raw material level.
- Process steps, Interim Inspection and test, final assembly and test: Look at the tasks being performed, the type of work, the duration or tasks, the equipment used, tools used and the total level of labor involved. This should provide a better understanding of the labor costs.
- Re-work processes: Look at the quantity, tasks, duration, equipment used, tools used, and level of labor involved. This provides you with a better understanding of their yields, scrap and re-work costs
- Pack and packaging: Look for the standards being used. This lets you understand whether your requirements are standard or unique and may carry an extra charge.
- Shipping area: Look at who their existing customers are for both the quality of customers they serve and as a source for reference check. Depending upon who the customer is and what you know about what they require from suppliers you may be able to either identify concerns which should be highlighted to provide a lead in for negotiating a lower price because of the perceived risk or having them provide assurance that there will not be problems. It also will tell you whether your requirements will be more or less than what they are accustomed to and whether your requirements may carry an extra charge.
- Customer warranty returns / repair area: Look at the quantity of returns to size the potential problems and their speed on repair, replacement, and the items being repaired or replaced. Highlight any excessive quantities to get concessions in terms or as an entry to negotiating further price reductions because of the perceived additional costs or risks to you

Have them present a representative product or project.

- What did they do?
- How did they manage the work?

While this is mostly useful to understand their understanding and capability to perform the work, any areas where you do have concerns should be highlighted so that you are showing a risk of doing business with them that may need to be offset with other concessions.

Review staffing issues and concerns

Many times when you are buying a service one of the most critical aspects is who will be performing the service. The same may apply in other areas where it may be important to understand who will be managing certain key aspects of the relationship. Understand whom they will use to manage the work for you and the relationship. If you are paying on the basis of labor, make sure that whom they propose not only has the required skills but are also being charged at an appropriate rate for their actual skills and experience. If the reason why they were successful on previous work was an individual and that individual is not assigned to this work or is no longer with the Company, highlight that as a risk.

Check references.

Always ask for the following references: 1) customer 2) Major supplier credit references, payment history, and 3) Bank references - credit lines, availability, guarantees given

There is no better way to find out about what the supplier does well or does poorly than to check with their existing customers and suppliers. Find out what the supplier included in the price to them and what may be optional cost. suppliers may want to charge you extra for things they do for other customers for free and this is one way to avoid that. Look for any area where there have been problems that you may need to address in your terms or that you may want to use as leverage from the risk you see in doing business with them versus their competition. If they have more perceived risks, those may need to be offset with other concessions.

Perform supplier financial evaluations

Look for information that will show where the supplier may have financial needs that you can use in terms of your negotiations. For example, if they have substantial cash and low cost of money, use that to get extended payment terms. If they have a shortage of cash or high financing costs, use that to get discounts for prompter payment commitments. Use any financial uncertainty to highlight risks in doing business with them versus their competition that may need to be offset with other concessions.

Review subcontractors, material suppliers.

Look at both the quality and cost competitiveness of their suppliers. Use any shortcomings as leverage to negotiate concessions or a reduction in price as a result of potential risks or cost impact that their use may create based on your past experience or knowledge.

Evaluate their product or service.

Instead of getting just what you need to evaluate the product from a technical perspective, get product to evaluate it from a cost perspective.

1. What are all the materials used and what is their cost?
2. What processes are used to manufacture to product? What do those cost?
3. How much labor was involved in manufacturing and testing the product?

If you can identify the materials and labor costs, you're half way through having what you need to negotiate cost, as all that remains is the manufacturing overhead, operating overhead and profit.

Gather the Information

After the reviews your team should be able to respond to the following 7 basic questions that will help you.

- How do they compare against their competition? Identify any areas where they unfavorably compare against the competition to use as leverage to drive concessions or cost reductions
- What is driving their costs? How much of the cost do they control and how much is controlled by others? If you understand what is driving cost, you better understand whether they will be able to provide additional discounts or longer term cost savings.
- Do they have processes and controls in place to manage cost and quality? Look for any areas where they unfavorably compare against the competition to use as leverage to drive concessions or cost reductions.
- Are there risks in doing business with them? Are they manageable? Use those risks as leverage to drive concessions or cost reductions.
- Do they have administrative processes and controls in place to efficiently meet our needs? Look for any areas where they unfavorably compare against the competition to use as leverage to drive concessions or cost reductions.
- Does our business and requirements fit within their target customer base? Will our requirements be more than, equal to, or less than what they do? If they are more, it will add cost; if it's equal, we should pay no added cost for what they already do as standard; and if it's less, it may burden their costs and impact the price if they are not be able to change it for their other customers and would have to manage our business separately.

- How efficient are they? Can the work be simplified? Look for issues to challenge them to reduce cost for increased productivity, elimination of un-necessary costs, etc.

Always look at pre-qualification of a supplier in three ways.
1. Are they qualified to do the work?
2. What is the cost impact of what I see?
3. How can I use the information I learn in the negotiation?

The traditional view would be to check to see that they have the necessary capability and capacity to do the job.

The cost view: Tour their facility. See what they are doing, how they manage the business, the tools they have. Look at who their customers are. Look at who their suppliers are to see their quality and character. Understand their process and quality steps. Look at capacity to understand how much they need your business. Look for indicators of problems (high volume in warranty or returns areas, large re-work area for production). It will give you a better understanding of the company and what is driving their cost. It will also give you an indication on how difficult it may be to drive the price down in the future if you plan on entering a long term relationship.

The negotiation view: Use all the areas where you have identified issues to either negotiate a reduction in the cost, or include contract terms and commitments to make sure that the cost of those problems aren't passed on to you. I've been in a number of negotiations where the supplier wanted to either charge additional costs because of our requirements, or fought against accepting our terms arguing that the terms required them to do something unique. If you tour their plant, you'll know what their standards are. Many times their standards were exactly the same as what we required or what they were already doing for another customer. If you don't tour their operation you'll never know what the baseline is to measure against in price in the negotiation.

CHAPTER 12 NEGOTIATION

There is no one best way in which arrange all the issues that you must negotiate. Some people recommend starting with simple, non-contentious issues to get the other party use to agreeing. That's fine when you have substantial time to negotiate or to change to an alternative supplier if you don't reach agreement. I tend to negotiate the most contentious issues first for both time management and to quickly force a decision. My rationale is that if the parties aren't able to come to agreement on those items that may be deal breakers, it makes no sense investing a large amount of time having to simply walk away. If I need to be negotiating with another supplier, I want to do that as quickly as possible. When something is critical from a schedule perspective, you may want to have parallel negotiations with multiple suppliers. What works best will depend upon how much time you have available and your circumstances.

Much of the negotiation involves two things – communicating and persuading. In a principled or win-win approach the same two things are required along with problem solving. In my blog there are ten posts on communication including learning how to sell positions. Several of those posts focus on asking questions that are needed to get beyond positions as part of problem solving under a win-win approach. They are also useful in a traditional negotiation to understand why the other party is taking their position. Many times one of the biggest problems in negotiation is communication. That's especially true in dealing with a new company. Many times there may be a misunderstanding about what you need or want based on the contract or specifications documents you provided them. I've found that going over documents to explain things conceptually helps reduce the number of issues. If there are multiple documents that make up your contract, explaining the relationship between the documents and how they work together can also help reduce the number of issues.

If the suppliers bid or quoted price is close to being acceptable, you should negotiate the pricing last. If you do it earlier you leave yourself open to the supplier saying that their price "didn't include this" so if you want it, they need to adjust their price. If their price is substantially off from where you need it to be, you could negotiate price first, with the caveat that you reserve the right to negotiate price further based upon what is agreed. With that approach if the supplier is never going to have a price that's acceptable, you don't waste time negotiating contract terms with them. If you have significant confidence that you will be able to come to agreement on the deal breakers and the pricing will be acceptable, then starting with less contentious items and working to more difficult issues makes sense.

When terms are dependent upon or linked to another term, you should negotiate that term first. For example many times the obligation to make payment and the warranty term are dependent upon the delivery and acceptance terms. If the supplier's wants warranties to start upon delivery of the product to the buyer you need to take that into account in your terms that are linked to that. If you agreed to a delivery term that is Ex-Works the supplier's dock in Asia and it takes 30 days for you to receive the material or equipment, you've already lost thirty days from the warranty. Similarly if the payment term is thirty days from the date of delivery, if you agreed to ex-works the supplier's dock in Asia, you may have to pay for it before you get it, can inspect it, or use it. So if you negotiate the delivery term first and agree upon ex-works, when it comes time to negotiate the warranty period instead of agreeing to 36 Months from the date of delivery you could demand 37 months to take into account the period of time it will be in transit. Instead of agreeing to pay 30 days after delivery you could demand sixty days after delivery so while the payment clock starts when they deliver it, you will have the material for a period of time before you have to pay for it and can determine that it's acceptable.

There may be other terms that you want to link together and those should be negotiated at the same time. For example I always like to link things like the supplier's requests to have flexibility to manage the activity however they see fit to the liability and costs they are willing to accept in the event they cause a problem. My attitude is if they want flexibility to do whatever they want, they need to accept the potential cost and liability for the problems they cause. If they aren't willing to be fully responsible, you need more control over what they can or can't do to help manage the risk. Let me give you an example of what I mean. The supplier wants the right to change their product at any time. The changed product may still meet the specifications. The changed product may no longer work in your application and could cause major problems and costs. So if you give them the right to make those changes at any time, how do you protect against that risk? The only way that I know of is to have control over changes to the product so you can test proposed changes to make sure they will work before the supplier starts shipping the changed product to you. If you can't get that, an alternative would be to require advance notice of the changes and samples so they can be tested to make sure they work, and have the ability to order an increased quantity of the current product that will allow more time to transition to another solution or to make changes where the newer version of the product will work with your product. I would also highlight that every time they change their product that adds to the cost of doing business with them. The message in that is if the supplier wants to be competitive, they need to manage the scope and frequency of any changes to keep that cost down.

It's probably best to address all "legal" terms separate from business terms. This can allow different parties to attend the different sessions. You don't waste your lawyer's time while you discuss business issues and maybe it will keep their lawyer away from the table when you negotiate the business terms. Ask your lawyer which terms they consider to be legal terms that they must participate in the negotiation or must review and approve versus the business terms. If you do this separation you can come to agreement in concept, and have the lawyers review and finalize the language. Where I have found this to be most useful is when one or both sides of the negotiation are represented by outside counsel. Outside counsel have the tendency to complicate discussions as a way of either showing that they are earning their fee or as a way to increase their fee. I was once asked to step into a negotiation that had been going on for about six months with no visible end in sight. What I observed was outside counsels for both parties arguing about minutia that wasn't important and issues that would never occur. At the end of the first session I met with the supplier's V.P. and told him that the only ones that were winning in the negotiation were the outside law firms and we needed to take control of the negotiation. He and I would agree upon all the business terms we needed to close the deal and we would have the lawyers simply write it up. We did that in two days and then called in the lawyers to tell them that this was what we had agreed and it was their job to simply write it up. We gave them two days to do it after which there would be no further fees paid. They weren't happy as it ended a fairly lucrative assignment. When they knew that anything over two days wouldn't be paid for they somehow were able to come to agreement within the timeframe. Since then every time I enter into a negotiation where a company is represented by an outside counsel I tell the supplier that I want to deal with Internal Counsel or I want to be assured that they will manage them. I don't want them wasting my time simply to generate more billable hours.

Another recommendation that I would make is if you have multiple documents that will make up your agreement always start with the one that has the highest precedence. That way you are dealing with issues from the highest priority downward and many times that can answer concerns or eliminate issues the supplier may have I reading the lower priority document on its own.

One of the key things to do in negotiations is to set and manage expectations with the supplier. You want to set expectations in advance of the negotiation on what its going to take to win the business. If that hasn't been done prior to the negotiation you need to do it as soon as possible in the negotiations. The reason for doing this is so the negotiator on the other side has the ability to set those same expectations with their management and internal stakeholders whose approval they may need for agreement. What you don't want to do is force your counterpart to have to go back to their management at the end of the negotiation having to explain what they needed to give and why. The sooner their management understands and buys into the fact that they may need to make those concessions the easier the negotiation may be. I've seen negotiators on the supplier's side hold firm to a position simply because they don't want to have to go back to their management to explain that they misread what it would take to win the business. Rather than put them in that position set the expectations so they can set expectations with their management.

In managing a negotiation the negotiator should have three tools available to use.
- **The Negotiation Plan** that you have prepared based upon all the information that you have about the supplier and the Commodity and what you have learned from the bid or proposal.
- **A Negotiation Action Item List.**
- **A score card where you track the value of all changes both plus and minus.**

   The Negotiation Plan. The purpose of the negotiation plan is to:
   1. Identify and establish the negotiation strategy,
   2. Establish the goals of the negotiation,
   3. Identify any items that will create a "walk away" situation
   4. Identify absolute requirements.
   5. Identify possible tactics the supplier will use.
   6. Create effective countermeasures. (How you will convince them.)

Negotiation plan contents:
  I. Proposed contract
     A. Description of product/Service
     B. Program, Project, Effort to be supported
     C. Type of Agreement proposed
  II. Sourcing
     A. Pre-negotiation Process
        1. Solicitation Effort
        2. Technical requirements.
        3. Business requirements.
        4. Legal Risk analysis.
        5. Business Risk Analysis.
  III. Pricing
     Bid/Proposal Analysis
     Basis for determination of acceptability of Price or negotiation of cost.
     Pricing Period required.
  IV. Negotiation strategy
     A. Target price
     B. Target total cost / life cycle cost
     C. Internal Cost Impact (Against standards or prior costs)
     D. Other Issues and Positions on each (Goal, absolute)
  V. Administrative details
     1. Place
     2. Timeframe
     3. Anticipated completion date
     4. Participants and roles of the participants

A negotiation plan can be as simple as a table with 4 columns that address all the key issues.

Item	Goal	Absolute	Tactics & Counter-tactics

The Negotiation Action Item List

A negotiator for any large agreement also needs to be a program manager to keep track of and manage all the issues that arise. To make sure that you don't forget something with all the various issues you discuss I believe that at the beginning of every negotiation you need to start an action item list where you capture the specific issue, what is required, who will provide it and when it will be provided. The supplier may not have all the buyer documents and specifications so you need to manage getting them to the supplier. Many times other individuals within the buyer or supplier will need to review and agree upon a number of documents that will become part of the agreement such as quality documents, so you need to manage that process so it all comes together when you want or need to have the agreement signed.

You can maintain a separate action item list, or you can annotate a record copy of the agreements to document and track status. My preference is to maintain a separate list that you review at both the beginning and end of each negotiation session. The review in the beginning is to track progress and get information disclosed. The review at the end of the session is to agree upon what was closed during the session and what new action items were added.

My action item lists usually contains seven simple columns.

#	Section #	Issue	Responsible party	Promised Date	Actual Date	Status

If an issue expands requiring multiple actions being required, you can assign new numbers with the information and close out the prior issue. Each buyer action and each supplier action should have a separate number to track status against. I also find that color coding both the information and status is helpful for management review meetings with buyer and supplier management that may occur during the negotiation. For example the text of all buyer actions may be typed in one color, all supplier actions are typed in a different color so its visually easy to see whose action it is and who has the most open action items. For the status column I use a simple open or closed for the written status but also color code the status column boxes as follows:

- White = open, but with no schedule impact.
- Yellow = open, starting to become critical.
- Red = open, late and/or impacting schedule
- Green = Closed

There are clearly advantages and disadvantages to maintaining an action item list from a negotiation perspective. The biggest disadvantage to the buyer is you can't avoid or not respond to a supplier generated question or issue as it tracks them. The biggest advantage to the buyer is it keeps things from falling through the cracks, puts a discipline in process where the supplier can't avoid things and allows you to better manage everything coming together when needed.

The Negotiation Score Card

As you proceed in the negotiation you need to be keeping track of what's been agreed and the risk, financial or cost impact to either the buyer or supplier of those agreements. You can do that a number of ways: annotate a hard copy of the agreement you are negotiating; add another column to the goals and absolutes list for the item; or maintain a separate sheet where you keep track of the impact. The time to use that is when you negotiate the final price. If there is an imbalance in terms of what you have agreed versus what they supplier has agreed you want to use that to drive the price down. You may have argued against a point based upon the cost or risk where they didn't agree and this is the point at which you show them the impact those changes have on your perception of value and the price you want to pay. In some cases they may want to re-visit those points to provide something better so the impact on pricing is less. If they don't, use that and all the other leverage you have to drive the price down.

The Negotiation Stage

The negotiation stage is where your strategy, tactics and knowledge come together to help make the negotiation successful. The knowledge that you have and the things that you have learned leading up to the negotiate through things like pre-qualification become tools to help say no, provide reasons why the supplier should agree, or to explain why what you are asking for is reasonable. If you took the time to understand the supplier and their process, that knowledge can be used when you negotiate things that tie back to their process. For example, if you buy a custom or unique item from the supplier and you know their process, you will know the point at which the item becomes custom or unique. You would use that for things like negotiating rescheduling rights or cancellation liability. If you find that you have previous agreements with the supplier you should review them for precedence. You should also contact the individual that negotiated the prior deal to understand their motivation for any concessions that were made. That prepares you to argue when past precedence should apply or why the deal different so as not to apply past precedent.

Summarizing agreement

At each point in the negotiation where you believe agreement has been reached, in your own words that what you believe was agreed to confirm that the other party has the same understanding. At the end of each session summarize all the points that were agreed and those issues that remain open and update and share the updated action item listing. If there is time, update and share the red-line version of your agreement.

Revisiting agreed issues.

Lawrence "Yogi" Berra a great New York Yankees catcher once said "it ain't over until it's over". My rule in negotiations is similar – "nothing is finally agreed until everything is agreed". You can easily have a situation occur where the current point you are negotiating would have an impact on something that you may have previously agreed. You can always make agreement to that new point be conditional on changing what was previously agreed. You link them together so if the supplier wants agreement on the current point, they need to agree to re-negotiate what was previously agreed. If they don't want to re-open the previous point then they don't have agreement with the current point. Doing this will also identify which of the two issues are most important to them.

Whose contract should you use ?

The real answer is going to depend upon how much leverage you have in the relationship and how much the supplier wants your business. buyers should always try to use their standard contract template for several reasons. From a negotiation perspective it's best to work off your position rather than the other party's position. It's best to work with a document that you know, understand, and can begin to build competence in negotiating. Working with a supplier's standard form contract or a third party contract form such as a professional association standard form is more difficult. It requires you to not just look at what's there to determine whether or not that's acceptable, but it also requires that you look for what should be there, is missing, and needs to be inserted.

Should your contract include a number of "throw-aways"?

That answer depends upon the point in the process at which you provide the proposed contract. If you provide it in advance of the supplier providing you a quote and set the expectation that they need to price their proposal based on those terms, "throw-aways" aren't necessary. If they want to change the contract you have the ability to demand that they also reduce the price as the price was based on the contract. If you introduce the contract after the proposals have been received, you may want to include "throw-aways" to counter the suppliers push to re-price based on the introduction of new terms or requirements. If you don't include "throw-aways" you need to set the expectation that this is what you need and will consider only limited changes that can be justified.

Where should you negotiate?

I've always been of the opinion that face to face negotiation are best as they allow you to read the body language of the other party and send your own body language that helps your cause. There are advantages and disadvantages to whether you do it at the supplier or buyer's location. At the supplier's you may have less access to key resources you need and you may be giving them an advantage with their access to all the resources they need. At the buyer's location while you have access to resources, you also may be subject to interruptions or having individuals want to attend the negotiations that you would rather not have attend the negotiation. If you are going to have the negotiations at the buyer's location, make sure it is a place where you will not be interrupted. More important, closely manage the people who will attend and meet with any attendees in advance to set expectations on their role and behavior in the negotiation. If you don't manage their behavior, they can unintentionally damage or weaken your position. Early on in my career I had several negotiations that I had to call for a recess, and tell team members that they were no longer welcome at the negotiation because their actions or comments were damaging the negotiation.

Can I use the supplier's specifications?

If you want to use the supplier's specifications and make that part of your contract, there are several things that need to be managed. The first issue is the order of precedence that is given to those specifications. What you don't want to do is create a situation were terms in the supplier's specifications have a priority over the terms that you have elsewhere in the contract. So you need to give supplier specifications one of the lowest priorities, if not the lowest priority, in the order of precedence. The second issue is that the order of precedence clause only deals with conflicts between the terms. If the supplier specification included terms that were in addition to, and didn't conflict with all the other documents that have a higher priority, those additional terms would apply. They would apply as they were incorporated and they didn't conflict with the rest of the document. For example, all the other documents may simply not address how the buyer may use the product or service that they are purchasing. If the supplier's specifications included use restriction terms that prohibited the use of the item in certain manners or applications, that use restriction would apply to the buyer's purchases, and that could cause potential problems. If you want to use the supplier's specifications you would need to review them in detail and strike out all potentially problematic language, and only then incorporate that in your contract, or you need to establish language in your contract that effectively prevents the supplier specifications from adding any terms or restrictions to the contract.

Who should I be negotiating with?

You need to be negotiating with someone that can make a commitment on behalf of the supplier. If you deal with someone at a lower level, they won't have the authority and the message they give to their management may not be consistent with what you want them to say. Dealing with individuals at a higher level has the advantage that they have different measurements, more flexibility and have a greater ability to look at it from the big picture of the value the deal may have in other areas. Make sure that the entity you are contracting with has the assets and resources to stand behind the contract commitments they are making. A further consideration is price. If you negotiate with a subsidiary, 99% of the time you will pay more as the subsidiary purchase the product at the supplier's transfer costs and needs to add their overhead and profit on to the price to recover their costs.

In negotiation there are some myths that you need to understand aren't true.

"Terms should apply equally to both parties." In most cases the buyer has one obligation under the contract that is to pay for conforming goods and services that are provided by the supplier. The buyer may have other obligations, and the impact of not performing or delayed performance may be far less to the supplier than what the impact would be to the buyer if the supplier fails to perform. The supplier has a number of obligations that a buyer simply will not have based on the commitments made in the contract, their warranties and representations. It's simply not equal in terms of the

obligations, it's not similar in terms of impact, and so most commitments shouldn't be equal or mutual. In some cases there may be no sound reason for something being mutual. For example, a buyer may be liable for the actions of the supplier as a form of agency could be implied from the relationship where the buyer is the principal and the supplier an agent. Agents are never liable for the actions of the principal so there is no need for a supplier to ask for things like personal liability indemnities to be mutual. The goal isn't to treat each party as equal; it must be based upon the legal differences between the parties, what has been committed and what the impact will be to the other party if they fail to meet their commitments.\

"Dealing with a subsidiary is the same as dealing with the Parent. Each subsidiary is a separate legal entity in which the supplier owns a majority of interest. As a separate legal entity, the supplier is not responsible for the actions or liability of the subsidiary and the Subsidiary is free to make its own decision and agree to its own terms. The only problem is when it comes time to collect damages, require performance or seek indemnification when the subsidiary may not have the assets or resources to stand behind the commitments make in the contract. Even if both entities signed the same contract, the parent would not be liable for the actions of the Subsidiary unless they agreed to be "jointly and severally liable" (meaning that they would be liability both individually and jointly for the actions of the other. Many times a supplier may want orders to flow through a separate subsidiary for tax reasons and may not be able to jointly sign the contract with the supplier in which case if you want the assets and resources of the supplier standing behind those purchases, you would need them to agree to accept liability for their subsidiary by providing what is called a company guarantee.

"It will never happen". I was in a negotiation where I was negotiating a contract for an order-consolidating center and the last remaining point was the term for termination for convenience. The Business Manager told me to not worry about it, as it would never happen. I proceeded to close the contract making sure we had the termination for convenience provision. Less than a week later I was informed that there was a management change in the direction of the business and we needed to terminate the contract. When someone says it will never happen, my response is if it won't happen, then you won't mind agreeing to terms just in case it does.

"We can sort it out later" While you may be able to sort things out later, it will usually cost more. The time to establish what you will pay or what your liability will be is when you have the most leverage, which is before you sign the contract. If you can't agree on the specifics because certain information isn't available, consider limiting your risk by establishing the things you do agree upon and how you will establish those open items such as including a formula, establish a maximum, or establish terms that will provide future leverage. For example, assume that you were in a new product development situation where the cost of the product cannot be established until the design is finished. You could establish what the pricing will be exclusive of the unknown items, so those costs are firm. You could establish the formula or method by which the cost of the unknown items will be agreed. To retain leverage, you could make any volume commitment for the purchases subject to your final agreement on price.

"They will fix a problem". Every problem is really an investment decision. To fix a problem requires the supplier to invest resources, capital or both to resolve the problem. Since it is an investment decision, it will be weighed against all the other investment decisions the supplier has under consideration for its limited investment dollars. Investment decisions are made based on what will generate more profit first, if the investment won't reduce their costs, they probably won't make it unless they are incurring pain in other ways such as the actual or potential loss of business. If there is something they need to correct, get a firm commitment that they will correct it and make sure you include remedies where the bigger the problem it becomes to you, the more it will cost them. If they don't fell the pain they won't make the investment.

"We can rely on their word. "Commitments from supplier executives last only as long as that executive remains in that position. If it's not a contract commitment, successors simply do not have to honor it. If it's important make sure its part of the contract.

"This is standard in the industry" In many industries there are associations of suppliers or contractors that may create things like standard documents, standard specifications, standard policies, etc. Most standards such as these are designed to limit the supplier's liability, cost, or risk and are against the interests of the buyer. These "standards" are simply tactics designed to give certain legitimacy to them. If the supplier wants your business, the vast majority of them will work off the buyer's documents.

"This is our Standard Term" Most suppliers sell through multiple channels. For example a supplier could sell to: an Original Equipment Manufacturer (OEM) Channel; a Value Added Reseller (VAR) Channel; a Distribution Channel, and a Major customer Direct Sales Channel. Within a Channel they could also have multiple tiers that are based on the volume of business and importance of the customer. For each channel and each tier they usually offer both different pricing and terms. For example, the Tier 1 OEM may get the best terms and distribution may get the least favorable. For the most part they have no single standard, as they adjust their terms, prices and risks they accept based on the size and importance of the customer. I've found few standards that can't be changed if it comes down to them potentially losing important business.

"It's non-negotiable". Saying that something is non-negotiable is simply a tactic. If the supplier needs or wants your business, they will find a way around the non-negotiable position if that's in the way of getting your business. I was once in a negotiation where the supplier told me that their warranty was 90 days and that was non-negotiable. To change it to the 1 year I wanted would require approval by an executive committee that met quarterly. My position was that as we offered our customers a 12-month warranty we needed a full 12 months on their product that we were going to resell. If they wanted us to resell it, we needed the 12 months. What we settled on was their 90-day warranty plus a 9-month, no charge maintenance contract that provided me with the equivalent of 12 months warranty. They maintained their position of only providing a 90-day warranty. We received the protection we needed for the year.

"Requesting a "Best and final price" will get you the best pricing". A request for best and final price primarily does one thing; it cuts off your ability to negotiate further. It doesn't guarantee you that you will get the best price. It only guarantees that the other party will look upon it as the final price. Never do something that eliminates or can be interpreted to eliminate your ability to negotiate further. Most best pricing clauses aren't worth the piece of paper that they are printed on. To have a best pricing clause that works for the buyer, it must be auditable and few suppliers are willing to provide the right of audit. Most suppliers also need to have the ability to respond to different conditions and competitive pressures, so if they are willing to agree to a best pricing provision. It will be watered down so its ineffective, such as saying that it will be best pricing for like terms, quantities and products. This is like trying to align the earth, moon, sun and all the planets of the solar system. Few buyer terms and requirements will be similar. If you want the best price, you need to negotiate it and not wait for the supplier to voluntarily give it to you because of a term in the contract.

"You have to give something to get something" Concessions are tied to leverage. The more leverage you have versus the supplier in the negotiation, the less you should have to give to get what you need or want. The more leverage the supplier has in the negotiation, the more you may need to give to get what you want. Even in situations where buyers have maximum leverage, suppliers will have a walk away point where they would no longer be interested in the sale. If you are at that point in the negotiation you may need to give something of value to them to get something of value to you so they stay above their walk away point.

"It needs to be a win /win" All that is really needed is the other party needs to think it's a win for them which means they met their goal. It doesn't have to be a real win, or what you would consider to be a real win on their side. They just need to meet their goal. I've dealt with companies that in their end of quarter or end of year chase for revenue would consider just getting the order so that they can book for revenue their win.

"To make it a win/win you can expand the pie" Expanding the pie is a concept that is described in books about win-win negotiation strategies where the parties refer to BATNA (best alternative to negotiated agreements) to avoid zero-sum negotiations. The first I read about it was in Fisher & Ury's book "Getting to Yes". The problem with expanding the pie is in many procurement situations you may not be able to expand the pie. In others you may not want to expand the business with a particular supplier for a variety of reasons. The simple fact is most suppliers are not best in class across the breadth of their products or services and business. Expanding the pie can mean being forced to purchase products or services that are not best in class to expand the pie.

"You can use problem solving to negotiate contracts. For you to get concessions the supplier must need or want your business. If they could care less whether they get your business or not, they won't be prepared to make the investment of time to either negotiate or problem solve with you. If they need or want your business, they will be motivated to do if it helps them win the business. Problem solving is a useful tool /tactic to be used in resolving obstacles. If you start with it as a process to conclude the contract, it makes the discussion more of mediation than a negotiation.

"Concessions are of equal value to both parties". As no two companies are alike the value of a concession is seldom going to the same between the buyer and supplier. For example, a buyer that has significant resources and assets may have a low cost of money. A supplier that is smaller may have a higher cost of money. So if the buyer pushed for a payment term of 60 days versus 30 days, the benefit to the buyer with the lower cost of money would be less than the cost to the supplier that has a higher cost of money. In that situation the buyer would put a lower value on that concession than the supplier.

"The one who makes the first move loses" The negotiation approach you use may need to be adjusted to the amount of time available and waiting for the other party to make the first move can add time that you simply don't have. Your counterpart's time may simply not be as important as yours and they simply may be in no rush. It's not where you start, its where you end up that counts. Sometimes to expedite the process to a go or no go decision, its important to make a well positioned first offer and establish the fact that you aren't going to spend significant time on it. If they want the business they have a deadline to respond to force quicker action.

Using "no". Use the tactic of saying no to the other party's request in a limited way. The more times the other party simply hears "no" the more they will have the tendency to dig in and refuse to make concessions which can jeopardize your ability to close the negotiation. When you want or need to say no and you can give a good reason or explanation of why, share that with them so they understand why you are telling them no. You can say "no" and then give a counterproposal of what you would be willing to do or agree to. Both of these help keep the discussion open. If the supplier is the one that is saying no, probe to understand why. If all you hear from a supplier is no and they don't want to share why, there can be several reasons. One is they would like your business, but only at their terms. A second reason could be the negotiator doesn't have the knowledge or authority to do anything different. In the first case I would take all the no's and put a cost impact on all of them and tell them they either need to reduce the price or you will need to find something that will be competitive. In the second case I would escalate the lack of progress up to the supplier's management as they can take a different view of the issues as they have a different perspective and different measurements.

Avoid barriers to communication. Since so much of any negotiation is communication, you need to manage your actions and behavior in a manner where you build credibility and trust and avoid anything that can be a barrier to

communicating. Communication is difficult enough. I once read that there are six outcomes to any communication:
Your communication may be:
1. What you wanted to say (but may not have)
2. What you thought you said (which may not be what you said)
3. What you actually said.

The party communicating with you may have heard what you said three different ways:
- They heard what they wanted to hear.
- They heard what they thought they heard .
- They heard what you actually said.

When you build a barrier to communication by your actions or behavior a fourth dimension is added to how they hear what you say. They may not hear anything you say because you angered them, you no longer have credibility, or they simply don't trust what you are saying.

Negotiation Types.

There are a huge number of books on negotiation. In the past most books and training were focused on strategies and tactics based upon what's called zero sum negotiations where for one party to win, the other party must give something up (lose). In the early nineteen eighties Roger Fisher and William L. Ury of the Harvard Negotiation Project wrote a book called "Getting to Yes – Negotiating Agreement Without Giving In" in which they describe what they called "principled negotiations" or what others call win/win. Almost thirty years later its still a best seller for books in paperback. Individuals that have been part of the Harvard Negotiation Project have gone on to expand upon the original premises of principled negotiations or to put forward additional or different theories. For anyone that plans to negotiate procurement contracts for a living I believe that you need to learn both approaches as the circumstances surrounding every negotiation will be different. What may work in some situations may not work in others. If you only focused on principled negotiations and win up dealing with a party that is focused on zero sum negotiations and getting as much as they can, you may lose simply because you were not prepared for it. There will be times when a principled negotiation may work extremely well and if you can use it and meet your goals it makes the negotiation easier. There will always be times when you need to use other strategies and tactics to meet your goals. In my blog I recommend a number of different books that I recommend reading. The majority of the material in my blog is about negotiation and was intended provide additional information about the negotiation.

In preparing for negotiating contract terms there are three specific posts that you should read as a refresher. "Contract Drafting with Precision" dated April 6, 2011 contains important information you need to manage during the negotiation of contract terms. The blog "Writing in the Active Voice" dated December 12, 2010, contains important information to make your documents and especially the commitments contained in the contract clear. The blog "Compatibility – Managing Compatibility in Documents" posted April 7, is suggestion to follow to avoid conflicts between documents as conflicts can create problems.

John C. Tracy

CHAPTER 13 THE REMAINING PHASES OF NEGOTIATION

The Bid document or RFP, when used properly, is another tool in the negotiation process.

- It is used to set the expectation on what you want to buy.
- It defines the terms that you want to buy under (further setting expectations)
- It also allows you to gather additional information you will use in the negotiations.

Just as you will use "what if" questions to probe specific issues in the negotiation, the RFP or Bid document can be constructed in a manner where those "what if" questions are establish in the form of options you want the supplier to price, and various alternatives for which you want to see the impact. This type of an approach is sometimes referred to as option bidding. Option bidding or "what if" is to understand the potential variables of cost. It can help identify where requirements are adding costs to the relationship. It can also provide you with a greater understanding about the supplier or the way they operate. For example, one supplier may want to limit the amount of change that occurs by either limiting the amount of change or charging premiums for change, whereas another supplier may be more flexible in nature and be willing to accept such changes with minimal limitations and no premiums. One supplier may be willing to offer a substantial discount for a longer delivery schedule (either because of other work they have or their lack of confidence in the schedules) whereas, another supplier may not be willing to offer anything because they want the work in that period or they have solid confidence in meeting the dates. One supplier may be willing to charge minimal costs for extending warranties because they have high degrees of confidence in the reliability of their product, whereas another may want to charge substantial amounts for extended warranties because either they don't have the same confidence in the reliability of their product, or their business model wants them to sell items with short warranties so they can sell on-going maintenance and repair contracts sooner.

As each supplier's capabilities, motivations and business models may be completely different, some amount of option bidding or "what if" also allows you to flush out a better understanding of what's important to them and how they operate. Once you understand what is important to them, you have the ability to change your negotiating tactics to use can use what's important to them in negotiating or trading off certain items under negotiation.

The option bid sets the assumptions to be used for the bid or proposal and then asks for options for changes against that baseline. The key is that it allows you a more disciplined set of responses for evaluation. Everyone must bid against the baseline and options are evaluated against the baseline. A number of options can be bid.

Option Bidding is also tool to get a better understanding of how the supplier feels about certain issues. For example, if they price the cost of extended warranties high, it's a red flag to either be concerned about their product's reliability, or to be concerned with the life cycle cost of their product. It can also give an indication on how confident they feel about an issue. For example, in construction we would bid major contracts with or without liquidated damages. If a supplier was willing to provide a large discount for not having liquidated damages, it was generally a signal that they weren't confident in meeting the dates. If a supplier offered no discount for not having liquidated damages, it was usually a sign that they were highly confident that they would finish on time. It also gave you and indication about your schedule. Sometimes if you took the amount of the credit a supplier offered and divided that by the daily liquidated damages rate, it helped understand how much longer they thought the work would take above the scheduled date.

If you competitively bid work, whom you include in your bid can also affect how successful you'll be in the negotiation. Suppliers know whom they can effectively compete against. If you include a supplier who others know they can't compete against, there is a strong likelihood that those suppliers will either not bid or will provide only a complimentary bid and not their best shot. The other supplier may wind up pricing their work higher because of the competition they see. You will get the best results in a competitive bid when all suppliers feel they are capable of winning and will respond accordingly.

The negotiation phase

This is the aspect that many people consider to be the only part of negotiations even though the actual negotiation may have commenced much earlier. It involves the Seven Steps that most books refer to as the negotiation phases. In procurement the negotiation falls into several key buckets – the price of the item, the terms of purchase, and who bears what risks in the relationship. This means that to be successful, in addition to understanding tactics you need to understand cost, the terms, the potential impact of any proposed or requested changes and what the risks are and the impact of accepting the risk. Tactics are to help you get your desired positions.

Mobilization

The mobilization phase is the period between execution of the contract and commencement of work. During this period negotiations will continue to occur, but in a more subtle form. The types of negotiations that occur in the mobilization phase are usually request for product or material substitutions, changes to specifications, change to the list of approved subcontractors or material suppliers. These "negotiations" are usually couched in requests based on the need to change because of availability of the items and their potential impact on the schedule if the change is not approved. It will also include proposals of an item as an "equal", when the specifications allowed "or equal" substitutions. Many times the intent of the supplier is to get the buyer to approve changes to the requirements simply because they have found a better deal. If you agree it will allow them to charge the same, but make more. The key in negotiating changes in the mobilization phase is to understand the value of what you have and, if what they propose is worth less or presents a greater risk, hold out for them to either provide you with an appropriate credit based on the difference in value, or require them to meet what they committed in the contract.

The production phase

In many types of purchases the negotiation in the production phase is more of what we refer to as supplier management. It is the documenting and managing the supplier's performance, quality, deliverables and continuous improvement in accordance with the terms and conditions of the contract and managing change that occurs. I've see purchasing organizations who spend most of their time contracting with the supplier and little time actually managing their performance. *If the supplier is allowed to do less than what was committed, you are getting less or it's costing you more.* Most of the negotiation in the production phase is in getting the supplier to perform to their commitments. In some types of purchases a major focus of the negotiations during the production phases are the changes that occur. For example, in construction it's not uncommon to have hundreds or even thousands of change orders that are negotiated.

Production phase changes

There can be changes to the scope, design, and implementation. There can be changes required because of different conditions. There can charges for all new work, reduced work or changed work. There can be negotiation of cost for things added or credits for work eliminated. There can be negotiation of value of abandoned work or the impact of cancellations or for the re-work of items to establish amounts to be paid. Unless you have previously agreed unit prices for changes, each change requires it own negotiation and even it situations where you do have unit prices you may still need to negotiate volumes of units. To negotiate fair changes in the production Phase, you need leverage. In many situations once the work has started, it becomes difficult to change suppliers and that results in a loss of leverage for the buyer. To prevent that from occurring, buyers should have their contracts establish how changes will be managed and how the costs will be established. If you don't you may be locked into the supplier and be in a position of having little leverage to negotiate acceptable pricing of terms for changes or your option may be to either 1) not make the change, 2) terminate the supplier and live with the impact, or 3) accept the supplier's position. If you can't easily and cheaply switch suppliers you need to pre-agree how costs will be established with a formula where you have the ability to verify the cost of materials, the amount type and cost of labor, the cost of any incidental charges and what the agreed percentages will be for the supplier's overhead and profit.

Project Close

Project close out is similar to supplier Management except the focus is on managing delivery of critical items such as warranties, spare parts, training, transition services etc. It is also during project close out that claims and counter-claims are identified that may also need to be negotiated. In many activities the last 5% is the toughest.

Warranty

Managing claims against warranties can involve another different series of negotiations as seek to prove that the failed material or product is covered by the warranty, that it is not excluded by certain exclusions and that it is the supplier's responsibility to meet all the contract warranty obligations.

Claims

Claims represent just another form of negotiation in which you seek to establish the validity of the claim (duty to perform, failure to perform, cost), and the supplier seeks to challenge the validity of the claim, the validity of the costs or seeks to negotiate a reduced settlement.

Important thoughts to re-emphasize on Negotiation Phases:

1. How well you manage all the negotiation phases leading up to the formal negotiation will impact how successful you will be in that negotiation and whether your tactics will work.
2. If you manage what is disclosed you'll get a better deal and have your tactics work.
3. Tactics may be useless if your team undermines you by showing the supplier that:
    a. There isn't competition
    b. There is a need and they are the only ones that can meet it
    c. They are clearly preferred or only they can meet deadlines or delivery schedule.
4. What you ask for from the supplier in the early stages of the process can provide valuable information to use in the negotiation.
5. How well you manage the negotiation phases that occur after the formal negotiation will determine how much of the bargain you negotiated you'll keep.

CHAPTER 14 BUYER AND SUPPLIER NEGOTIATION GOALS

Irrespective of what each party's stated goals may be for entering into a contract, there are always some basic goals that each party will usually have:

The supplier's goals will be to:

- Reduce their costs or transfer certain costs to the buyer
- Reduce the risks they assume or transfer certain risks to the buyer
- Avoid making commitments that create potential liability or added cost.
- Limit their potential liability
- Have flexibility they need to effectively manage their business
- Since most Suppliers' negotiations are managed within their sales organization, their goal will be to make the sale or have terms that help make the sale.

The buyer's goals are to:

1. Reduce their costs or transfer certain costs to the supplier as part of the price.
2. Reduce the risks they assume or transfer certain risks to the supplier
3. Get the supplier to make commitments that create potential liability or cost to the supplier and minimize their commitments
4. Limit their potential liability
5. Ensure that the have the tools to manage any risks they assume and the overall performance
6. On the buyer's side, as contracts are negotiated by procurement people, their goal is to reduce the price of their purchases, the life cycle cost, and to have as much flexibility as possible to deal with changes.

If it seems like the majority of the goals are in direct conflict with each other, they are. So it's very important to understand what you are agreeing to and what that will mean to both you and the supplier from a cost, risk, performance or liability perspective. Let's talk a little about each of the basic goals and how the supplier tries to meet their goals.

Reduce their costs or transfer certain costs to the buyer.

There are a number of ways a supplier can transfer cost to the buyer in the contract. For example:

- **Payment terms.** The shorter the payment term, the more of a cash flow cost the buyer has.
- **Delivery terms.** For example, an origin based delivery term will transfer all the cost and risk of shipping to the buyer at the delivery point.
- **Warranties and Representations**. What they warrant, how long they warrant it, what's included or excluded from the warranty, how warranties are redeemed and who pays the cost of returns all has a potential cost. Classic examples of this that you may find in a supplier's standard warranty terms would be that in the event of a claim, materials will be

provided without cost, but it becomes the buyer's responsibility to pay for labor. Another is when a warranty has so many limitations or exclusions that it significantly reduces what's covered.
- **Limitations on liability** on both the types of damages that may be claimed and/or limitations on the amounts of damages will all transfer any excess cost over the limitation amount to the buyer.
- **Termination rights** of the parties. In termination for cause I've seen suppliers want buyer's to pay them for termination costs when they were the cause of the termination. For termination for convenience you negotiate the cost of any termination.
- How **disputes** will be managed and where there will be heard can impact buyer's cost to pursue a claim or defend against a claim.
- **Manage indemnifications** provided for personal injury or property damage or IP infringement.
- Provisions for recovery of **Attorney's fees** in the event of a dispute would be a cost to the buyer to pursue a claim against the supplier or to defend against 3rd party or wrongful supplier claims if not permitted.

Reduce the risks they assume

Most risks to the supplier come from the commitments that they make for their performance and inherent risks associated with their product or service. The manage those risks by the standard of commitment they try to make, by including terms that allow them to remedy or cure the problem before assuming liability and by limiting their liability. For example to transfer the risk of non-performance on a delivery date to the buyer they may want to include language that says that they will make reasonable efforts to complete the work by a certain date. In any termination section they would also want to include a fairly long period after a breach, which allows them to cure the breach and which gives them more time to complete the work. Finally they could try to negotiate liquidated damages or limitations on the amount of damages so the majority of the risk of performance is transferred to the buyer.

Avoid making commitments that create potential liability or cost.

Suppliers try to limit their liability in the language that they want to use to establish their commitments. For the supplier to be liable they must have failed to meet their commitment, so they will want to use language in making commitments that reduces the potential that they will fail to meet the commitment. For example instead of making a firm commitment that they will do something, they may want to make the commitment that they will use commercially reasonable efforts to do it. As long as they used commercially reasonable efforts, they won't be liable it doesn't occur. The standard of commitment that they make will also impact their costs. If they make a firm commitment to do something, they have to spend whatever it costs to do it or be subject to damages if they don't. If they only made "commercially reasonable efforts" to do it, in effect they would not have to spend any more than they would normally spend and if it added cost it wouldn't be commercially reasonable,

Limit their potential liability.

Suppliers will attempt to limit their liability in several ways. Liability can be limited by the commitment they make, in the limitation of liability section of the contract where they would try to limit both the types of damages that may be claimed and their per incident or maximum liability amounts for their liability. They may also seek to limit their liability in any sections of the contract where the buyer includes a remedy for the supplier's non-performance. One way that is done is to have language included with the remedy that says that it is the sole and exclusive remedy for the breach of that provision. Another its to try to limit their liability to the cost of the product or some small multiple of the cost of the product or relate liability to the amount of the purchases.

Have flexibility they need to effectively manage their business
Most buyer contract boilerplates will limit the types of changes the supplier can make. As this limits the supplier's flexibility the may want to include things that provide them with more flexibility. For example, they may propose that they can change the product as long as it doesn't change the "form, fit, or function of the product". The problem with that is a change that doesn't impact the form, fit or function could reduce the quality, reliability and performance of the item increasing the buyer's costs or risks. A change that met the requirements of form, fit or function could also cause the product to no longer work in buyer's application. Other areas that supplier frequently will want to change are any provision that would limit their right to make other changes such as end of life or a product changing the design of a product, changing the process use to make the product or perform the service, changing suppliers or subcontractors. What supplier's view as flexibility to manage their business, a buyer will view as adding potential additional cost or risk to the relationship? For example, if a supplier wanted to end of life a part that they make to replace it with another newer part, that new part may not work in buyer's application and it would in a production setting require the buyer to make a last time buy of the part to cover both production and service needs. If they guess wrong on the low side of the volume it could impact their ability to ship their products or provide service. If they guess wring on the high side, it creates obsolescence. In both cases the buyer would have inventory carrying costs of the purchases adding to the cost.

Make the sale or have terms that help make the sale.

There are a number of ways that a supplier may use to try and force or protect sales and virtually all of these can add to the buyer's cost.

- Minimum order quantities. This can be applied with respect to the quantity of products purchased or the total value of the order. Either will force you to buy at least the minimum quantity.
- Vendor multiples. This is when items are sold in set quantities usually driven by package type. For example, when was the last time you were able to by a single AA battery at a store? Most come at least 4 to a pack which is a form of vendor multiple.

- Non-cancellable / non-returnable orders. These force you to complete the purchase irrespective of whether you need it or not.
- High termination costs can force you to continue to make the purchase as the alternative is to make the termination payment and get nothing where you get no value for your spend.
- High Restocking fees. A high charge a supplier may have for them simply to discourage buyers from making returns.
- Step pricing with bill backs for failing to purchase the required quantity will mean that even if there is another supplier with a lower price, you'll need to take into account what the impact would be of the bill backs as those would effectively be added to your cost of doing business with the alternative supplier.
- Volume of business related discounts. This is structured in a way where the discount you get for next years purchases will be based on this year's volumes and it forces you to take into account the potential impact to the discount any alternative sourcing would have, especially if there are some products or services that you must buy from the supplier next year
- End of life notices. What an end of life notice does is force you to make a last time buy to cover any potential future needs.
- Short warranty periods on products or services in many cases are designed to force you to purchase maintenance service contracts.

On the buyer's side, the buyer's boilerplate contract template should provide you with most of the tools you need to meet the majority of your goals. If you use your own template it forces the supplier to try to change, delete or insert terms to meet their goals and it makes it more obvious when they are attempting to change the sharing of the risk and cost that your boilerplate represents. If you work off the supplier's standard form it makes the job more difficult. Not only do you have to worry about what's included in their standard document, you also have to be able to identify what's missing. Unless you're an expert I would always recommend working off your own standard form for that reason alone.

CHAPTER 15 COMMUNICATING IN NEGOTIATION

15.1 General Communication

What does a communication have to do with negotiations? The answer is simple; negotiations absolutely require good communication. If you are unable to communicate with the opposing party in an effective manner, your likelihood of success is substantially reduced. Good negotiator need to be able communicate. I once read that each party can have six different interpretations of a communication

- What you wanted to say (but may not have)
- What you thought you said (which may not be what you said)
- What you actually said.
- They heard what they wanted to hear.
- They heard what they thought they heard
- They heard what you actually said.

Communication is successful only when what you actually said is what they heard and they fully understood it. For example, if you were familiar with negotiating with Japanese suppliers you would know that culturally they have difficulty saying no. So instead of saying no they will tell you that something will be "very difficult". If it was your first time negotiating with a Japanese supplier you could interpret "very difficult" as meaning that it is something that they will try to do but feel that it is difficult. If you understand the Japanese culture you would understand that what they were effectively telling you is no. What they wanted to say was no and what you heard may be more of what you wanted to hear which was yes.

If you negotiate internationally one of the first things you need to do in learning to communicate is to learn the cultural rules associate with communication in any country you do business in. In negotiations with English speaking counterparts you will find that the meaning of certain words will be different between America, Great Britain, Canada and Australia. The same words can have entirely different meanings. Even in negotiating within a country, different sections of a country may have different variations of language and it doesn't stop there. Most industries and many commodities have a form of language of their own. Many of the terms may be unique or may have a unique interpretation in an industry or commodity. Let me give you a simple example of what I mean. The insurance industry speaks in terms that are frequently unique to only the insurance business. To the outsider, it's extremely confusing. For individual consumers, laws were written that required insurance companies to provide "plain English" documents so consumers could better understand what is being communicated. Business does not get those consumer protections, so if you were ever to negotiate the procurement of various types of insurances for your company, you need to either be able to speak the language or have someone on our team who understands and can speak the language. Many companies also have the tendency to develop their own internal language and acronyms that are unique to them and which, if used with a 3rd party that never has done business with that company, would be confusing at best. Many times the point at which the confusion manifests itself is in the negotiation of contract terms that also may be slightly different or unique in the terms their use to that company.

Negotiations that both parties want to succeed can fail simply because one or both of the parties failed to communicate. When "Fisher and Uhry" in their book "Getting to Yes", talk about focusing on interests and not positions, I believe that part of what they are talking about is the need for the parties to communicate to find a common ground. Most people aren't clairvoyant, so they don't know what you need or want and won't understand it unless you tell them. Even when you think you have told them they may still not understand because of the common problems that exist in communication.

To make sure there is an understanding, don't just tell them what you want, explain it to them and give them examples so there is no uncertainty. That way what you wanted to say thought you said and actually said will all be the same. When they are speaking you need to be a good listener to make sure that it's not just what you wanted to hear, but its both what you thought and actually heard. To make sure you are communicating you need to question and confirm both understanding and agreement. Confirm any point where they apparently agreed. Confirm your understanding and agreement on their points.

There are five aspects of communication you need to focus on to be a good negotiator.

1. You need to set and manage the suppliers expectations

2. You need to speak like a negotiator and make it clear what you want.

3. Throughout you need to make sure that there is a meeting of the minds and that both parties understand and agree the same thing. Most problems that may occur during the performance of a contract are the result of the parties not having the same understanding.

4. Learn how to sell you points.

5. You need to learn the power of questions as part of both preparing for and conducting the negotiation.

In my blog Http://knowledgetonegotiate.blogspot.com there are a number of tips on communicating that you should check out: Communicating in the Bid or Proposals Stage; Communication - Interviewing; Communication - Internal Questions To Ask In Prep; Communication - Learn To Sell Your Positions; Communication - Setting and Managing Expectations Communication - Types of questions; Communication - Using questions; Communication - Using The Right Words; Communication Basics; and Communication - Manage Your Team's Communications

15.2 Using Questions in Negotiations.

Questions are a great negotiation tool, and the use of questions to help in the negotiation will start well before the formal negotiation process begins. As part of their selling activity, salespeople may spend substantial time probing to determine the buyer's need, interests, timing, volumes, etc. They ask questions to determine the acceptance of their product versus the competition, whether any unique features they have are needed or desired by the buyer that may reduce the competition. They may also probe to find out who the competition may be, so they get a better understanding of the competitive environment based on where they know they will stand their competition from their recent dealings. All this questioning by the supplier needs to be managed so it doesn't impact their perception of competition and the uncertainty in their getting the business.

As part of the buyer's pre-qualification of the supplier, the buyer should also be questioning the supplier about what they do, how they do it, who their customers are, etc. to gather information they may be able to use in the negotiation. This questioning should also try to uncover the supplier's motivations, needs and hot buttons. For example, a simple question on their capacity and current business load may show how much they need the business. During any visit you should look at and question what they do as a standard and check for signs of potential issues or problems and ask questions to see if there are any issues or problems that you may want to raise during the negotiations to get an advantage. For example, I've seen suppliers want to change extra for a step in their process that they performed for all their customers. That meant it had already built into the product cost they quoted. For example, if you found a large amount of product returns, you might question what is causing them or why the amount is seemingly large, and then use that in negotiating quality levels, warranty replacement turnaround time, or controls over changes.

In the actual negotiation, questions are used for a wide variety of purposes:

As Fisher & Uhry say: "Focus on interests, not positions".
- Asking questions allows you to have an open discussion on the point(s) instead discussing and listening to their position(s).
- Questions force the supplier to talk, which helps you learn about them and the underlying issues or concerns.
- Questions can provide a break in your discussion and can keep you from potentially saying too much too soon.
- Questions force the supplier to think about their position or their argument and what they really want, which may be different.
- Questioning can narrow the supplier's focus to a specific issue or issues.
- Supplier's responses to questions become their proposal that makes it easier for them to understand and agree upon if you like what you hear.
- Questioning helps identify what the real problem, issue, or concern may be that needs to be addressed. Sometimes the stated problem or issue isn't their real or primary concern.

- Questioning and listening attentively shows that you are interested in what they have to say, which allows better communications as you are respecting what they have to say.
- Questioning buys you time to mentally formulate your next steps, approach, tactics or next question.

The right string of questions can help lead the discussion and supplier to a position you want.
- Question can solicit information to understand the underlying problem or reason for their response.
- They can invite joint problem solving
- They can help clarify information you received.
- They can verify that the information you have is current and accurate.
- They can check whether your current understanding is correct.
- They can be used to rephrase to determine whether there was agreement.
- They can probe for the degree of importance of an issue
- They can be used to share information or knowledge that will help you.
- They can help set expectations.
- They can show problems with their position or strengthen your position.
- They can use the supplier's information against them.
- Questions can help understand how close or apart you are
- Closed ended questions can be used in making conditional concessions
- Questions can be used to introduce specific tactics.

Questions are structured as either close-ended or open ended. Closed ended questions should be used when you want to direct the discussion and limit the possible responses. Closed ended questions call for a simple response like yes or no. E.g. "If I do X, will you agree to that?"

Open-ended questions allow for an open response and are used to try to get at issues, motivations or invite problem solving. "What if" is an example of an open-ended question.

Questioning is also a way to introduce different tactics. For example, asking the supplier "Do you understand the impact this will have on your competitiveness?" introduces the competitive nature of the activity and the use of total cost impact as part of the negotiation.

Most of the time you want to move from broad open-ended questions to narrow closed ended questions to continue to narrow the focus, but that's not necessary. You may need to ask several closed ended questions just to effectively set up the right open ended question. For example, you could ask a number of closed ended questions to have the supplier acknowledge that there is a problem, they understand it, and they understand the impact, before you ask they an open end problem solving type question like "how are we going to solve this problem?" or "What have you done with other customers to get over this same issue?"

Keep your questions simple and don't ask multiple questions at the same time as the supplier can then select which one it will answer, and that may not create the flow you want. Script out most of your questions in advance so you are careful to not ask a question that you may not want the answer to or which could hurt your position. Never ask a closed ended question when you are down to one issue and the response could leave you without any other options. After you ask the question stop talking and listen. You don't learn anything by talking, you learn by listening. Listen to not just the words, but what they say, how they say it, the conviction they have and look at the body language during the response. This helps you understand the degree of importance or the pain they have with the issue.

Here some questions you'll hear in many negotiations:

- What if _____? (Open-ended probe)
- If we do ____ will you do _____? (If, then tactic)
- Do you understand the impact this has on your competitiveness? (Competition tactic)
- Are you aware that your competition provides this? (Competition)
- When you purchase from your own suppliers:
- What terms do you expect?
- Would your Procurement people accept this?
- Could you effectively manage your business with this?

All provide validity to your position by comparing it to what they do.

- Who else do I need to talk to get agreement on this? (Escalation)
- Can you explain why ____?

Here's an example of using questions:

Assume the supplier is offering only a one (1) year warranty, but all their advertising and marketing for the product says that the product has 100,000 hours of reliability and you want a 3-year warranty term. Your questioning could follow these lines:

Doesn't your Specification show you as having a reliability of 100,000 hours? If your product has 100,000 hours of reliability, doesn't that mean that it should fail on average in 11 years? If the product has 11 years of reliability, how do you explain why you are only offering a 1-year warranty? Is there a problem with your reliability you haven't made us aware of? Are you having a higher incidence of failures in the initial years that would drive up your financial exposure above the normal statistical rate? If you don't have a reliability problem, and you aren't seeing excessive early failures, what are you seeking to avoid? If your product were as reliable as you say it is, wouldn't both the risk and cost be minimal for years 2 and 3? If it isn't a cost or reliability problem, what's the real reason behind this?

Do you understand the impact this may have on:
- o Your competitiveness?
- o Your getting this business?
- o Your product being restricted in our use of it?

CHAPTER 16. AVOIDING ENFORCEABILITY PROBLEM COSTS

One cost that's within the buyer's control is the costs that can occur simply because the contract wasn't properly drafted or checked before execution. Drafting problems with contracts can affect the interpretation or requirements, the coverage and the enforceability of certain terms. Doing a great job of negotiating the deal can be quickly lost if you don't ensure that you have a solid, enforceable contract. Here are several things to always check in your drafting of contracts or purchase orders:

Terminology. The terminology used in your contract and attachments needs to be consistent. For example, if you define the other party as "Supplier", the term "Supplier" should be used in all places where you are referring to them. To help with this, learn how to use defined terms so it always has the meaning you defined.

Be consistent use of the Defined Terms. For example, if one document refers to an Epidemic Defect Rate, the other documents addressing the same thing should also refer to Epidemic Defect Rate. If you define the term "Product", every time you want to describe a commitment that applies to the entire product you purchase, make sure you use the capitalized defined term "Product" and not "product". For any words that have a dual meaning, used the defined term to define the intended meaning.

Check to ensure that you **closed the loop on establishing requirements**. If one document defers to another document to establish a term, make sure the other document actually establishes the term. This may seem like common sense, but I've seen many problems arise because commitments have not been properly established. For example if you used a master agreement it would defer a number of items to be established in a Statement of Work. For example it could defer to the SOW to establish:

Definition of the Products and Services	Warranty period for defects in materials and workmanship
The price	Minimum order quantities
The delivery terms	Lead time,
The payment term	Flexibility,
Period for acceptance	Cancellation rights
Quality levels required to reject lots	Epidemic defect rates

If the contract points to an Attachment to further define the item or requirement, check to ensure that document referred to properly establishes the commitments. For example, if the contract says that the delivery terms will be specified in Attachment A, Attachment A should be called Attachment A and should include the specific delivery term and the delivery point such as: Delivery shall be FOB Origin, supplier's Dock at Penang, Malaysia. Create an **"Order of Precedence"** between all documents to eliminate conflict and make sure it establishes the correct priority. The contract and all documents incorporated by reference into the contract are looked upon as a single document that is complimentary with all requirements having the same weight unless the contract specifically establishes precedence between documents. As there is always a potential for conflict between the two, you need to define which of the documents has priority. If your contract is made up of several documents like a contract and a statement of work, establish the priority between those documents. If you have a drawing and written specification that defines the requirements of your purchases, you should establish the priority between those documents in the event there is an inconsistency between the two. If you incorporate supplier documents as part of your contract its especially important to ensure that they do not conflict with or diminish the commitments being made under your contract and one way to do that is by placing those documents at a lower priority in the order of precedence.

If you have language that says "In no event will either party be liable to the other party for any lost revenues or profits, incidental, indirect, consequential, special or punitive damages" that would limit all damages to only direct damages and would preclude any damages that you might want to recover that are incidental in nature. That may not be what you want to do, as there may be certain specific incidental damages you would want to recover. Be especially careful with dollar caps on liability. If you have language that caps the total dollar liability of a party under the contract, that will cap items that you may not want to have a dollar cap on such as 3rd party claims for Intellectual Property infringement or claims for personal injury claims. To prevent that you could include a limitation in the specific section so it applies only to that section or you could refer to the specific section(s) that are excluded from the cap on liability.

Tailor documents to your needs. Most standard templates are designed assuming that:
- The purchases aren't for complex products or systems.
- There are alternative sources where the supplier may be easily replaced
- The supplier presents minimal risk.

This means you may need to tailor your contract based on the potential risks involved with: a) what you are purchasing; b) the impact to you if there are problems; or c) any concerns you have with the supplier, the supplier's product or services or their potential performance. The more dependent you are on them and the greater the potential risk, the more you may need to add alternative requirements or additional remedies in the event of a problem. For example, if a sole sourced supplier fails to ship product, a remedy of cover (having the supplier pay for the incremental cost to buy from another source) may provide you nothing, as there may be no other feasible source.

Avoid Ambiguity. Words can confuse or mislead and many words have multiple meanings that can allow for multiple interpretations that creates ambiguity. One of the best ways to avoid ambiguity is through the use of very precise terms that leave no room for misinterpreting what was meant or agreed. If you can't find a precise term and a word has multiple meanings, create a "defined term" providing a precise meaning for that word so that every time that word is used and is highlighted as a defined term (by using Caps) it has only that precise meaning contained in the definition. If you have possible confusion of difficulty making it precise, use examples to describe exactly what is meant so it is clear to all that read it. Leave no interpretation to chance. When writing is ambiguous and could be interpreted multiple ways, when things are good they may interpret it the same way as you, but if there is a problem and they are seeking to avoid liability or cost, suppliers may choose to interpret it using the definition that is in their best interest.

Product or service definition. The definition of the product or service is critical as it defines what the supplier is obligated to provide. It establishes the basis by which you can accept or reject the product. It also determines what the product or service must do in situations where the product fails to work under warranty or defects situations. The contract should clearly establish the product specification or definition of the services to be performed. That specification should take priority over all other attachments and the contract should not conflict with it. The specification or definition of services is an area where you need to make sure the requirements are not ambiguous. When you are dealing with both specifications and drawings that define requirements the two could be in conflict so you need to make sure that as between those two documents there is an order of precedence and you need to make sure that the document that has priority is unambiguous. Having worked in government contracting doing construction contracting I found that a number of suppliers would have people on staff who specifically focused on looking for problems or conflicts between the documents as that presented an opportunity to make money through the change order process. They would bid low by taking the most favorable interpretation to them, and then when someone wanted it changed, there was always a cost.

Acceptance Requirements. For activities that require a development activity, you need to include all the specifics regarding the development such as the plan, critical milestones, checkpoints, interim deliverables, ownership rights, acceptance and test criteria for completion of the development, and any specific requirements of the development including testing (component, function, system, application, performance, or compatibility). You would also include any management requirements to help manage the development such as reports, documentation, design standards, certifications, customer requirements, operating environment, and requirements for samples or prototypes. Even if there isn't a specific development activity involved, you may establish specific acceptance and test requirements that must be done for acceptance based on Function, System, Application, performance, and compatibility. This is to ensure that their standard product you are buying meets your needs. Your requirements for acceptance should always have priority and not allow for supplier requested loopholes like their product will "materially comply" with the requirements.

General Specifications. In addition to the specific product specifications there may be a number of other specifications that you may want to require such as workmanship standards, quality standards, general requirements, packaging, packing and shipping specifications. For example in many cases supplier try to sell FOB Origin or EX-works where all risk of loss of damage in transit transfers to the buyer. If you agree to such terms and assume the inherent risk, the buyer should have the right to specify how they want the product packed and packaged and whom they want to use as the carrier to reduce and manage risk.

Quality Management Requirements. In buying products for manufacturing, intense quality management is required and this may require quality specification(s) and separate quality agreements or specifications. To ensure you get the product you ordered in consistent quality every time, contracts and quality specifications normally establish a formal change process which controls changes to the product itself and provides formal notification / approval for changes to the process that could affect quality. This may include approval over subcontractors, product acceptance criteria, shipped product quality levels, reliability levels to be met, and specific process change approvals or notifications required.

Unique Business Terms. Depending on the nature of what you are buying and the frequency or purchase, your contracts may need to have product unique business terms that may vary from product to product. Every unique business term needs to be made part of the contract either by amending the contract, the statement of work that's made part of the contract, or by some other document or process that is authorized by the contract. If its not made part of the contract the contract terms will not apply. If there are a number of changes you should work with your Law Department to legitimize the use of E-tools to do certain tasks like adding a part number or changing a price.

Process and Administrative Issues. Every contract needs to address Invoicing requirements, returns for defective products, RMA process for warranty returns, requirements for change notices, end of life notices and other notice requirements.

Performance Management Terms. In addition to the product specifications, deliverables, milestones, acceptance and test criteria, you may also need progress reviews, scorecard reviews, management escalation processes, to manage the Supplier. You may also need specific performance related remedies and damages that are authorized (such as liquidated damages) to help drive the supplier's performance. If you don't include management terms as part of the contract making it an obligation, the supplier wouldn't have to do anything you request. The supplier is only obligated to provide what they committed to provide in the contract.

Service and Support Requirements. Most purchases may require some degree of on-going support or service such as the ability and cost to purchase FRUs, Spare parts, Repairs, Maintenance, Support, Support Services and End of Life Purchases. It may also require the inclusion of hours of operation, response times, and problem escalation processes. If you are providing self-maintenance it may also require all of the above plus things like options to make end of life purchases, purchase of back-up support and service maintenance training. If you need future support and service, make those commitments part of your contract.

Change Management Requirements. As a change to the supplier's product could case that product not to work in the buyer's application, or changes to the supplier's processes could also cause quality problems or impact reliability or cause other problems such as form, fit, or function problems, buyer contracts need to address change order processes, product modifications, and process change requirements such as notices and approvals. The last thing you want to buy is something that meets the specifications but doesn't work in your application because a change occurred.

Documentation & Training. Depending on what you are purchasing the contract or specification should also define the requirements of manuals, operating instructions, product and maintenance documentation, translations, user manuals, record keeping, training, and end-user training.

Other Requirements Other requirements could include: buyer deliverables, coordination or integration requirements, rights to enhancements, upgrades, exclusivity commitments, escrow of materials, qualifications for those performing the work, designated suppliers or materials to be used, and security requirements, It could include special requirements dealing with supplier risk. If you will be dealing with supplier subsidiaries or affiliates it could include company or parent guarantee for those purchases. For single source items there could be requirements for things like second sources, manufacturing licenses, items held in escrow, disaster recovery commitments.

If its important to you, **make sure that its performance is measurable!**

- Product has specifications,
- Services have specifications or statement of work
- Performance has agreed quality, reliability levels or standards
- Delivery performance is established (lead-time, on-time delivery)
- Warranties are committed
- Changes that can impact quality and performance are controlled
- Basis for pricing and discounts is clearly established
- Methods for determining applicable remedies are clearly defined
- Required protections such as Indemnities or Insurances are clear

- Rights of termination by either of the parties are clearly defined.
- Flexibility commitments are established

Every commitment needs a time established for its performance. This includes the contract term, period of product availability, delivery lead time, acceptance time, replacement period for rejected products, warranty period, time for payment by buyer or supplier, period for warranty replacement, time to issue return material authorizations, end of life notice periods, time to exercise options, time for other notices, time standards for performance such as promptly, cure period for any breaches, frequency of performance for things like services, response times for services or problems, and times and levels required for problem escalation. Time commitments may be expressed in a number of different ways:

1. A specific number of minutes, hours or days to perform
2. A specific number of minutes, hours or days after an event to perform
3. A goal that is used in conjunction with a "no greater than" commitment. In this the supplier will try to meet the goal according to the standard of commitment they agreed, but they must meet the no greater period.
4. A period within another period to perform (e.g. X days in total in which to complete the work, with the requirement that once work commences it will be completed within Y days to minimize disruptions).

One of the most important factors in establishing time for performance is to define the measurement. For example, if its hours, is it clock hours or business hours. It its days, is it calendar days or business days? The difference between the two in both instances can be substantial. 70 business days equals at least 98 calendar days and probably more when you take into account holidays or other non-business days. If it's business days, which of the parties' business days are used to calculate the number of days? Business days will be different from company to company and from location to location. Use calendar days whenever possible.

Avoid anything where you leave the decision between alternatives to the supplier, unless every option is equally acceptable to you. Left to their decision they will decide the alternative that's best for them, and that could be the worst for you. If you can't reach agreement, consider limiting the options available. For example, for in warranty defective products the alternatives could be to repair, or replace the product or, provide a refund or credit the purchase price. If what you purchase is custom, and it's repairable, the supplier will not want to provide a refund or credit and be stuck with the product. They will want to repair it and return it to you. If the product isn't repairable, the only difference between replace or credit is the supplier will lose the contribution to overhead and profit that was included in the price. If the buyer needs the item to be replaced, they may not want the supplier to provide them with a refund or credit. For example if you purchased a spare part to a piece of equipment and it was defective, providing you with a refund or credit may leave you with the situation where the equipment doesn't work because you don't have the part or you can't to a repair because you don't have the part.

Avoid language requiring mutually agreement, because there is never any guarantee that it will be agreed. If you must commit to something being mutually agreed, require that:

- The agreement will not be reasonably withheld or delayed.
- The negotiation must be conducted in good faith.
- When possible establish parameters for agreement in advance such as a third source, benchmark, industry data, etc.
- Create a default position if there isn't agreement so you aren't forced to accept less. For example, if the parties fail to reach agreement on pricing for the next contract period after negotiating in good faith, the default could be that the buyer may continue to purchase at the same price and terms for X days thereafter to allow the buyer to transition to another source.

Contracting Party. For major agreements or agreements with substantial risk, contracts should be written with the parent company or major operating division that owns the business and not sales subsidiaries or third parties. Supplier subsidiaries may not have the resources and assets to stand behind their contractual promises (e.g. warranties, indemnifications) and third parties have even less. The parent company is not obligated to honor the promises of the subsidiary or the 3rd Party. If you must buy from a subsidiary or 3rd party there are two approaches you can take: 1) Write contracts with the parent company and have the parent company designate the subsidiary or 3rd party as an agent to perform certain functions such as receiving orders, issuing RMA's (return material authorizations) etc. 2) Write contracts with the supplier subsidiary or 3rd party and have the parent company execute a "parent or company guarantee" or other document where they agree to be responsible for certain liabilities for those purchases. For example if a supplier only want to sell through distribution, you can still have an agreement with the Supplier where for those purchases they make certain commitments directly to you. The full legal name for both parties should be used in the contract and that all future amendments, correspondence, etc. You may identify and define the parties to a contract by a defined term that will be used throughout the contract to simplify references to the parties rather than having to spell out their entire legal names each time they are referred to.

Effective Date. Each contract requires the establishment of an Effective Date. Putting the Effective Date in the first paragraph makes it easy to find after the contract is signed and also makes it easier to describe the contract in other documents in a precise way, such as "with an Effective Date of December 21, 2012".

Incorporating Documents by Reference. Documents that are not a part of the contract need to be incorporated into the contract. Simply attaching them to the contract does not make them part of the contract. To properly make them part of the contract they should be incorporated by reference within the body of the contract or within the body of another document that has been properly incorporated by reference into the contract. Incorporation of a document by reference is done by: stating the incorporation by reference in the body of the contract where the specific document is referred to, or incorporating those documents in listing of Attachments within the contract.

Examples:

Pricing is set forth in Attachment A, entitled "product and Price List", five (5) pages, dated January 2, 2002, which is incorporated by reference into this contract.

Section ___ Attachments.

The following Attachments are hereby incorporated by reference into this contract:

Attachment A, entitled "product and Price List", 5 pages, dated January 2, 2012

Attachment B, entitled "Cancellation and Rescheduling Terms", 1 page, dated January 2, 2012

Attachment C, entitled "supplier Quality Agreement", 5 pages, dated December 31, 2011

This Statement of Work adopts and incorporates by reference the terms and conditions of Base Agreement #_____).

The key thing you need to do is make it very clear exactly what document(s) you are incorporating by reference. To do that each document to be incorporated should have a name, title, or reference number. Documents should have a date, or formal revision number so you know the exact version of the document that is included. If the document consists of multiple pages or if all pages of the document are not intended to be incorporated, list the number of pages, or applicable page numbers. Check to ensure that the title of the document you want to incorporate is exactly the same in both places.

Exhibits. Exhibits can be used to explain things in either the contract or in an Attachment. If they are to explain something in the contract, they should be incorporated by reference into the contract. If they are to explain something in an Attachment, they should be incorporated by reference into the Attachment so that it is clear that it applies only to that specific Attachment. Exhibits should have the following on each page: a title; a date; reference to the contract or SOW number it applies to, or reference to the Attachment to which it is an Exhibit; and page numbers.

Incorporation of Exhibits may be done in the same manner as incorporation of Attachments where they are either incorporated where they are first mentioned or listed within the document they become an Exhibit to.

Example of incorporating an Exhibit where first mentioned:

(As set forth in Exhibit 1 entitled, "Lead-times", 2 pages dated February 23, 2012)

Example of Listing Exhibits:

Exhibits.

The following Exhibit are attached to and made a part of this Attachment:

    Exhibit 1, entitled "Lead-times," 2 pages, dated February 23, 2012

Pen and Ink Changes. When a change is required to a contract sent for signature, sometimes parties will strike out or write in changed language. While the cleanest way to manage these changes is to re-generate the contract with the changes and have it re-signed, it is also legal to make pen and ink changes. All such pen and ink changes to the contract must be initialed by both of the individuals who are signing the contract. If only one party initials the change, the change has not been formally agreed upon.

Initialing all Pages. If there is any concern about the integrity of the supplier, you may want to take the additional step of having both parties initial each page of the contract, Attachments, Exhibits and all other documents that make up the contract. This prevents the unscrupulous supplier from removing a page and substituting a page with different content where it could be difficult to prove which page was placed in the contract.

Use of Defined Terms. When terms used in a contract have a specific definition / meaning, they are usually defined either in a definitions section of the contract or, they may be defined in the contract by adding language that makes it a defined term. Example: (hereafter referred to as "Product"). The first letter of Defined terms is always capitalized. Some people will capitalize the entire word or term. In drafting and reviewing contracts you need to check each ime a defined word is used throughout the contract and any associated documents to ensure it is used properly as a defined term. If it should be a used as defined term, the first letter must be capitalized ("Product"). If it should not be used as a defined term, the first letter must be lower case ("product"). This is important because many terms may have multiple meanings such as material, and the use of the defined term will determine which meaning applies. In reviewing your contract, also ensure that the defined terms are used consistently throughout. For example: If "Products" is a defined term used in the contract and the contract points to another document that will specify the Product its important in that document to refer to them as Products using the defined term. The reason for this is commitments in the contract may apply to Products (such as Product Warranties). If you purchase something that is not described as a Product you would be purchasing a product, not a Product and the contract coverage may not apply

Make sure that you define and explain any acronyms or technical terms used and try to avoid using internal acronyms unless they are fully defined.

Dates/ Date Numbering Convention. In writing dates, the recommended approach is to spell out the date – February 23. 2002 and not use abbreviations such as 2/23/02 or 2.23.02. The reason for this is that different countries have different date numbering conventions. The US numbering convention is month/date/year. Other countries have numbering conventions of day/month/year. For example we have 02/07/02, in the US it means February 2, 2002, but in other countries with a different date numbering convention it could mean the 2nd of July 2002.

Numbers. When a number is used in the body of the contract it is recommended that you spell out the number both alphabetically and numerically. This is to eliminate any confusion and in the event of a problem the written word will have priority. This is not recommended for price lists that contain many prices. For example: "The non-recurring charges shall be One Thousand US dollars (US$ 1,000.00)." "Supplier shall provide the replacement part within five (5) calendar days."

Currency. To avoid confusion on currency, it is recommended that you spell out the currency (Ten Thousand U.S. Dollars (US$10,000.00)) where used or through a clause (e.g. "All amounts and prices listed in this contract shall be in U.S. Dollars").

Applicability of other documents in amending or changing the contract.
There can be a number of other documents or correspondence between a

buyer and supplier. It is important to understand that those documents cannot change or amend the terms of the contract unless they are identified as an amendment to the contract, reference the contract and are signed by authorized representatives of both parties or the parties have agreed that other actions, documents or writings may constitute an amendment. Why is this important? If a product or service hasn't been properly added to the contract, it will not get all of the protections that the contract provides, and coverage would be limited only to the standard purchase order terms.

If there is a document that is signed by authorized parties to the contract after the Effective Date of the contract with the same contract number listed, you have a later writing between the parties to the contract and later writings have priority over earlier writings. This could amend the contract. When you do have a writing signed after the Effective Date, you must make it very clear what the writing applies to. If the change only applies to one product or Service or a group of products or Services, you need to make that clear. Otherwise your later writing could amend the requirements for all products or Services. WA's issued after the Effective Date may alter the terms of the contract for those purchases made under those WA's. One thing to remember is that the Order of Precedence clause only deals with establishing the precedence between documents when there is an inconsistency. It does not deal with additional or new items that aren't consistent with the existing contract.

Manage Lists. When you use lists in the contract, check to determine whether it is meant to be all-inclusive or not. If you don't intend it to be all-inclusive, the list should be preceded with language that shows that the items listed are just examples by adding wording such as "This includes, but is not limited to"

Make it Clear.
1. Avoid using internal acronyms or abbreviations.
2. Avoid repetition. Repetition creates the potential for conflicts or confusion.
3. Make sure the word or examples you use only have one meaning. If there are multiple meanings, create defined terms.
4. Write short sentences.
5. If something is meant to be binding use words such as "shall" or "will"
6. Write the clauses so they are clear and unambiguous.
7. Use words that are direct, precise and would be commonly understood.

One of the best ways to make a contract clear is to write in the active voice. In my blog you should read Contract Drafting – Using Active Voice with the blog date of December 12, 2010 to learn more.

Check the Document. Check spelling; paragraph numbering, and all cross-references both manually and with your word processor's spelling and grammar checker. Have someone else read it.

CHAPTER 17. HOW SUPPLIER'S ATTEMPT TO MANAGE THEIR LIABILITY

In their Proposal suppliers will normally:

- Manage the quotation and any representations made before or during the contracting process to only those things that can be clearly delivered.
- Ensure that their response to quotation is clear, and states any necessary assumptions or clarifications including the clear definition of deliverables by both parties.
- Review the requirements as to suitability of what is requested / proposed.

In the negotiation of contract terms, suppliers will attempt to:

1. Not assume risks or seek terms that transfer the risks to the buyer
2. Provide a reduced standard of commitment.
3. Ensure there are clear definitions of deliverables and dependencies.
4. Ensure there is a clear definition of responsibilities for all parties.
5. Include limitation of liability provisions, and specific disclaimers to avoid certain types of damages such as incidental, consequential or special.
6. Accept only those terms that can be reasonably performed and managed.
7. Seek relief from performance for problems caused by parties not under their control, such as non-performance by buyer specified suppliers or subcontractors, or defective buyer supplied items.
8. Require clear measurement criteria and acceptance tests.
9. Ensure any warranties and performances are tied to what they can reasonably manage and that appropriate exclusions are included.

During the performance execution suppliers will attempt to:
- Transfer risks contractually to their suppliers and subcontractors.
- Perform qualification of subcontractors and suppliers.
- Flow down responsibilities and liabilities (so each has clear deliverables).
- Manage the activity and deliverables.
- Ensure that customers, and other parties not under their control, are held to their commitments.
    a. Implement detailed change control and management.
    b. Ensure all parties involved meet their performance requirements (delivery & performance to schedule, quality, and compliance to specifications)
    c. Periodic reviews of performance.
    d. Implementation of corrective actions.
    e. Document all requested changes and buyer instructions, and supplier requests for waivers.
    f. Documentation of all delays or performance problems having an effect on performance.

In this Chapter we'll focus on the two parts of the negotiation / contracting process that suppliers frequently attempt in trying to reduce their potential risk and liability. The first is reviewing forms of softening / qualifying language they may use to limit their commitment. The second is a subset of that which is the standard of performance there want to commit to by the words they propose.

17.1 Qualifying / Softening Language

Most supplier proposed contract changes fall into several categories.

- They may want to strike an entire section or concept. When that happens it's very easy to see and understand what has been changed. If you understand what the language was intended to provide, you'll understand the impact of the deletion.
- The supplier may want to add additional language in terms of additional rights or remedies for the supplier or additional obligations of the buyer. For the most part, that's also easy to see and understand the potential impact of these types of changes.
- The third type of change is when they use qualifying or softening language. Qualifying or softening language is subtler. The addition or change of a single word can change the entire meaning of the section, the rights or remedies you may have, and what the supplier's potential responsibility or liability may be.

In negotiating contracts you need to be on the lookout for qualifying words and their impact and understand when to use them. What are qualifying of softening words?

All the standards of commitment words other than will or shall are qualifying words such as: best efforts, reasonable efforts, commercially reasonable efforts, intend, may, good faith. Here's a list of a number of other common qualifying words you may find in contracts.

1. Conditional commitment (If X happens then we will do Y)
2. Material
3. Materially adverse
4. Unreasonable
5. Knowledge
6. Substantially
7. Form, fit and function
8. Promptly
9. Including without limitation
10. Direct
11. Gross
12. Willful
13. Finally
14. Arising out of

15. Related to
16. Out of pocket
17. Sole or sole and exclusive
18. At its sole option,
19. May, but shall not be obligated to

Suppliers use qualifying words to lower the standard of their commitments and reduce their potential risk and liability. For example "reasonable efforts" lowers the standard from an absolute commitment to only have to use reasonable efforts. They may also raise a standard to make something more difficult for them to be at fault. For example: gross or willful when used with negligent behavior for which they would be liable raises the standard that is needed for them to be liability for their acts. Qualifying words can be used to delay their obligations, such as inserting "finally" into when they are obligated to pay based on a judgment. They are also used to limit exposure such as only being responsible to pay for "out of pocket costs" (which would exclude any buyer internal costs). Having a remedy be described as "sole and exclusive" would exclude all other remedies.

In addition to qualifying words there are other qualifiers such as

- Exceptions or carve outs
- Trumping of precedence provisions
- Conditions precedent
- References to the ordinary course of business
- References to consistent with prior practice
- Floors or ceilings
- Exclusions to avoid doubt
- Point in time language
- Triggering events

Qualifying words or qualifiers inserted by a supplier that are related to a buyer's commitment are most frequently used to increase the level of commitment made by the buyer to the supplier. Qualifying words inserted by a supplier that relate to the supplier's commitments or obligations are done to reduce the commitment as part of their trying to manage their cost, risk, and potential liability. Most qualifying words do not help clarify things in the contract as the two parties can easily disagree on what each party considers to be reasonable, material, prompt, or substantial.

17.2 Exceptions and carve outs

Exceptions and carve outs are frequently found in standard contract language. For example, most Intellectual Property Indemnification provision will provide for exceptions to the indemnity for infringements that may have been caused by the buyer. Most Limitation of Liability provisions will include a carve out of the limitation so that for the breach of certain specified clauses, more than just direct damages may be recovered. Exceptions or carve outs make the language not absolute between the parties for all situations. For example "except as provided for elsewhere" is an example of a carve out which would override the commitment in the section where it is used. There can also be what's called basket exceptions where certain acts are allowed within certain agreed parameters so a restriction is not absolute. For the supplier the goal of a carve out or exception is usually to expand or broaden the exception or add new carve outs or exceptions to avoid being responsible or liable. For the buyer a common use of carve outs or exceptions relates to firm commitments. For example a buyer could agree to purchase all of its requirements for a particular item, as long as the supplier meets certain requirements or goals in terms of cost, quality, delivery or technology. That provides the buyer with an exception to the commitment if the supplier fails to meet those requirements or goals.

Materiality: Materiality is a common qualifier that suppliers want to include. For example a supplier may want to insert language that allows them to take certain actions without the buyer's approval as long as that doesn't materially impact the buyer.

Material adverse affect. Material Adverse Impact would allow the party to do or not do something unless the other party could show that not only were they impacted, but also the impact was both material and adverse. As a buyer you may want to use the concept of material adverse affect in some instances. For example, a requirement for indemnification may be timely notice on the part of the buyer of a claim. If you failed to provide timely notice it could void the indemnification. To prevent that, you could include language to the effect that "buyer's failure to provide timely notice shall not relieve the supplier of its responsibility to indemnify the buyer provided that such delay in notice does not _materially adversely affect_ the supplier's ability to defend against such claim.

Unreasonably withhold consent. Most of the time supplier's want to be free to manage their own business in the way they best see fit and want to avoid provide the buyer with the right to require consent over certain actions that it may want to take. There are also certain actions where they simply will not be willing to agree to consent of the buyer such as with things like a change of control where they agree to merge with or be purchased by another company. If they are willing to agree to buyer's consent, they will want that subject to a reasonableness standard so the buyer can't withhold their consent without good reason. In many agreements the buyer may want to place controls over what the supplier may do as change may cause problems. For example if you were buying something that was heavily personal focused such as an individual team doing your work, you may want consent prior to any changes being made to the team. For products you may want consent prior to any changes in the product that could affect quality or it's working in a particular application. If who does the work is important to you, you probably want to have consent over subcontracting the work or assignment of the contract to third parties. Whether you prohibit something completely or agree to not unreasonably withhold consent really depends upon the importance of the action to you and the leverage you have in the relationship. It may be reasonable as a part of giving your consent to require additional commitments or considerations. When I did construction contracting much of the equipment and materials that we would specify would be a specific brand product and part number "or equal". Contractors would be required to submit to for our approval any materials or equipment they were proposing using as an "or equal". If we felt it was acceptable for use, but of lesser cost or value we would require a credit as a condition of providing that consent. If we were concerned with its reliability we might require an additional warranty period on the item as a condition of the consent.

Knowledge. Another common qualifier that supplier's may want to include is a "knowledge qualifier". This occurs most frequently in warranties or representations, where they may want to insert it in a number of situations to water down their commitment and reduce their potential liability. For example, your language may say:

> "Supplier warrants that the product does not infringe the Intellectual Property rights of any third party"

Their proposal back could be:

> "To the best of supplier's knowledge, supplier warrants that the product does not infringe the Intellectual Property rights of any third party"

The difference between these two commitments is significant. In the first case you have an absolute warranty against IP infringement. In the second case, if there is an infringement, but at the time they signed the contract they had no knowledge of it, they will have met their commitment and not have breached the warranty. Another knowledge qualifier is actual knowledge. The impact that it has is the party may only be liable or need to take certain actions if they have actual knowledge of a fact. If they don't have actual knowledge they have met the commitment.

A knowledge qualifier can be in buyer's interest. For example, assume that a supplier wanted to include a restriction on the buyer where the buyer must take certain acts in the event certain facts occur. The buyer may want to insert qualifying language to do two things. One may be to require actual knowledge as a pre-condition to their taking action and the other could be to make it clear that buyer is under no obligation to manage the item, so they only must take action if and when they have actual knowledge. For example, assume the supplier wants to include language in the contract that limits the use of their product to use solely in buyer's products. You wouldn't want to breach the contract and be liable if you find out that somewhere in the supply chain the product is being used in other ways. So you would want to qualify your commitment with language such as:

> "Buyer shall not knowingly allow the use of supplier's products in products other than buyer's products. Buyer may, but shall not be obligated to, verify the use of such products. If Supplier provides notice of situations of unauthorized use or Buyer has actual knowledge of such unauthorized use, then Buyer shall ___"

In writing it that way, the only time you would assume potential liability is if you have actual knowledge and then fail to take the agreed actions.

Substantially in the form of. This allows for changes to me made that can allow something like a new contract to be different as long as the difference isn't "substantial". I'm not fond of agreeing to agree in the future and suggest that if you are going to use something that talks about a new contract to be substantially in the form of something that, you take the time to narrow down the issues that remain to be agreed. Most of the time, the further out in time you go in coming to agreement, the less leverage you have. You may have eliminated other options or invested too much money, time or effort to walk away.

Form, fit, and function. This is frequently used when a supplier wants to be free to make changes without the buyer's approval or consent as long as the change doesn't affect the "form, fit, or function" of the product. You can have changes that don't affect the form, fit or function that can affect the quality, and reliability or a product and whether it works in a specific application.

Promptly. This is used to avoid agreeing to a specific period in which to take action. As parties can easily disagree on what promptly means. If response were important to you I'd always include firm commitment and look upon promptly as a goal and include the firm commitment. For example "Supplier shall promptly notify Buyer of any planned end of life actions and all ends of life notices shall be provided at least 12 months prior to the planned end of life date."

Substantially all, substantial portion. This waters the commitment down from being absolute to something less. For example all that needs to be done is for the work to be substantially complete for a payment to be released. It its important for it to all be completed, if you agree to do something based upon something being "substantially" done, make sure that you have the right to retain enough money until it is all completed.

In the ordinary course of business. This opens the contract interpretation up to what occurs in the ordinary course of business, which may conflict with what the parties agreed in the four corners of the contract

Consistent with prior practice. This opens the contract interpretation up to what occurred in prior practice, not what the parties agreed in the four corners of the contract.

Trumping / precedence provisions –precedence over others. An example of a trumping provision is "Except as otherwise provided for in Section ___ of this contract". This would have a commitment in the section where it is used be overridden by the other referenced section

Floors and ceilings. A "floor" is usually described by the words "not less than" and represents a minimum. A "ceiling" is usually described as "not to exceed" or "not greater than" and represents a maximum. Every buyer should be aware of two common qualifiers that are frequently used with pricing, but which may be used in other areas. Those are "Not to exceed" and "Not less than". For example in what I call two stage commitments you may include both a goal and an absolute and the "not to exceed" qualifying language would be used to set the absolute. For example:

> "Supplier shall use reasonable efforts to deliver the Product within five business days, but delivery shall not exceed Ten (10) calendar days.

Without the "not to exceed", the only commitment you would have is that they will use reasonable efforts to delivery in five days. If they don't deliver, but used reasonable efforts they met their commitment. The "not to exceed" establishes an absolute commitment.

"Not less than" is also a qualifier you may want to use. For example assume that the supplier wanted to cap certain liability at a multiple of the value of the past year's purchases. That may be fine, but what if there were no prior year purchases or you encounter a situation after the contract has expired or the purchases have stopped and there are none? In that case a "but not less than" qualifier provides you with protection that, no matter the circumstances the amount will not be less than that amount. For example

> "Supplier's annually liability for the breach of this section shall not exceed five times the prior years total purchases by buyer from supplier, but shall not be less than US$____ Millions dollars"

Suppliers may want to insert "floors" when it comes to buyer's commitments to them so the level of purchases will not be less than a certain amount. More frequently they will include ceilings in areas of liability where they want to cap their liability at a specific amount. For example in negotiation of a limitation of liability provision they will traditionally want to limit both the types of damages that they may be liable for and they will want a ceiling for the total amount of the damages that they may be liable for. buyers may use ceilings to cap their maximum upside price and payment liability.

Formula. To avoid confusion or misinterpretation the parties may decide to include a formula in as a qualifier.

Exclusions to avoid doubt. This is used when the parties agree that there is a specific exclusion that they both agree upon and want to spell that out so it's clear that the exclusion in the contract does not apply to it. Many time an exclusion to avoid doubt can take the for of a disclaimer such as the one that suppliers will routinely want to have inserted in a warranty provision to exclude implied warranties or merchantability or fitness for a particular purpose such as.

> **SUPPLIER DISCLAIMS ALL OTHER WARRANTIES, EXPRESS OR IMPLIED, REGARDING SUCH PRODUCTS, INCLUDING BUT NOT LIMITED TO ANY IMPLIED WARRANTIES OF MERCHANTABILITY, FITNESS FOR A PARTICULAR PURPOSE OR NON-INFRINGEMENT.**

Including without limitation. This is used to usually expand / not limit what be required or what they may be liable for. If you provide a list, it is used to ensure that the list isn't considered to be all-inclusive. A buyer may have language in their contract that requires the supplier to reimburse the buyer for certain costs. The language in the buyer's contract may say:

> "supplier shall reimburse buyer for all costs and expenses, which includes but are not limited to, _____" (where the blank would include a listing of all the different types of costs and expenses.)

To make sure that the expenses are not limited to only those included in the list, the buyer inserted qualifying language "which includes but are not limited to". The supplier in their response may propose striking the qualifier to later argue that the list was inclusive and or may want to list only those specific types of costs that will be reimbursed, or they could include their own qualifier such as "may include only". In using the broad open-ended qualifier you don't need to list all the possible different things, as the list isn't limited. If you agreed use a limiting qualifier, your list would need to include all possible different types of costs or expenses, because if you didn't list it, you wouldn't be able to claim it.

Point in time language. Point in time language is usually used in things like warranties or representations to avoid the warranty or representation from continuing through the life of the contract. For example, "Upon the execution of this contract, supplier warrants that the products don't infringe the Intellectual

Property rights of any third party". If you agree to point in time language, they only need to be in compliance at that specific time. So in the example, if there was a claim made the day after the contract was signed, the supplier would not be responsible for that as all they warranted was that there was no claim at the time of execution of the contract.

Gross negligence. This is used in commitments about negligence and indemnification. It requires a higher standard to be liable. Instead of liable for simply being negligent, the standard of negligence needs to be gross negligence.

Willful misconduct. This is similar to gross negligence in the fact that it requires a higher standard for the party to be liable. Instead of being liable for misconduct, the misconduct must be willful.

Trigger events. Language that establishes trigger events is most frequently used in things like termination or when license rights would be provided. For example if a clause said "If either party breaches a material provision in this contract and the non-breaching party notifies the breaching party in writing of the breach and the breaching party and fails to cure such breach within thirty (30) calendar days, then the non-breaching party may terminate this contract for cause." In this language there are multiple triggers. First there must be a breach. Second the non-breaching party must send a notice. Third, the breaching party must fail to cure the breach within the 30 days. Only then does non-breaching party have all the completed triggers that give them the right to terminate. The goal of a party proposing changes to trigger events is usually to make it more difficult for the other party to accrue those rights.

Conditions precedent. A condition precedent is language that makes the commitment or duty not firm until the named condition precedent has been met. For example if the Patriots are in the 2010 Super Bowl, I will pay you $10,000 to cater my party. The language "If the Patriots are in the 2010 Super Bowl" is a condition precedent and the obligation to pay the $10.000 for the party catering would not be effective unless that condition precedent is met.

Final or finally. Suppliers frequently try to insert these in contracts in language that deals with when there is an obligation to make a payment. For example the difference between a supplier agreeing to pay all costs awarded versus all costs finally awarded is substantial. The term "finally" would mean that payment would be made only after all appeals have been exhausted making the award is final. As appeals could go on for many years, the net present value of the difference between paid immediately versus getting paid in maybe 10 years from now would be substantial. At low interest rates the value would be about 50% in higher rates the value of that late payment would be basically pennies on a dollar.

"Arising out of" versus "relating to" In using the words "arising out of" requires that there be a direct causal relationship. If you use the words "relating to" it does not require a cause, it only must be related to the act.

"Sole" or "sole and exclusive". The words "sole" or 'sole and exclusive" are frequently used to limit the remedies that a party may have. For example, in an on-time delivery provision in a buyer's contract the buyer may list certain specific remedies for the failure to deliver on time such as the right to cancel the order or have the supplier pay for any premium freight costs. suppliers may propose language that to the effect that those remedies be the sole and exclusive remedies for the failure to make a timely delivery. If the buyer were to agree to that, buyer would not be able to terminate the contract or sue for damages as they by the language agreed that the listed remedies would be the sole and exclusive remedies.

At its sole option. This is frequently used when there are a number of potential options that may be available and the party wants to have the right to pick which option they want. For example, if a supplier shipped the buyer defective product the buyer might want to have the right to have the item repaired or replaced or has a credit or refund of the purchase price. The supplier may want to change that from the buyer's option to their option. What's the impact? In most cases it means that the supplier will not want to provide the buyer with a credit or refund so the buyer will be forced to wait until the supplier either repairs of replaces it. What it can also do is create a situation where the buyer really needs the repaired or replacement product, but the supplier could opt not to provide it if was simpler or cheaper for them to just provide a refund. I would never give the supplier the sole option to take steps that could negatively impact the buyer and with faced with this issue might simply split it where it would be supplier's option to decide whether to repair or replace the item, but that any refund or credit would require the buyer's consent so I couldn't be forced into getting a credit or refund when what I need is for them to delivery the product.

May, but shall not be obligated to. In situations where, as the buyer, you want the option to do something but do not want to be obligated to do it, you could use a qualifier such as:

"buyer may, but shall not be obligated to," or

"buyer may, in its sole discretion,"

This provides the buyer the right, but not the obligation to take the action. For example, not every time the supplier breaches a contract may you want to terminate the contract with them. So in your language on termination, you would probably have language that doesn't force you to terminate, as much as does provide you the right to terminate if you so desire.

Direct. The word direct is used this frequently is used in conjunction with a discussion on damages. For example suppliers will use it when they want to limit their potential liability on an item to only direct damages and not be subject to claims for incidental or consequential damaged.

Out of pocket. This expression is used in conjunction with the language around the recovery of costs or damages and is used to try to avoid having to pay for internal costs. "Out of pocket" would mean amounts that they had to pay to others, not costs that they incurred internally. When there is a problem the majority of the costs may be internal, so before you agree to accept "out of pocket" as a qualifier, understand what the impact would be on your recovery.

Other words to watch out for

All, only For example, if a supplier inserted "all" or "only" to a commitment on buyers purchases it could create what's called a requirements contract where the buyer would be obligated to only purchase that type of product from supplier or to purchase all of its requirements from the supplier. The buyer's language may say.

"buyer shall purchase capacitors from supplier".

The supplier could counter with

"buyer shall only purchase capacitors from supplier" or

"buyer shall purchase all of its capacitor requirements from supplier"

Both are examples of adding qualifying language that would limit buyer's ability to purchase capacitors only from the supplier.

In negotiating contracts, you need to always look at the intent of any language inserted to understand the potential impact and what that word or words mean. For example what's the difference between these two commitments?

"Supplier shall pay all expenses, cost and damages awarded"

"Supplier shall pay all expenses, costs and damaged finally awarded

Or

"Supplier shall reimburse buyer for all direct costs related to...

"Supplier shall reimburse buyer for all direct out of pocket costs related to

If you read the chapter 2 that discussed Total Cost you should be know that in the first example, the insertion of "finally" would allow the supplier to not pay anything until those costs are "finally awarded" which means that the supplier would have to exhaust all legal appeals before they are obligated to make payment. That could take many years and financially that would mean the difference between getting paid now, or ten years from now when the net present value of the payment would be substantially less.

In the second example the insertion of the qualifying language "out of pocket" would allow the buyer to only collect for costs that the buyer actually had to pay to others. That would preclude the Buyer from being able to recover any costs that the buyer may have incurred on its own.

17.3 Commitment Standards

In establishing performance there are many promises and conditions. There are Express Conditions that are those that are spelled out in the contract. There can implied conditions that are necessary to perform the work. For example if you contract with a supplier to perform construction on the interior of a building, the implied condition is that you will provide them with access to perform the work. There may also be constructive conditions that would be supplied by the courts if the intent of the parties weren't clear. The key in creating express conditions is to understand the standards of commitment as the commitment varies based on the language you use to establish them.

You can:

1. Intend to do something
2. Agree to agree in the future
3. The party can make a commitment that they may do something
4. Agree to agree in the future with both parties acting in good faith
5. Agree to act in "good faith"
6. Agree to do what is "commercially reasonable"
7. Agree to do what is "reasonable"
8. Agree to do it with "best efforts"
9. Make a conditional commitment (If X happens then we will do Y)
10. Make an absolute commitment ("shall, will")
11. Make it a representation
12. Make it a warranty.

Intent. A statement that the parties "intend" to do something is not a firm commitment on its own as the parties are free to change their intent.

Agree to agree is not a firm commitment as there is nothing that forces the parties to agree and if you don't agree, there is not commitment.

Saying that a party **"may"** do something does not obligate the party to do that. It provides a right, but not a duty. For example, in most termination provisions we may terminate the contract but we are not obligated to terminate it

"Should" also does not require performance. It merely describes what a party should do, not what they must do.

Agree to agree in the future with both parties acting in good faith only requires the parties to act in good faith in seeking to agree. If there is no agreement and you can't prove bad faith (which is difficult) they met their obligation

Agree to **act in "good faith"** only requires that they act in good faith, if they did and you didn't get what was promised they met their obligation

Agree to do what is **"commercially reasonable"** requires them to act in a manner that would be customary for their industry. If something would cost them more to do it may not be commercially reasonable.

Agree to do what is **"reasonable"** only requires them to assert reasonable efforts to perform, but requires more than commercially reasonable

Agree to do it with **"best efforts"** is frequently interpreted to mean that they are required to asset their best efforts irrespective of cost to do something which has in some cases been interpreted to mean up to the full extent of their assets.

None of these guarantee you will receive performance, they only require the party must exert that committed level of effort to perform.

Making a **conditional commitment or pre-condition** (If X happens then we will do Y) is an absolute commitment only if the condition is met. If the condition is not met there is no commitment.

Using words such as **"will" or "shall"** are the only unconditional commitment to perform.

If you need or want something done, the language that requires it must be in clear, unequivocal terms. For example saying that a supplier "should" do something does not require that they do it! It only says that they should. If they chose not to, they met their obligation.

If it isn't practical or economically feasible to require a firm commitment, you may consider a two-stage commitment approach. For example, the supplier shall use best efforts to do X within __ days, but X shall be done in no greater than __ days. This provides a best efforts commitment to meet a target or goal, but also an absolute requirement to provide it by the no greater than date.

Only agree to use reasonable or commercially reasonable efforts when absolutely necessary and always try to get a 2-stage commitment when using them. For example, supplier shall use reasonable efforts to perform repair or replacement of Defective products within X days after receipt, but in no event shall repair or replacement be provided in more than Y days.

As the impact of problems can vary, consider language adjusting the standards of commitment depending on the magnitude of the problem. For example:

"Supplier shall use reasonable efforts to perform repair or replacement of Defective products within X days after receipt, but in no event shall repair or replacement be provided in more than Y days. If the percentage of Defective products exceeds A%, supplier shall use its best efforts to perform repair of replacement in N days, and in no event shall the repair or replacement be provided in more than ___ days. " (Where each period allows less time because of the magnitude of the problem)

When time is important to the commitment, use language that makes the time period clear an unequivocal. For example the difference between a lead-time of 90 days is substantially different whether it is 90 calendar days or 90 business days (which equates to at least 126 calendar days). Define Days as Calendar Days so it clear. Simply saying the supplier must do something in 5 hours could mean either business hours or consecutive hours. If you called at Friday as 3:00 and the supplier was open 8-5 Monday thru Friday it could mean that it won't be done until Monday at 11 when you may need it by 8:00 PM on Friday.

Make it clear what you want. For example requirements for bi-monthly reports could mean twice monthly or every other month. Use specific dates like on 1st and 15th day of the month

Except for the Payment obligation (which in most cases will be conditioned on the receipt of conforming goods and an acceptable invoice). **Buyers should resist making firm commitments to perform.** If the buyer makes a firm performance commitment, the buyer may be liable if it fails to meet its commitments. For example, if the buyer is responsible to provide materials or approvals to the supplier by a certain date, the buyer could be subject to claims from the supplier for damages the supplier sustains if the buyer fail to meet that date. If you are forced to make a firm commitment, always address and limit the supplier's remedies for your potential failure. For example:

"buyer shall provide its acceptance or rejection within 10 calendar days after receipt from supplier. If buyer fails to provide such approvals or rejection in a timely manner, supplier shall be provided a day for day extension of the performance period as the sole remedy for buyer's failure to respond on time".

-or-

If buyer fails to delivery the materials on time, supplier may cover and buyer's sole liability shall not exceed _____.

One of the important things to manage in the negotiation of the contract is to manage how commitment standards and conditions are used within the contract. For example, it's not uncommon for a supplier to want to include a precondition before a commitment or liability so if the pre-condition were not met they would not be responsible. For example I've seen suppliers who as a part of their commitment to indemnify the buyer against third party claims wanted to require the condition of buyer providing them with timely notice of the claim. If you accepted that it would eliminate that protection completely if you failed to provide the timely notice to meet that condition. There are several problems with this. First, the parties can and probably will disagree over the meeting of timely notice. The failure to provide notice may not have any impact on why the claims was made and may not have had any impact on the supplier's ability to defend against the claim. You don't want to release a supplier from liability unless your action caused the problem or you inaction prevented them from being able to manage the risk. If the Supplier insisted on prompt notice as a condition of the indemnification a good counter might be to add something like "Failure by the Buyer to provide prompt notice shall not exclude Supplier's responsibility to indemnify Buyer unless such failure materially prejudiced Supplier's ability to defend against the claim. In doing the failure alone wouldn't excuse them , there would need to be both the failure and it must have impacted their ability to defend against the claim.

In addition to specific performance commitments a contract will also have warranties and representations regarding their performance, their product or service or specific facts that the buyer may be relying on to enter into the contracts.

Material representations. A material representation is another form of commitment. A material representation is a convincing statement made to induce someone to enter into a contract that would not have agreed without the representation. If the material representation is included in the contract and proves not to be true or misleading, the party that received the representation in the contract can rescinded or cancels the contract without liability. For example if you said, "supplier represents that supplier has all necessary governmental licenses to perform the work." that would be a material representation If that representation proves to be untrue or misleading, the buyer may terminate the contract without liability.

Warranty commitments. A warranty is the highest level of commitment a supplier can make and the breach of a warranty has the highest potential ramification to the supplier. If the supplier makes a warranty and that warranty is breached and not cured by the supplier, the breach of a warranty is a material breach and the buyer would have the right to both terminate the contract and sue for any damages they sustain.

Implied warranties. In addition to the specific warranties or representations that may be spelled out in the contract, there may also be implied warranties that may exist under law unless they have been specifically disclaimed in the contract. The **implied warranty of merchantability** means that the goods are fit for the ordinary purposes for which they are used. They are or average quality and they are adequately packaged, and labeled. The **implied warranty of fitness for a particular purpose** is when the supplier knows the purpose for which the product will be used and knows that they buyer is relying on the Supplier's skills and judgment to select that product for buyer's purposes. It is not uncommon for supplier to want to disclaim all implied warranties.

Rights and duties. In specifying acts, there are rights and duties.

1. A party who has a **right** does not need to exercise the right. For example, either party may terminate the contract as a result of a "Material Breach" by the other party. They are not obligated to exercise the right. For example rights can be defined using "may". For example Buyer may extend this agreement for a period of one (1) year by providing notice to the Supplier on or before December 20, 2012. The Buyer has the right but not the obligation to exercise the right.
2. **Duties** are mandatory and the language used to describe duties needs to affirm that the action is mandatory. As actions in a contract are mostly future actions the words *will* or *shall* are used to establish duties.
   "Shall," states a future obligation.
   "Will," states a future fact that must exist.

For example:
   "Supplier shall provide repair or replacement for any Product returned under warranty within ten (10) calendar days from receipt of the defective product from Buyer."
   "Supplier will continue to make spare parts and provide repairs for the Product for five (5) years after the last Product purchase."

CHAPTER 18. BUYER'S MANAGEMENT OF RISK AND POTENTIAL LIABILITY

For the buyer to not assume the risk and the resulting liability or cost, the buyer must ensure that all representations made by the supplier are clear and are carried forward and made a part of the contract. The buyer in negotiations should avoid assuming risks they can't manage or control or, assume liability. The buyer should seek to avoid supplier disclaimers and other tactics used by suppliers to try to disclaim or limit potential liability.

When specific sub-contractors or suppliers are required, the contract must hold the supplier responsible for their sub-contractor's or suppliers' performance. The supplier needs to manage the activity and deliverables. The supplier needs to ensure the sub-contractor is held to their commitments. The buyer needs to ensure all parties the buyer controls meet their performance requirements (delivery & performance to schedule, quality, and compliance to specifications). The buyer needs to institute and use management controls and built those into to the contract such as scheduled meetings, management reviews, problem escalation processes, performance measurement & documentation, change management documentation, etc..

Buyer's can further manage some of the potential for risks by elect the right supplier by pre-qualifying them in advance. The most important task a buyer can perform to increase its chances for success is a thorough pre-qualification process of the supplier to uncover any areas where there is a high degree of risk in using the supplier. The buyer needs to verify that the supplier can produce the product according to the product specifications, in volume, and that the supplier is capable of managing the other aspects of its business to ensure a smooth flow of product. Many times a supplier can have a high quality product, but their business and fulfillment processes may be so bad that there is a significant cost and risk to use them. When possible, use industry standard parts instead of custom parts so there are multiple sources that can be quickly qualified in the event of a problem. Consider establishing a second source to reduce risk.

Buyers need to:
- Create contract terms that protect the source of supply;
- Insert clauses that provide guaranteed periods of availability of product and out of warranty repair services;
- Place limitations on the supplier's ability to make changes to product specifications or the manufacturing process and/or move the manufacturing location of the product without your consent.
- If you allow the supplier to "end of life" a product or service, require sufficient notice to allow you to establish and implement an alternative strategy including the rights to make an end of life purchase of the product.
- Create supplier liability for damages if the supplier fails to perform and meet contract requirements such as: product specifications, delivery performance, warranties, etc.
- Make the supplier responsible for costs if they fail to deliver, or if you are required to satisfy your requirements using other source (which is called "cover") where the supplier is responsible to pay for any incremental costs associated with buying the replacement product from another supplier.

- Require suppliers to manage their business using proven business methods (such as adopting quality management. programs and standards, provide periodic performance reporting, conduct product cost management reviews, etc.)
- Require the supplier to provide information and establish the necessary tools to manage the supplier's performance (such as performance reporting, scorecard reviews, problem escalation processes, and responsibility for increased costs caused by problems).

Where risks cannot be transferred, where it doesn't make sense to transfer or where the supplier is unwilling to assume the risk, your contract terms need to provide you with the tools to manage performance and drive the supplier's behavior to mitigate the cost or manage the risk and the associated costs. Your contract terms define any exclusions or limitations on the supplier's liability, the costs or risk they assume. If you are forced to assume more of those costs and risks by the contract terms the supplier is willing to agree, you are getting less value and the price you pay should be less.

In negotiating responsibility for risk and the resulting cost impact, a simple maxim to follow is that the party who has the greatest ability to manage or control the risk should be the one who should assume the risk and resulting costs. Buyers should not assume risks over which they have no control, especially if the supplier has the ability to control and manage the risk.

In virtually every instance, the buyer already assumes some level of risk and the resulting cost for problems. For example:
- In many cases, buyers don't look to suppliers to assume full responsibility for costs until the problems (such as defects or late delivery) reach a certain thresholds, so buyer already assumes a degree of cost attributable to supplier non-performance.
- Even with a supplier's payment for some costs, buyer will never fully recover all their costs. If a supplier delivers defective products or fails to deliver product, buyer will never be made whole because, in most limitation of liability provisions, the buyer may have agreed to not hold the supplier liable for buyer's lost profits or consequential damages even though those may be out of pocket losses to buyer. A late shipment of a .10 cent part could cause buyer to lose a million dollar sale due to a delayed final product shipment and there is no way buyer will be able to recover those damages.

A contract may address all of the potential liability areas for a supplier with the exception of strict liability. For example, it may contain contractual liability for failing to delivery on time. It could include a general indemnification provision for dealing with the supplier or their employee's negligence. If there was reliance or if there was no disclaimer of the warranties of merchantability or fitness for a particular purpose, those could be included. Most contracts will contain specific warranties giving rise to supplier liability. A contract could include a material representation, which if proven untrue could be the cause for termination of the contract, against creating liability.

CHAPTER 19 CONTRACT NEGOTIATION EXAMPLE

In a negotiation the supplier's goal is to make the sale, but at the same time their goal is to reduce their cost, risk, and potential liability. One of the ways a supplier can reduce their potential liability exposure is to limit or reduce their commitment. That is done by:
- Including a lesser standard of commitment.
- Making the commitment conditional (such as requiring that they agree or must verify something as part of the process).
- Limit the remedies for the commitment.
- Including certain fairly open ended carve outs from their commitment.
- Using qualifying or softening words.

19.1 A red-line example

Here is a red line of a clause that I received from a supplier as part of a negotiation. It provides some great examples of how suppliers try to attack a commitment and limit their potential liability. I'll explain what they are doing in the second column. **Bolded** language was added. Language was struck was deleted:

"Epidemic Defect" shall mean a product (individual part number) that experiences a **confirmed** similar defect of the same root cause for one or more of the following during the Measurement Period: (a) At a rate of one percent (1%) or more in product delivered during any given thirty (30) day rolling period. or (b) At a rate of one percent (1%) or more of total purchases under warranty period plus two years (the "Measurement Period," hereafter referred to as "Installed Base Epidemic Defect"). or

> The addition of the word "confirmed" makes it a conditional commitment. They are only obligated if they confirm the defect. If they don't confirm the defect they have no obligation. There is no requirement that they take the steps to confirm it promptly or that they act reasonably or in good faith in doing their confirmation, so it may never be confirmed and without confirmation they have no liability.

(c) An **inherently dangerous** defect that can cause personal injury or substantial property damage (hereinafter referred to as a Safety Epidemic Defect). or

> With the insertion of "inherently dangerous" they sought to add a higher standard to their obligation so that it must not only have caused injury and property damage but it must be "inherently dangerous". If something wasn't inherently dangerous, they would not be obligated.

(d) recalls

> They deleted the entire concept of a recall so they would have no liability for recalls

In the event of an Epidemic Defect, buyer shall provide supplier with notice of the Epidemic Defect and supplier will commence its performance hereunder within five (5) calendar days of buyer's notice of the Epidemic Defect. **All Epidemic Defects shall be subject to verification by supplier. Epidemic Defects Verification shall not include failures due to buyer or customer misapplication, misuse, neglect, tampering, disassembly, repair, alteration, utilization of parts not approved by supplier, or chain failures induced by internally or externally integrated sub-assemblies.**

> The requirement of verification makes it a conditional commitment as previously noted. The verification language includes a disclaimer from being responsible for a number of issues that are vague and could be argued to relieve them of liability.

For Epidemic Defects confirmed by supplier, supplier will, at buyer's discretion: (i) refund or credit the product Price, or replace or repair the products at no charge in a timely manner, and

> This again requires their confirmation as a pre-condition to their obligation to provide the remedies.

(ii) reimburse buyer for all actual and reasonable **third party** expenses incurred by buyer related to the Epidemic Defect

> The third party expenses language would eliminate the buyer's ability to recover any internal costs.

and agreed to by supplier including, without limitation as to types of costs, costs associated with repair or replacement, field costs, problem diagnosis, and field and finished goods inventory related costs **subject to the limitations set forth below.**

> This makes the amount that is to be paid subject to their agreement, which again makes the obligation conditional. They have no obligation to pay until they agree, but there is nothing that requires their agreement, or that they act promptly and in good faith to agree.

buyer shall make every effort to mitigate damages and costs due to Epidemic Defect and supplier shall not be responsible for any items hereunder that can be or could have been mitigated by buyer.

> They want to impose very high standard ("every effort") on the buyer to help mitigate any liability, but they made no commitment to pay for buyer's costs to mitigate the liability. In fact they specifically excluded they buyer from recovering costs by limiting it to out of pocket costs. They also disclaimed liability if the cost could have been mitigated.

supplier's maximum liability under this sub-section shall not exceed the amount paid by buyer to supplier for the affected product during the six (6) consecutive months prior to the incident giving rise to the liability.

> Here they sought to limit their liability by placing a cap on liability based on what would be a very limited base. It was six- months spend, and only for the specific product (part number) that caused the damage.

The remedies set forth in this section are buyer's sole and exclusive remedies in the event of an Epidemic Failure.

> Here they want to eliminate any other remedies that the buyer could have so the only thing they would be liable for is the very limited amount they have reduced their liability down to. This would exclude their obligation under warranty so in effect all they would be paying you is the cost of the product (which you would already get under warranty) and provide you with no other costs. It would also exclude any remedies for other damages that may have been caused by the defect such as personal injury or property damage.

As you can see from this example there are a number of ways the supplier can and will try to attack the commitments to reduce their risk, potential liability and cost.

To ensure the best position for your company, you need the terms that you put forward to be clear and unequivocal and clearly place the desired risk, liability and costs on the supplier when that is appropriate. In the negotiation of the terms, the goal should be to get your terms or get applicable consideration for any term that will lessen the supplier's cost, risk, or liability.

19.2 Dealing with supplier proposed changes

The best ways to deal with the supplier attacks on risk, liability and cost are:

- If you are in a power position, simply say no.
- If you have those terms from their competition, remind them of the competition and let them know that if they want the business that's what they'll need to agree as that is the standard.
- Tell them of the cost impact of the change and what it will now take for them to be competitive. This way you move potential risk and liability issues to real cost issues they need to deal with if they want the business. They may be more willing to assume the potential risk (which may never occur) versus changing their price.
- Link your agreement on the concession to them providing you with something you want of equal or greater value to you that they may be more willing to provide.
- Move them from extremes to acceptable degrees of commitments and positions by simply tying it to the award of the business so it becomes a situation of either agree to the change or be prepared to lose the business.

Let's review the ways supplier's try to attack things

- Make conditional commitments versus firm commitments in our example this was the tie to "confirmed defects" so their only obligations was to defects they "confirmed:
- Require conditions or approvals of things required for them to be liable in our example this is their approval of all the expenses.
- Make commitments subject to their actions with no obligations that they take the necessary steps to perform those actions. In our example this applied to both the confirmation of the defects, approval of the expenses, and the requirement that everything be subject to their verification
- Reduce the degree or standard of commitment being made. In our example this was the insertion of the standard that it be an inherently dangerous defect rather than simply a defect that caused personal injury or property damage
- Reduce or limit the potential liability for not meeting the commitment. In our example this what the limit of liability where they limited it first to the amount within the previous six month period which both limits the potential exposure but could provide no recovery if you had a situation where there were no purchases in the prior six month period prior to the defect occurring. They further limited it by limiting it to only the specific product that caused the defect so it wasn't all sales for six months but only the sales of those products for six months. The then further limited their potential liability by making the specific remedy the buyer's sole and exclusive remedy for epidemic defects.
- Impose costs and standards on the buyer In our example this was the requirement that the buyer use "every effort to mitigate the damages and costs. Not only did it place the mitigation responsibility on the buyer, it also

transferred the cost of those mitigation efforts to the buyer as there was nothing that had the supplier commits to reimburse buyer's actual and reasonable costs associated with mitigating the damages.
- Exclude the buyer's ability to recover its own costs. In our example this was the language that had the supplier only reimbursing the "actual and reasonable third party costs incurred by buyer" which then excluded the right of the buyer to claim and recover its own costs as the buyer costs would not be third party costs.
- Transfer costs and risks to the buyer by the terms used.

As we learned in total cost there are a number of different costs in a supplier relationship and by the terms suppliers will want to negotiate into the contract, they will want to push some of the costs back to the buyer. When you are negotiating a term you always need to think about what is being proposed from a total cost perspective and how it will impact your costs. Some attempts are easy to spot and some a more subtle. One of my favorites in the not so subtle category is when a supplier proposes to share the freight costs of warranty returns where the buyer pays to send the item back to the supplier and the supplier will pay to ship the item back. The problem I have with that is I paid for them to ship me a good product. I probably paid the freight to get it to me. Because it turns out to be defective, why should I have to pay again? I've also had suppliers want to charge me a No Problem Found or No Defect Found charge for every time we ship a product back to them that's not defective. My response has always been that if they will agree to pay me for all my costs when they ship me a defective product, I'll be glad to pay them their costs when I ship a good one back. None of them have every wanted to agree.

There are direct costs that they may try to transfer and the classic one is driven by the delivery terms, that is the cost of freight, duties, fees and insurance to cover the risk of loss while it is in transit. For example, ever wonder why some supplier's have a very short warranty period? In some cases it may be to transfer the warranty cost to you, but in many cases it's to force you to purchase support and maintenance at an earlier period to add to their sales and profit.

Terms will also drive indirect costs. For example, the longer the lead-time, the more likely it is that the buyer must carry more inventories with an inventory carrying cost. The longer it takes for repair or replace a defective product, the more inventories you'll have.

A lot of negotiation is common sense where you can look at what is being proposed and recognize whether it increases your direct costs, indirect costs, inventory levels, quality cost, or forces you to buy or pay for things before you need them. If they do, and there is no good business reason for it, the supplier is trying to transfer the risk and cost to you. Here's another example. The supplier tells you that a certain product is non-cancelable, non-returnable. To me there are two types of non-cancellable orders. One is where it is truly non-cancelable and the supplier can do nothing to stop it or mitigate the cost once started. The other type is to simply force the sale to occur, where the supplier could stop work for a cost of less than the sale price, but they won't. In that second type the buyer is forced to pay the full purchase price even though they may no longer want or need the product, which means they now assume the cost and risk of inventorying it until it can be used or attempt to resell it for whatever value they can derive. In this case you might push for flexibility that would allow you to make changes or cancellations at a lesser cost based upon the point at which it becomes unique to the buyer which should be one of the few reasons to agree to a non-cancelable, non-returnable term.

19.3 Who Decides?

One of the most frequent battles in contract negotiation is who gets to decide upon an item.

- Who decides whether a product or service is defective?
- Who decides what remedy will be provided?
- When there are multiple possible alternatives to correcting a problem, who decides which of the alternatives is acceptable?

Buyer's are always concerned that if they leave the decision open to the supplier, the supplier may never decide; the decision will not be reasonable or equitable; or the supplier will decide in the manner that is the least expensive for the supplier but most expensive for the buyer.

Here are several examples:

A buyers warranty redemption provision allows the buyer to decide upon whether the buyer wants to have the defective product repaired, replaced or have a refund or credit. The supplier wants the decision to be at their option. Both have good reasons for wanting the right to decide.
- The supplier wants to have the right, because if the buyer has the right to return product for a refund, they can't recognize the sale as revenue.
- The supplier may also not want to be forced to do a repair if providing a new one is less expensive.
- The supplier may not want to have to replace it, if the item can be repaired.
- The supplier may also be concerned about the buyer using the right to return for refund or credit as a way in which the buyer can reduce its inventory levels at the supplier's expense.
- The buyer may need to have the product repaired or replaced, as they need it for their or their customers use and getting a refund of credit isn't acceptable.
- The buyer may also have a history of bad experience with repaired products not being acceptable or causing further problems.

Who should decide?

This may be a situation where the right to decide shouldn't be only with one party. When faced with this situation, a middle ground may be structured to meet both parties' needs.

> "supplier shall have the right to repair or replace the product, or with buyer's approval to refund or credit the price, provided however that if a product that has been repaired is found to defective be defective a second time while under warranty, supplier shall replace that product with a new product."

This approach would allow the supplier to decide whether to repair or replace it, but they would need to replace it if it subsequently became defective. This also allows the buyer to require that the supplier repair or replace the item if they still need the product rather than have the supplier want to provide a credit or refund. If you were concerned about not being able to use a credit, you could also include a commitment where if the credit is unused for a certain period of time, the supplier must pay the amount of the credit.

Here's another example of who should decide. Most intellectual property indemnification provisions contain multiple potential remedies

1. Obtain the right to continue to use and sell the products and Services.

2. Modify the products and Services so they are non-infringing

3. Replace the products and Services, with non-infringing ones; or

4. At buyer's request, accept the cancellation of infringing products and Services without cancellation, and refund any amount paid.

Who should decide which of these would be done?

For the buyer you would want the supplier to work their way down the list and only move to the next option if that option can't be done. The reason for this is the lower down on the list you go, the buyer's costs increase, as does the potential impact to the buyer and potentially their customers. The supplier on the other hand may want to look at it from strictly a cost perspective and as such want the right to choose whichever option is the most cost effective for the supplier.

How would you resolve it? If you had all the leverage in the world you could demand it be done your way. If you don't, what would you do? One approach could be to remove the least desirable option (#4) and offer to let the supplier decide which of the remaining 3 options to choose provided that each of the options has to be cost neutral to the buyer. For example, in the situation where they get a license, the buyer will have no costs. If they want to either modify or replace the product they need to assume buyer's reasonable costs associated with the activity that buyer has to do to replace the product at their or their customer's point of use.

In any place in the contract where the supplier wants to make or control the decision you always need to look at the potential impact. For example, if the supplier only wants to provide warranty coverage after they have verified the product or service is defective, what's the potential impact? What if they never verify it? What if they take a year to decide? What if their decision is arbitrary?

If you are going to allow the supplier to decide anything, it's best to put parameters and safeguards in to protect you. For example if they want to verify a defect prior to providing warranty repair or replacement, you want the act to be done reasonably and in good faith so they can't be arbitrary in their decision. You want the act to be timely, so you want the action to not be unreasonably withheld or delayed or require a specific time frame where if they haven't verified it by that time they lose the right to decide. You might also want the right to have their decision or finding reviewed by an independent third party in the event that you don't agree, with the decision of the third party being binding upon them and with the cost of that review being at their expense if they are wrong.

CHAPTER 20. NEGOTIATING CONCESSIONS

To be successful in negotiating concessions requires;

- **The supplier must want or need your business.** If they don't want or need it, they will want to do it on their terms, not yours.
- **The supplier must believe there is competition they have to beat.** If there is no perception of competition, there is no threat of losing the business to a competitor. Competition is what that drives a supplier to make concessions. Expectations of competition must be set early so the salesperson sets the same expectations with their management. If their management thinks it's an easy win, they won't support concessions.
- **The supplier must perceive an immediate benefit.** They are in no rush to concede today for business in the future. supplier's who are generally represented by their sales team concede to meet their immediate needs like revenue, quotas, and their bonuses.
- **The buyer's team must support the competitive nature of the activity.** Comments showing lack of competition or preference will impact success.
- **The buyer's team must show conviction in their positions.** Everyone must show the conviction in getting the concession. If suppliers perceive they get the business without a specific concession they won't make it.
- **The negotiator must be able to successfully explain why it's needed and the impact to the supplier if it isn't met in terms the supplier can quickly understand and relate.** Good explanations will:
    o Highlight the immediate impact on their competitive position (The threat of losing the business);
    o The potential impact the position has on current or future business and volumes (The threat of getting less business)
    o The Total cost impact that would require additional price reductions (Tie pricing to terms)

The successful explaining it is part of persuading.

There are four primary elements in every form of persuasion: the source, the message, the channel and the receiver. (From "Persuasive Business Proposals" by Tom Sant)

- **The Source.** The key with the source is it must be credible.
- **The Message**. The message must be tailored to the needs and circumstances just like a sales person will tailor their sales presentation depending on who they are presenting to. The message comes in two parts
    o What is the problem or need?
    o What makes it worth solving?
The things that make the problem worth solving is usually either the potential loss of business or the ability to increase business.

- **The Channel**. The channel is the method by which you deliver the message.

- **The Receiver**. The receiver must be able to receive, understand and process the message in a way that will get action and be one that is able to look at the big picture.

Here's an example of persuasion in negotiating a price reduction:

The Source may be a highly respected consultant or benchmark study that would be readily accepted by the supplier as credible.

The Message would be the supplier isn't competitive (The Problem). What makes the problem worth solving could be described as likely results: At the current price their volumes will be reduced or they won't get the business. If they offer a reduced price they will keep and possibly increase their volumes.

The channel for the message would be conversations with the supplier about future business. In those discussions you begin to set the expectation of the need for a price reduction. You could provide your credible information in advance to reaffirm the expectation. Most parties do not like or respond well to surprises during the negotiations, so its not recommended to wait until the negotiation to provide the message. The exception is in situations where there is newly discovered information.

This leaves **the Receiver**. Many times procurement negotiators don't do a good job of managing the receiver part of persuasion. To be successful the receiver must be able to receive, understand and process the message in a way that will get action and also be one that is able to look at the big picture. If you deal with too low a level within the supplier's organization, there is a strong likelihood that the individual you are dealing with cannot make the needed concessions. Most sales people at lower levels are armed with a standard playbook they are told to manage to, and anything different requires higher level of management approval. They may not see or even care about the big picture unless they are personally impacted or benefit. For example, if they already made their sales quota for the period, they may not want to push their management for the exceptions you need, because it simply doesn't do anything for them. Your deal, the annuity stream that it may represent may be of little importance to them simply because they look only at what's important to them personally. In managing the receiver, it is important that if you don't feel that you are being heard or adequately represented to the supplier's upper levels of management, involve them or request an escalation to be heard at the next higher level within the supplier's organization. Understand that there will always be levels whose job it is to tell you no, and you need to get around them to decision makers that can look at the potential revenue and risks and look at it from the bigger picture.

They will be able to weigh it on how it fits into the overall scheme of things. I've seen things that were treated as major issues at lower levels in a supplier's organization that vanish when you deal at the right level. The key it to make sure you're selective in escalating issues and only bringing forward what's really important. Don't waste their time on what they will view as miniscule or nuisance points.

The other frequent problem in managing the receiver is if the negotiator hasn't set the right expectations along the way. Setting the right expectations early on is very important with the receiver. Frequently the receiver will also need to report to and set expectations with their management on the business. If you don't set an early expectation of what you need, they will not have relayed that issue or problem to their management as an obstacle they need to overcome. If your position in the negotiation then conflicts with the expectations they have set with their management, it creates a problem for them with their management. It may be easier for salespeople to say that they lost a deal than it is for them to have to go back to their management to admit they had misread their customer and additional unplanned concessions are required. The point at which you sit down at the negotiating table should not be the first time a supplier has heard a specific issue or goal. Set the expectations of what you want and need early and often. If they know it's a problem in advance they can deal with it. If it comes to them as a surprise at the negotiating table, the odds of getting it will be reduced. The more frequent and earlier you can channel your expectations and needs to the receiver, and the higher up you go in their organization, the more likely you will be in achieving your goals.

CHAPTER 21. NEGOTIATING COST

Cost is cost, right? As they say in the Hertz™ commercials, "not exactly". In Chapter 2 we reviewed all the different types of costs that can exist in a supplier relationship. If you negotiate something based upon the supplier's "cost", you need to understand what they actually mean so you understand the formula that makes up the cost. There are a large number of terms used to describe cost. The saying "figures never lie, but liars use figures" is important to remember when you negotiate anything based on "cost".

21.1 Common Cost Accounting Terms Used In Negotiations:

Actual cost is the actual expenditure for labor and material.
Allocated cost Is the cost of supporting departments that may not be directly attributable to the product or Service. It is shared by a formula.
Annual and administrative expenses are usually allocated on the basis of total cost of products (i.e. labor plus materials plus manufacturing overhead).
Budgeted cost is based on a budgeted amount that is carried in the estimate.
Capital assets are items that must be depreciated over defined depreciation schedule.
Cost analysis is the review and evaluation of a supplier's proposed cost or pricing data to determine what the cost should be, assuming reasonable economy of scale and efficiency.
Costs are expenditures for material, labor, and burden (expenses) incurred in the production and sale of an item or service.
Contingencies are not costs, they are reserves (when accounted for) or allowances (when built into the prices) to cover events or situations that *might* occur, such as possible increases in material prices, lower yields, higher labor costs, delays in the schedule. When the contingencies occur they result in cost. If the contingency called for never occurs and they were treated as an allowance, they become an addition to the suppliers profit.
Direct costs are those costs that have been incurred and which can be directly traced to a given product or service. Direct costs can be charged directly to that of a given order, job or product or service. The most important direct costs are labor and materials.
Direct labor is the cost of all labor performed upon the product which changes the shape, form, or nature of the materials that are used in the product or service and includes: wages, fringe benefits, payroll taxes, bonuses, and other compensation.
Direct material is the cost of raw materials, purchased parts, and subcontracted manufacturing or services that become part of the manufactured product or service.
Expenses are purchases that may be expensed in the year purchased.
Fixed costs are not affected by production quantity or volume-period costs. Examples of fixed costs are depreciation, rent, and executive salaries.
Incremental costs are the costs to produce more of a unit or product, labor, material, etc. This is an important way to view costs particularly in the pricing of changes in work, material or scope or changes in production quantity or volume. Only the incremental costs should be relevant.

Indirect costs are those that do not result from the manufacture of a specific unit or lot or performance of the service, so that they cannot be charged directly, but must be allocated or apportioned to that product or service by some method of approximation.

Manufacturing or production overhead is indirect expense incurred in the manufacturing, conversion, or service delivery process. Manufacturing or production overhead expenses include indirect labor, maintenance and operating supplies, and fixed or period charges (i.e. expenses not affected by quantity or volume of production) Among manufacturers, indirect labor would broken down into sub-categories such as production foremen, group leaders, clerks, and production material handlers, quality control and process engineering, procurement, materials and production control, including scheduling, receiving, and warehousing, industrial engineering, supervision, cost accounting and industrial relations. Non-labor expenses in manufacturing overhead include maintenance materials: spare parts, operating and repair materials, work performed by outside maintenance and repair contractors. Operating expenses such as building maintenance, depreciation, all perils insurance, taxes, fuel and non-production fuels and electricity, non-capital equipment and tools including expendables, office supplies, postage, rentals, non-production travel, depreciation and amortization, dues, memberships, obsolescence of raw material, auto expenses.

Material acquisition rate would be a charge applied to the materials cost to cover the associated overhead and expenses that may not be directly attributable to the item. It's an allocation of costs against each purchase expressed as a percentage of the direct material cost.

Non-manufacturing overhead - all other indirect costs, such as selling administrative, engineering costs, research and development expenses, sales commissions, travel expenses, advertising, insurance on finished goods, taxes on finished goods, officer's salaries, office personnel salaries office stationery legal and accounting expenses, office supplies, telephone and related expenses, losses on bad accounts, contributions, etc.

Opportunity cost is profit lost from not taking a particular action.

Overhead costs are indirect costs that cannot be charged directly to a unit of product or service. They may be accounted for in one general account, or may be broken down and allocated against a more direct accountable function or department using an activity measure such as direct labor hours, machine hours or units produced. The approach used for assigning overhead can be extremely important as they can be used to unreasonably burden the cost of a product. Overhead cost and overhead rates can also be actual, expected or budgeted. Suppliers may have manufacturing or production overhead, selling, administrative, and engineering overheads.

Period cost is a cost that is recognized in the period in which they occur.

Profit is not a cost. Profit is the return on the supplier's investment for risk-taking, use of their capital, and for managing production and operating performance. suppliers profit goals may be calculated different basis depending on the supplier:

- Profit on sale - gross margin (GM),
- Profit before taxes (PBT)
- Profit as a rate of return on assets (ROA)
- Rate of return on investment (ROI)
- Profit as a percentage of cost
- Profit through over-absorption or over-recovery of cost

Product costs are costs assigned to the product produced.
Relevant cost are costs that differ with alternatives.
Semi-variable. Semi-variable costs are a combination of variable and fixed. A certain portion is fixed and another portion varies based on the level of production.
Set up or tear down costs are associated with setting up the equipment for production and tearing down the equipment after production has been done. Set up and tear down costs are usually established in standard labor hours to perform the tasks and then should be allocated or spread over the production run.
Standard cost is a predetermined measure of cost based upon time and motion study, past costs and production experience, expected costs, theoretical costs or some combination thereof. Cost Accounting systems may employ either actual or standard cost data.
Start up costs can be a hybrid between the variable cost and fixed costs of overhead, which result from a particular project or production run. They include:
    Special engineering from design or production.
    Special Tooling - tools, dies fixtures.
    Special set up costs such as purchase and installation of special machinery.
    Rearrangement of physical manufacturing plant.
    Loss of use of facilities during set-up.
    Training costs for employees to implement / use new process.
    Start-up costs may be accounted for in standard overhead accounts, but as the buyer you would want them to be segregated. This is to avoid their being treated as recurring costs, rather than one-time or non-recurring expenses. You want to pay for the start up costs once, and not be paying for it over and over as part of some overhead rate.
Sunk (costs already incurred)
Unit costs are costs of a unit of product as incurred cumulatively through the production and/or distribution cycle or delivery of the service.
Variable cost. The cost will vary directly with production quantity or volume. Common variable costs are direct labor and direct materials.
Variances normally apply when standard cost approaches are used and Variances represent deviations of the actual cost incurred versus the standard cost. Variances may be favorable (i.e. actual less than standard) which represents additional profit to the supplier or unfavorable (the reverse) which represents additional costs to the supplier.

21.2 How Costs Are Described:
Costs may be described based on their nature or the impact of volume.
- Fixed Cost (cost does not change with volume)
- Semi-variable cost (cost has both fixed and variable components)
- Variable cost (cost changes as volume increases or decreases)

Costs may be described based on the relationship to the task.
- Direct (cost can be directly traced to the item or task being provided)
- Indirect (cost that cannot be directly traced and must be allocated).

Costs may be described based upon when they are recognized.
- Product (costs assigned to the product produced).
- Period (recognized in the period in which they occur).

Costs may be described differently in decision analysis discussions.
- Relevant (costs that differ with alternatives)
- Sunk (costs already incurred)
- Opportunity (profit lost from not taking a particular action)

When you talk about manufacturing costs, the costs are usually described as:
- Direct labor (see below)
- Direct materials (see below)
- Factory overhead (see further explanation below)

Service cost is usually described as including the following:
- Direct Labor – the time spent delivering the service.
- Materials and supplies – the tools used in providing the service
- Technology – depreciation, maintenance contracts, and support and repair costs, expense items for the technology used to perform the service.
- Occupancy- depreciation, rent, repair and maintenance, janitorial, landscaping, security, utilities, insurance, property taxes.
- Service Overhead – Other resources supporting service personnel

Costs may be described by functions that generate them such as:
- General and Administrative (G&A)
- Marketing and Selling
- R&D
- Manufacturing
- Service

Cost may be based upon:
- Unit Cost (the cost of one unit of measure of the product)
- Total cost (the aggregate or fully burdened cost of the product with all cost included).

Cost will usually include allowances for losses based on the process or un-saleable returns. That allowance may show up as materials cost or in allocations.

Costs may be described as capital asset or expense. For equipment purchased with a value over the amount established for expense items, the following would be part of the capital cost for that item: purchase price, broker commissions, duties, sales tax, insurance, freight, site preparation, installation, upgrades, and labor costs for set up, travel for you or consultants to review, test, install, initial, training costs to use the equipment. For that same piece of equipment the following would be expensed: maintenance supplies, maintenance contracts, ordinary repairs, operating supplies and minor tools and post installation training.

All costs will be **Variable, Fixed or Semi Variable.**

All costs will also be **Actual, Budgeted or Standard.**

For any allocated costs you need to understand what's included and the basis of the allocation. For example, if you pay labor cost based on what the laborer was actually paid, it would be an actual cost. If you pay a rate irrespective of who performs the task, it's probably a budgeted cost. If rates for a class of laborer are established without a link to their specific compensation, it's probably a standard cost.

21.3 The Cost Shell Game

A game that you've probably seen on the streets of a major city or on TV or the movies is the "shell game" where there are 3 shells or cups and an object is placed under one. The shells are rapidly shuffled, and then you have to correctly guess which of the 3 shells contains the object. When you negotiate cost you also have to be concerned about a variation of the same shell game. The shell game occurs when a supplier uses the pricing formula to move costs from one area to another area where they will get an advantage. In negotiating the cost of a product, a large percentage of the product's cost will be the cost of the materials. If you establish a pricing formula based on the "cost" of those materials, you need to ensure that the supplier isn't burdening the cost of materials with costs that should have been covered by another cost factor. For example: If a supplier requires the delivery for raw materials to be to destination versus origin or requires extended payment terms or includes requirements in their supplier contracts such as special packaging or packing requirements, logistics programs or special services, those requirements will all increase the cost of the material. They will also decrease the supplier's manufacturing overhead. The costs the supplier would normally have under the "shell" of manufacturing overhead or the "shell" of operating overhead then winds up under the "shell" of material cost. When this happens, the supplier is paid more for the material cost, but they may also get compensated more for all other costs as certain compensation like overhead and profit may be based on a percentage of direct materials cost or on direct cost, of which materials cost is usually a large percentage. The net effect is the supplier winds up being compensated more while their actual costs have gone down as they have transferred those costs from them to their suppliers. A further "shell" game that suppliers can play is the apportionment of cost that occurs with manufacturing overhead and equipment or tools costs. For example, if you are using equipment or a tool that will also be used by other supplier customers, you want the apportionment of those costs between customers to be reasonable and based on standard accounting practices so they don't unnecessarily burden your cost. In negotiating based on "cost", you need to avoid paying double. For example, the initial price may include certain one-time or start-up costs that were amortized into the product cost. If costs were amortized, you need to know what they were and what the amortization formula was to be able to back them out of the formula before you start negotiating the subsequent pricing. If you don't, you could be paying them over and over again. When a supplier agrees to amortize one time costs into their price, there are usually two motivations behind their offer. One motivation is to help make the sale. The other is in hopes that the buyer will forget what costs were included in the price, and that will provide them opportunity in their future negotiations.

If you plan to negotiate on a cost plus basis, it's important to have at least three things: 1) a formula that determines what is included in each element of cost and 2) agree upon how those costs will be established (for example it its an allocation how the allocation is calculated) and 3) agree upon how those costs will be documented and verified. Otherwise there are a number of games a supplier can play that impacts the cost such as front end loading certain costs or burdening your costs with a disproportionate share of a cost to the benefit of other business.

21.4 Cost Models Used in Negotiations

A cost model is tool used to predict the cost of a product, service or their elements to assist in negotiating the cost or the cost of the elements. Here are a few common types of cost models:

- **Bottom-up Models** estimate each component of cost separately and the results are rolled up to produce an estimate of the entire product or service.
- **Top-down models** estimate the overall cost and effort but may not consider all the components of cost separately.
- **Algorithm based models** look at key variables considered to be the major cost drivers to estimate the cost.
- **Predicted cost estimates** are amounts achievable based on economies and efficiency based on historical data. For example learning curves would be used in predicted cost estimates
- **Comparison / analogy** uses similarities between two or more elements, where the cost of one is well known.
- **Parameter cost** is based on statistical relationship of costs to attributes or performance of the product or service.

Competitive bids are not a cost model, as it doesn't attempt to address what the item should cost; it addresses what the supplier is willing to sell at. In every cost model there are common elements:

1. **There are the processes that are performed** - the sequence of activities described in terms of tasks, events, work products, resource use, and the relationships between them
2. **There is the work structure / tasks** - A work breakdown structure is a listing of tasks for production of the product or Service. A work breakdown structure defines the tasks to be performed and relates the tasks of work to each other and to the end product. For example, a work breakdown may include standard labor hours for specific tasks. If may also include the quantity and cost of materials used in the process, with allocations for scrap, waste, etc.
3. **There are metrics** - Quantitative analysis values calculated according to a precise definition for each of the tasks and used to compare costs for supplier's tasks against known benchmarks. (Benchmark cost to previous costs, other supplier's costs, expert analysis, etc.)
4. **There are costs**. The costs allocated to each of the different tasks, exclusive of contributions to overhead or profit. Cost may be expressed a number of different ways as we already discussed.
5. **There is overhead** the rate or rates to be allocated to the total direct cost to cover all expenses not considered as direct costs.
6. **There is profit** the rate to be allocated to the total direct cost for the supplier's contribution to their profit.

Cost analysis requires you to look at what you're buying and understand how the products are manufactured or the service performed. Once you understand how it was made or performed, you can do cost analysis to figure out what it should cost on the basis of materials used, the processes, and the amount and types of labor involved in processing. The same also applies to Purchasing Services, where there are a limited number of processes and skills required to perform the work.

21.5 Negotiating Cost Using a Price Analysis / Price Comparison Model

A price analysis / comparison approach is used when you may not know the individual items or value of parts that make up a product. In performing a price analysis you would look at all the features of a product to compare it to prices charged for similar products. Since most suppliers will try to make their product unique in some way, the estimated price you should pay will be adjusted for additions or deletions based upon the features it contains. In some instances you could assign a specific cost based on the known cost of the additional feature. An example of price analysis would be in the purchase of a PC. Each manufacturer produces a unique configuration to differentiate their product. In doing a price analysis you would compare the cost of competing products at the lowest level, and then analyze what the difference should be for any added features based on your knowledge of the cost of those features. So for a PC you would try to compare the cost of stripped down versions of the same chip version and operating software. In doing that you would compare each of the features between the PC being benchmarked and the price analysis PC such as memory, hard drive, communications, cd/dvd, graphics card, loaded software, and warranty and would make adjustments (+ or minus) for the value each difference to identify what the PC being benchmarked should cost

21.6 Algorithm or Cost Formula Models

An algorithm or cost formula type of cost model is used when there is a known or standard formula for the cost and the only thing you need to negotiate are the specific variables to the formula. Once you agree on the variables, the formula will establish the cost. For example, you could have a manufacturing situation where the only variables are the cost of the material and the number of standard hours associated with a task and all other variables such as material acquisition rates, labor rates, overhead and profit charges could be pre-agreed. Once you negotiate and agree on the raw material cost, and the number of hours, the formula would establish the price.

Parametric cost formulas are ones where certain of the parameters are closely related between from one product to another so if you can calculate the cost/per parameter against the other product. The argument is that the cost/per parameter shouldn't change, only the volume. E.g. For a semiconductor purchase the parameter could be something like a cost per gate for a specific technology and density chip. Parametric cost formulas work best when there is a close link between the item that you based the historical cost where know the parameters and the new item. If there are significant changes to the product, its functionality, or underlying technology used to make the product, a parametric formula may not work.

21.7 Using price comparisons as a tool

This approach compares the price to a known competitive historic price for the same or almost equivalent product or service. For this to work you need to assure that the comparison is valid (consider differences in specifications, requirements, industry costs, volumes, market dynamics, etc.). The previous price must be valid base and a steady downward trend in price is not sufficient unless it parallels the market. Industry price sources may be used if there is confidence in the validity of the source. Use this technique when time is a constraint and sufficient benchmark data is available.

Steps:
1. Identify or establish the price benchmark
2. Request quote / proposal from supplier
3. Compare proposal to benchmark
4. Negotiate for the supplier to meet or beat the benchmark

20.8 Using feature-value assessment as a tool to negotiate pricing.

To do this, compare product or service price and features against other similar but not equal products or services. This requires that you have the ability to both identify the differences between the products or services and also can assign a price or value to the differences. Use this technique when the only known solution to a requirement or product / service has features or value not offered by a competitive product or services. A feature value assessment is slightly different than a price analysis approach in that you focus on the value the item provides to you as you may not need or want all the features.

Steps:
1. Establish benchmarks for:
2. Comparison product / service / system price
3. Feature-value assessment
4. Evaluate the price based on higher or lower value of the features provided in the product/services/system.
5. Negotiate for the supplier to meet or beat the equivalent price.

One of the reasons why it's important to understand and be able to use these tools is because the process of competitive bidding can easily be flawed and simply not produce the best cost. In a suppliers market of excess demand all a competitive bid may do is identify what price the supplier is willing to take on the additional work which has no resemblance to what their costs may be. In a buyer's market of excess demand, there's still no guarantee that a competitive bid will get you the best price, as there are a number of dynamics that can impact it. Even in a buyer's market your success will be dependent upon whether your bidders have excess capacity, not whether the market has excess capacity and there are other factors that can impact it. I once was asked to manage the procurement of construction of an office building in Munich, Germany. We were strongly advised that we should negotiate the work, but our company policy was that work should be competitively bid and my management insisted that we bid the work. We went out to 5 contractors and bid the work. When we received the bids they were far above what we wanted to pay which wasn't much of a surprise based on the advice we received. We then checked with the Bidders to understand whom they planned to use as their major subcontractors for the work and found that in every instance a large percentage of their subcontractors were all our other bidders. This is exactly what we were warned about and why negotiation was recommended. Armed with that information I was able to get agreement that we could negotiate the work. We wound up saving several million dollars making only minor changes to the specifications and the other Bidders still wound up as subcontractors on the job. To this day I can't say if there was collusion in the bidding process, but it clearly wasn't a competitive environment and it taught me that competitive bidding could easily be flawed. You need to know how to negotiate!

21.9 Negotiating Services Cost

In negotiating services on a cost basis, many of the same elements exist.

- What are all the tasks involved?
- The materials used?
- Cost of equipment and tools used (for allocation to the service cost)?
- Labor types involved in each task
- Standard hours allocated per task
- Labor rates by type
- Facility cost
- Utilities cost
- Consumables
- Cost of sales
- Gross Profit Allowance
- Material acquisition costs
- Contribution to Overhead/ SG&A Expense

For example if a supplier has an hourly rate the charge for an individual is the rate variable of fixed depending upon the term of the commitment? Is the rate their actual, budgeted, or standard cost? Is the rate unburdened or burdened (such as with allocations for benefits)? What is included in overhead costs and what will be billed separately?

21.10 Preparing to Negotiate Cost

To assist you in the negotiation, in soliciting the bid or proposal you should request:

- A detailed breakdown of the cost, rates, processes, quantities
- Assumptions on things such as scrap, expected performance improvements, process improvements that will reduce costs, pricing at various volumes etc.
- A description of what is included in each of the different costs factors (as no two methods of allocation may be the same)
- The basis for all cost factors (budget, actual, or standard)
- The method of all allocations.
- All assumptions and contingencies that have been built into the price.

The more information you can get the better.

Part of negotiating cost is to think of all costs in relationship to Price. The more relationship costs are passed on to the buyer, the less the buyer should spend on the Price. If the buyer can save internal costs by having the supplier perform certain supply chain activities, the more the buyer should be willing to share some of those savings in the price they pay. In addition to the unit rate, you need to understand what the cost drivers are. Most businesses within an industry are similar from a cost perspective and what drives their costs. Their costs are driven by the cost of the materials, labor and processes.

To reduce costs you must understand the nature of the elements of the cost, and question why each is needed, to identify what portion or portions of those costs may be impacted by change. The more you understand what is driving their costs, the more you can question: 1) whether it is needed, 2) whether the cost or rate is appropriate and 3) whether it is competitive. The supplier's quoted price may assume that you need certain materials or processes that simply may not be required and that may be changed to reduce cost. Your specification may call for materials and processes that simply aren't needed or could be replaced with lower cost approaches providing opportunity to reduce the cost. Where there is waste or inefficiency in the supplier's operation versus others, use that information to drive them to eliminate that to reduce the cost.

21.11 Negotiating Using Cost Analysis

Negotiating using cost analysis is a form of "divide and conquer" approach, where you attack each of the individual elements of cost. Each process step will have a cost based upon:
- The amount of time and cost to set up the process.
- The amount and type of labor involved to perform the process.
- The machines, tools and equipment used to perform the process
- The materials consumed in the process
- The amount of time and cost involved to tear down the process.

For all costs you attack:

- The need for the activity.
- The elements of the activity.
- The quantities.
- The rates.
- The basis for the rate.

For each operation, check to make sure the costs reflect the labor rate for the type of labor required to perform the process. In times of excess capacity suppliers may want to staff jobs with individuals that are over-skilled for the work. Adjust the labor cost based on historic or expected learning curves improvements. The Learning Curve theory says that as quantities go up, unit costs tend to come down because of greater efficiencies in production. The efficiencies in production can occur as a result of more efficient labor, higher yields in the process, or the implementation of changes to the process allowed by new equipment or tools. For example in plastic molding "soft tooling" is used for low volume production and "hard tooling" is used for higher levels of production. While the cost of the hard tool is more, it is more efficient and easier to set up or take down thereby reducing the amount of labor required. Review the kind of production or management talent demanded - production calling for an unusually high degree of design, engineering or production skill or production carried out under unusually difficult circumstances will be the basis for the supplier seeking a high enough profit to keep their management interested in the buyer's business. One rule of thumb that they may use will be to take a look at what type of profit level those resources would return if they were invested elsewhere in the Corporation. On the other hand, subcontracted components frequently require less effort from management and should justify a lesser profit margin.

In negotiating labor rates there is a funny thing that happens when negotiating rates for professional services. The supplier may be totally unwilling to reduce their rate, as that may bathe standard by which they measure themselves. It can be an ego or pride thing to bill out at that rate. If this occurs, focus on the other side of the equation, which is the quantity of hours required to perform the task. The argument to work with their ego is that for someone at that rate, they should have the experience to be able to perform the tasks in a shorter period. For you, the net result is the same - a lower price.

In negotiating labor rates you also need to be aware of what is called "billing increment". Billing increment issues also occur in other purchases. What a billing increment does is establish a minimal amount of billing time for each activity or task or a point where the service is rounded off to the next increment. For example, a law firm may charge $300.00 per hour for a principal of the firm. The billing increment may be 20 minutes. This means that every activity, whether it takes 1 minute or 20 minutes will be billed at the 20 minute billing increment of $100. Over 20 minutes to 40 minutes it will be billed at 2 increments or $200. Anything over 40 minutes would be billed at 3 increments or $300. If the lawyer handles ten different clients over the hour, because of billing increments they could potentially bill out as much as $1,200 an hour for that one attorney. Always negotiate billing increments as low as possible, and preferably based on actual time.

Other things to check with Labor:

1. Category and skill of personnel performing the work check for right level and skills:

    a. Too little skill = less productivity and more waste

    b. Over skilled = no more productivity, but added cost

2. Rate for person performing. Is it consistent with level of skill required?

3. Basis for rate is it actual or standard hours. If standard hours are used, what are the assumptions behind standard. Non-billable downtime? Learning curve?

In challenging materials costs, you look at the quantity, rate, and basis for standards, scrap etc. Review the Bill of Materials and ask:
- What type of material is required?
- What are the dimensions, amount or weight of material needed?
- What portion of those materials should be allowed for scrap?
- What price should they pay for the material at the volumes they are Procurement?

Consider the risks involved in materials procurement. If there are high, or unusual risks involved in the procurement because of the nature of the product or the length of the delivery schedule, supplier will seek a higher profit. There argument is the more risk they take, the more profit they should receive. Material Procurement risks can be dealt with in a variety of ways to avoid the supplier requiring a higher profit or building in a contingency in the material cost. For example there can be pricing reviews, consigned or advance purchase of materials authorized, firm quantities committed allowing the supplier to get firm pricing, etc. Adjust the materials cost for Cost Improvement Curves. E.g. higher yields, less scrap, improvements in raw material cost. Finally in negotiating material costs, always consider all the possible discounts they could be getting.

20.12 Attacking Overhead.

Check the rates, basis for allocations and when possible compare it to a competitive benchmark. There is no standard formula for allocating overhead! Different types of expenses have different basis for the allocations. This is important for negotiation, as cost breakdowns from different suppliers probably will be different depending upon their own internal method of allocation. When in doubt, ask for clarification on their method of allocation. Examples of Common methods of Allocating overhead are:

Expense Classification	Basis of Allocation
Depreciation of Building	Floor space
Depreciation of Equipment	Cost of the equipment
Fire Insurance Premiums	Value of the items
Custodial Services	Floor space
Supplies	Estimated Usage
Building Rent	Floor space occupied plus shares of any common
Power and Light	Floor space
Mandatory Insurances	Payroll involved
Stockroom expense	Inventory or requisitions
Payroll expense	Number of employees
Property Taxes	Space occupied / Space value
Personal Property Taxes	Valuation of equipment
Inventory taxes	Inventory
Small tools	Tools used, and their cost
Repairs	Actual cost per Department

Overhead rates may also be applied on a composite or blended average basis (e.g. covering all indirect expenses) against a direct cost factor. The composite or blended overhead can be applied against such items as direct labor dollars, labor time, process time, material costs, etc. Determine whether they reflect past or projected experience. Verify the reasonableness of the capacity utilization over which they are planned to be absorbed.

21.13 Attacking Allocated Cost

The cost of various supporting departments not be directly attributable to the product or service cost, may be shared by a formula. That includes procurement and receiving (if not part of direct materials cost), material handling, quality control, quality assurance, and support services such as IS, HR, accounting, and common areas and services like cafeterias, etc.

These types of allocated costs are determined by a process where you:

1. Determine the cost object to be allocated
2. Identify the indirect costs associated.
3. Select the allocation base over which to spread the allocation
4. Calculate the allocation rate (cost divided by base)
5. Assign the indirect cost allocation

Allocations are frequently based on the expected output for allocations or standard yield. Allocations will be impacted by capacity utilization as that may determine the allocation base. Allocations may be impacted by yield assumptions. Lower yields may mean a lower allocation base. In reviewing allocations you always check the basis for the allocation, whether it is reasonable and applies to what you are buying and be sure to check all the assumptions for allocations. Otherwise they may be allocating cost to you based on one set of assumptions and may be operating far more efficiently where they will make added profit from the allocations.

21.14 Review all contingencies.

Check the reasonableness of occurrence of the contingency. Check the reasonableness of the cost allowance. Review the suppliers or buyers ability to manage the risk and any costs associated. Because un-used contingencies which are treated as an allowance can quickly become added profit, the buyer should make sure that they understand the contingency, the risk, the potential costs and then make the business decision whether to treated it as a reserve which must be accounted for or treat it as an allowance which becomes the suppliers sole responsibility to manage, with the resulting potential that if they manage it well.

21.15 Additional things to check in negotiating the price.
- Remove anomalies, segregate out one-time costs.
- For extended periods, normalize the cost or adjust the cost to constant dollars -
- Review whether you are paying based on budget, actual or standard cost.
- Look for things that are different from the supplier's standard model that should reduce their costs .
- Look at their profit from a risk perspective.
- Look at profit based on the amount of value added to a product.
- Pay only for costs reasonably attributable to your product and relationship.
- Look for potential market price curves and supplier learning curves.

21.16 What if the supplier refuses to open it up to a cost discussion?
If you can't attack the individual cost elements, you have the more difficult task of negotiating the price. You may still use the cost model or benchmark as the definition of what is reasonable or competitive, and then use other tactics to drive them down such as:

- Where they have a unique product, let them know that you don't need or value the uniqueness, and other products (which are more competitive) will meet your needs. If they want to make the sale they need to do better.
- If the sale represents a substantial annuity stream to them, remind them that the only way they will get that annuity stream is by being more competitive.
- If you have leverage in other dealings, use that leverage to drive this cost down (Send the message that being treated unfairly on this activity will impact other dealings).
- Position the impact their cost will have on acceptance within your company. Show them:
  - Price / volume sensitivities to show the volumes they will lose if they hold to their price
  - The impact on future sourcing of their pricing.
- Help your negotiation of cost by showing them the problem and when possible the competition.
- Use a price / value approach
- If you have multiple suppliers, consider a reverse auction approach.

In a negotiation for plastic material that we used to build keyboards, monitors, computer and printer housings, we had a situation where the supplier was coming in for a price increase on top of a price that we already thought was too high. In preparation for the negotiation we did a detailed analysis of the costs. We used the costs that were in effect when we initially started to buy the product from the supplier, versus those same costs of today. The major elements of the cost were the raw materials, labor, electricity, manufacturing overhead, and general overhead and profit. For the material, labor, and electricity elements we did a slide-by-side comparison the cost then versus the cost today, and the result clearly showed that there was no cost difference between them. We then compared the Price between the initial agreed price and their current position and highlighted the significant difference. In summing it all up a single slide, we showed all of the costs that were equal and what they would be today. We also assumed that over time they would be more efficient, but showed their manufacturing overhead as being the same. This then graphically focused the entire cost difference on just one element – their overhead and profit, We showed what the initial contribution was based on our estimate and what it was under their current position. The graphic was clearly embarrassing, highlighting that all they wanted to do was increase their profits at our expense because they thought we were locked into using them. Then we dropped the bomb and explained that we had just completed the successful qualification of another supplier's materials and, if they didn't change, they would lose all the business. On its own, the embarrassment of the graphic may have driven some change in their position, but when we introduced competition back into the equation, they were then forced to not just respond, they had to respond to the competitive pricing of the other supplier or risk losing the business. There are two lessons to be learned from this story. One is the best weapon you have to drive cost is competition. The other is when you have the information to back up your position it's much harder for the supplier to defend something that simply can't be justified. They know that if they refuse to move they may win the battle, but they will clearly lose the war.

Now that you know the elements of cost and things you may negotiate, here's a number of different tactics that may used specifically to negotiate cost.

21.17 Additional Tactics to Negotiate Cost
Cherry picking. Picking the best of multiple prices for each individual major function. In situations where you are able to get detailed cost breakdowns or have bids based on different segments of the work, suppliers have provided you with ammunition to cherry pick and try to take the best of the best. Your benchmark becomes the sum of the lowest costs quoted for all items or segments from the combination of all of the suppliers. In negotiations you use the benchmark to drive individual supplier prices down to the benchmark price.

Competitive evaluations. Use non-price differences between suppliers to drive price down in non-price competitive evaluations you establish a number of decision criteria and assign weights to each of the items. Then you rank each of the suppliers based on the criteria, assign a score base on the weighting and create a weighed average or total number of points for each of the supplier. How you use it in price negotiations is to use the competitive weighting as the basis for getting the supplier to reduce their price. They know that if their price is the same as the other supplier's and the competitive evaluation is worse, they will probably lose the business. To offset the difference in the competitive assessment, they are encouraged to adjust their pricing, making them more attractive.

Total cost / total supply chain cost. Use past or expected performance and terms to drive reductions. The underlying concept is that everything either, from performance to contract terms, adds to or reduces the cost of the relationship and as such in making a decision; the cost of that performance or terms must be added to or deducted from the price (mostly deducted). So if a supplier's performance is less than their competition, their price also must be enough less to offset the difference. If the supplier's terms are less that the competition, their price must be less to offset the difference. The key elements in these price adjustments are cash flow, delivery costs (freight, duties, risk of loss), inventory cost, quality cost, and net present value of expected spending but there can be a number of elements taken into consideration and identified as a cost. How you use this in a price negotiation is to identify the impact that their performance or terms has on how they are viewed against the competition so that they know if their price is the same and their total cost is worse, they will probably lose the business. To offset the difference in Total Cost factors, they are encouraged to adjust their pricing, make firm commitments to improve performance, or make concessions on their terms to negate the difference. The simple fact is that the more uncertainty you can create in their expectations about winning the business, the more likely they will discount to offset any perceived shortcomings.

Life cycle / total cost of ownership. Net present value of all expected costs and impact that has on the competitiveness of the purchase price or cost of life cycle purchases. This approach is very similar to Total Cost, and takes into account all cost factors involved in the relationship from the initial purchase until completion of the useful life and the scrap or disposal of the item purchased. While total cost deals only with the supplier, Life cycle or TCO includes the cost of operation such as consumption of utilities, labor cost, set up, tear down costs, cost of maintenance, preventative maintenance, repair, calibration, scrap created, and consumables used in addition to the actual payments made to the supplier. The focus of a Life Cycle cost / TCO evaluation and use in the negotiation can be to benchmark costs between competing suppliers to drive concession from one to offset differences in the Life Cycle Cost. The information can also be used to drive concessions in the cost of follow-on purchases by things like extended warranties, price caps for spare parts, repairs, maintenance, or even trade in allowances for future purchases.

Return on investment (ROI). Evaluation of cost versus desired ROI to establish whether the investment at the supplier's price makes sense. Many suppliers try to use ROI or Value Based Selling as a way of getting their price, as what easier decision can you make than to pay for the purchase out of the savings the purchase will generate. When they use this tactic, buyers need to push for competitive benchmarking so the discussion reverts back to cost and not ROI. buyers may use ROI where they want to create an uncertainty about whether the purchase, contract, or individual element would be approved. If it fails to provide an adequate return, why make the investment? The ROI evaluation could be used for evaluating purchases representing internal investments or it can apply to whether it makes sense for you to use or tore-sell the supplier's product as part of a solution. This is intended to create uncertainty in whether you will make the purchase that must be overcome by providing you with something better that improves the ROI. To improve the ROI the supplier could reduce pricing, delay payments, create payment schedules more in tune with when you will receive value, or provide free service on a limited time basis or reduced service cost or anything else that will motivate you to make the purchase.

Horserace. Using multiple rounds and position at each round to drive improvement. This tactic is frowned upon by many buyers, which think the practice is un-ethical. In many businesses or countries it's simply common practice where you keep going around until no one is willing to beat the current offer you have on the table. This works best when it's either a buyer's market where everyone is chasing any business they can get, or when your business is substantial enough for multiple suppliers to fight over, and it can produce great results. The approach is to have multiple rounds and after each round you advise them of their relative position, always offering them the ability to come back to you in future another round to try to change their status. The goal is to show the competition where each as a perceived equal chance to win the work provided that the have the best price. The goal is also create uncertainty, so they are forced to act to control their destiny. Competition and uncertainty provide the greatest leverage to drive discounts. If successful, each round will result in a lower cost as suppliers try to adjust their status. A form of horserace is to have what's called a reverse auction.

Conversion cost, start-up cost. When there is a substantial cost to change from the use of one supplier to another, you need to show the conversion cost as part of a life cycle cost evaluation or ROI evaluation. While the proposed supplier's price may be competitive with the incumbent, the cost of conversion makes them less competitive on a life cycle cost or ROI basis and you would use that information to get a better deal from the proposed supplier in the form of reduce pricing or their commitment to pay for a substantial part of those conversion costs. Most suppliers will be willing to do this provided that there is an adequate commitment for the term of the contract, as they know that to replace them, the next supplier will face the same disadvantage in trying to replace them. In conjunction with this tactic buyer's may also want to pursue forms of bonuses for renewing the term of the contract as in these situations where it is expensive to replace the incumbent, there is usually a high selling cost to get the business that will be avoided by the buyer's renewal.

Delays in receipt of value. Similar to ROI, this approach is founded based on the fact that there is a large up front payment expected by the supplier, combined with the fact that it will take a substantial period for the items to become fully operational, fully used and returning the investment made. The goal is to create uncertainty in the decision to buy based on that delay in the receipt of value versus what the company is achieving with its other investments. The goal here is either gets the price reduced; the payment periods extended or get other compensation that offsets the delay in the receipt of value.

Contingency / understanding of the work. With this you approach the supplier to review their understanding of the work, to ensure that it meets with your understanding. If their understanding is something more than what you need or require, you will clarify the requirements or specifications accordingly and negotiate a reduced cost based upon the new understanding. Once you have an understanding of the work, you then ask the supplier to identify any areas where they have carried specific contingencies in their pricing and why. This allows you to evaluate the risks involved and whether the buyer should assume the risk completely, partially or allow the supplier to continue to manage the risk with the contingency included in the price. Identification of contingencies frequently will disclose situations where un-necessary contingencies are being driven by design requirements or other requirements that may not be necessary or may not be worth the contingency they cost and may be able to be eliminated without any major impact. For example, I once had a supplier carry a contingency to cover liquidated damages because they knew that the schedule was too aggressive and they wouldn't meet it and would have to pay the liquidated damages. By extending out the schedule we were able to eliminate the contingency, but still have the protection of the liquidate damages for delay if the revised date was not met.

What if? When you've exhausted every other strategy and still don't have the cost to the point where you want it, it's time to employ the use of "what if" to see if there are any changes that could be made to further reduce the cost. This allows the supplier to identify what is driving the cost. For example a tolerance on a specification may be so tight that it requires extra work, processes or additional scrap. contract requirements made without understanding the supplier's capabilities or processes can force them to add cost that may not be necessary. "What if" allows the supplier to identify areas that are driving costs that may potentially be eliminated. Sometimes with only a minor change that has no real impact on the product may provide an opportunity to reduce the cost. It allows you to use the supplier's expertise to help look for ways to reduce cost by eliminating unnecessary or wasteful requirements.

Price sensitivity analysis. If you have the ability to produce a credible price/volume sensitivity analysis, this is a great tool to help reduce price. It shows in simple terms the trade off between price and volume and what the expected volume impact will be based on the price. This works best when the supplier's product will be a significant percentage of the cost or what the buyer is re-selling. It works because it carries the simple underlying message that if they want the higher volumes (which every supplier wants), they need to offer lower prices.

Customer constraints. This is a last round tactic in which you use the internal customer (or sometimes the external customer) to sell the need to reduce the cost. It can be something as simple as explaining that it exceeds their budget and they can't go back for more funding. It could also be to explain the cost they need for the project it will be used in to go forward. Since it is coming from someone other than the buyer, it has more credibility and presents the salesperson with a problem they need to solve if they want to make the sale. This works best when there is no cheaper alternative to what you are buying where the response would be to offer the cheaper alternative to solve the problem.

Approval Hurdles. In every company there are controls on spending levels and purchase approval levels. The more you spend the higher level financial and contract approvals you must pass through. To a sales person, each additional level represents another possibility that the sale may be stopped. They also represent significant potential for delays in the purchase as the customer proceeds through the approval process. If the sales person is rewarded based on their meeting certain revenue goals for a period, any delays in the purchase can impact them financially. As a last round tactic, use those approval levels to drive a further reduction. For example, assume that you have negotiated the supplier down to a price of $103,000 for a piece of equipment. To get the supplier to cut the price to under $100,000, you explain that the magic number is $100,000. If it is above $100,000 the customer will need to get approval at the next higher level or the buyer may need to get approval at their next higher level. This provides the supplier with the choice. They can either: reduce the price to under $100,000 and get the order now, or if they want to stay with their price the decision will need to be elevated to the next higher management level which could delay or cancel the purchase or bring on another round of negotiations from the buyer's manager who will undoubtedly push for more reductions or concessions than what has already been agreed.

The business manager crank. This is a great tactic for when a supplier thinks that they are a lock for the business by what they have learned about the customer's problems, needs and preferences. What the Supplier doesn't know is all the other problems the business manager or CFO has or what investments are competing against the same dollars for their investment.

This usually is an ROI approach where the business manager tells the supplier that they have a number of other investments that they need to make and the ROI from their Product or Service is a problem with making the investment to purchase their product difficult to do against competing programs. The goal of this tactic it to once again introduce uncertainty where the supplier thought there was no competition. They may not have competition based on what they are selling but they do have competition for the investment budget dollars.

CHAPTER 22 DISCOUNTS

When most people think of discounts, they think of traditional business related discounts like unit volume, or sales volume. Discounts can come in a number of different shapes and varieties and may be based on the relationship, marketing activities, sales activities, or operational issues and may take the form of financial assistance for certain activities such as promoting the product and not as straight discounts. Either way it reduces your cost. Here are examples of a number of different types of discounts that could apply to a relationship.

Unit Volume. This is the most common of them all. This relies upon the premise which buyer's have that the more you buy of an item, the lower the cost should be because of the savings that the supplier achieves with the higher volume. The reality is suppliers usually offer price breaks for higher volumes not because they're warranted from a cost perspective but because buyers expect them and because they want to use them to drive the buyer's behavior. The buyer's volumes may not even impact the supplier's costs. For example, if a supplier produces 100,000 units of a product during the course of a year and you buy 10,000 pieces, how much of an advantage to their cost structure will your volumes actually provide them? Will the extra 10,000 pieces allow them to get a material cost price break point? Probably not. It especially won't if they have no guarantee that you will actually buy that volume. Will the extra 10,000 pieces provide them with a new process cost break? Probably not, in fact it could cost them more if they had to invest in additional capacity that won't be fully utilized. Will it reduce their per unit labor costs? Probably not. If they couldn't achieve significant productivity improvements at 90,000 pieces, any change for an added 10 percent is unlikely. Will it have a significant impact on their overhead allocations? Only slightly. Instead of burdening the allocated cost over 90,000 pieces they'll burden it over 100,000 which is an 11% impact, but that 11% is usually on very small percentage of their product's cost. Will it have a significant impact on their cost of sales? Not always, in fact if you are a high maintenance customer it could increase their cost of sales. If the real cost differences from changes in volume are only slight, why do suppliers structure their pricing based on volume and not based on the cost impact to them? Their primary motivation in their pricing structure is being able to manage their profitability. They also use pricing to drive customer behavior. For low volumes they want to drive the customer into their channels where they'll traditionally make more money, have less costs and assume less risk. You can't do that if you offer low prices on low volumes to everyone. For larger customers, they also want to create a form of customer loyalty that will impact future decisions. While you may be free to make spot purchase decisions, the right supplier pricing structures may force you to weigh the impact a spot purchase will have on the discount you will get on other purchases from the supplier. Most suppliers will either want to give you step discounts so you have to earn what you get before getting the next level of discount. They do that to drive repeat business. Alternatively they may want a chargeback mechanism where if they give you the higher volume price and you don't meet the quantities, they can charge you the difference between that price and what you would have paid at the lesser volume. That creates a clear impact of not sourcing from them. Their goal is to provide them with an advantage where you have to weigh the impact of sourcing from others against the impact that may have on your purchases from them. Where there's a significant difference in pricing based on volume, ask them to explain why. In most cases there really isn't a rational explanation for the differences, only that they have chosen to sell that way for their profit model and to try to manage customer behavior. Use that to get the best deal you can based on your estimated volumes and use it avoid step pricing or bill-backs. The argument is simple. If they won't be financially harmed from a cost perspective from not getting those volumes, why should you be penalized if you don't meet the volumes? In most cases they can sell it to you for the high volume price and still make a profit. They just won't make as much of a profit as they would like. Whether they'll accept that will be dependent on how much they need or want your business.

Combined Business Volumes This is the concept of leveraging the entire relationship you have with a supplier across all activities and not just an individual product or set of products. This type of discount usually needs to be negotiated at the strategic relationship level. Many OEM's will have customer volume based discounts so that the more business which you do with them, the deeper the discount. As with unit volume, this discount has little connection to any cost savings that are generated by volumes. It is based not so much on customer loyalty as it is the desire to win more business. Customers have the tendency of buying other products from the same company if they already receive the higher discount. Competitors try to avoid giving steeper discounts on low volume purchases. There is no real savings to a supplier from the combined business volumes that warrant the discounts. These discounts are more to lock you in to continuing to buy more and more from the supplier.

Value of breadth of sales capabilities. There is a value to a supplier in dealing with a buyer who has broad based operations that it will use to open up new markets and new geographies which they or there other customers couldn't reach. There is also a cost that the buyer encounters in opening those markets that should be rewarded by an incremental discount

Residual / annuity value. Many times when you help a supplier sell their product, what you are also doing is help them build an annuity stream from that sale in terms of follow on sales of parts, services, maintenance, upgrades, etc. Many times the value and profitability of that type of annuity business is far greater than the profitability on the initial sale. The annuity revenue that you create for the supplier for tomorrow should be recognized to you today. Use it to reduce today's price.

Signing bonus. When there are substantial costs associated changing suppliers, one of the things to ask for is a "signing bonus" to help you defray those costs. The cost of changing suppliers can be things like needing to re-write certain programs to accommodate the new supplier, making changes to your production line or product design to use them or, sometimes almost needing to start almost from the beginning with the activity. The time to negotiate a signing bonus is before you agree to switch. Once you agree to switch, you are locked into those costs and probably will be locked into that supplier, as there will be a substantial cost to switch to yet another supplier.

Customer loyalty. In many markets there is a substantial cost that a supplier incurs when they lose a customer and need to acquire a new customer or customers to replace them. If a supplier will spend the money to acquire a replacement customer, they should also spend money to retain you as their customer as it avoids those other costs.

Market conditions. Contracts are negotiated at a point in time based on the facts known at the time. During the period of a contract there can be substantial changes where the overall market drops, or where your supplier is impacted by another supplier who has a better product to offer or may have a less costly manufacturing process or overhead. When the market changes and there is a large incentive to change suppliers, a loyal customer shouldn't be penalized for remaining loyal. If the supplier will discount to others to get new business, they should also discount to those who continue to provide them with business, especially in down markets. Too frequently buyers rely upon "best pricing clauses" as their way of getting future discounts to deal with changes to the market conditions. Best pricing clauses are seldom implemented in a manner where the reduction is automatic. Most times they need to be forced by reviews or audits.

Better customer. This is a measure to look at actual performance not just against the contract, but also against their other customers. When your actual performance is consistently better that their other customers, you should be getting a better deal. For example you should be getting a better deal if:
- You pay sooner or more consistently;
- You have better accuracy on Forecasts;
- You have less activity with changes or cancellation or rescheduling.
- You have E-business systems that reduce their management costs and others don't.
- You use resources to work with the supplier to reduce their costs, improve their quality.
- You help them reduce costs not just for their dealing with you but also with their broader based business.

Stability / Risk involved. Suppliers have all types of customers. The more stable you are, the lower the risk they will have in terms of getting paid, the less you should pay. If you are a premier, low risk supplier, you should pay less even at the same volumes than other customers who are higher risk. While anti-trust laws would not allow discrimination on pricing for similar volume at similar terms, you might not be able to pay a lower price but they can make your total cost less based upon what they do to support you.

Customer base you bring to the table. When a supplier enters into a relationship with a premier buyer/ reseller, they are getting access to the accounts which the premier customer has spent years to build and which many times they or their other customers wouldn't be able to penetrate as accounts. There is a value to dealing with the leader and getting access to their customer base.

Value of your name as their customer. When you are a premier company in the industry the fact that you are a supplier's customer has significant value to the supplier for marketing purposes. If you let them use your name in their promotional customer list materials you should get compensated for that.

Reference account. Many customers don't want to buy a product until they see how it is actually successfully used. Without good references for a product it's much more difficult for a supplier to sell their product. References from top companies are like gold as it helps them sell to more customers. If you agree to help show customers on the value of the supplier's product, you should be compensated.

Leadership purchase / use. When you are the first to purchase or use a new product or technology and you are a premier company, it becomes an endorsement of that new product or technology. The supplier will use that to sell to others. If you are first or an early adopter you should get compensated for that endorsement.

Value of supplier qualification. When you are a premier company and qualify a supplier that acts as a form of "seal of approval" which is used by second tier companies in selecting the supplier. This represents significant value to the supplier. If you help them make sales you should get compensated for that.

Value of product qualification. Many smaller companies do not have the resources nor do they want to spend the money to qualify products. They will wait until a major customer has purchased the product knowing that they have qualified it. The value that a product has passed our qualification requirements is a significant value to the supplier for use in marketing the product to these "me too" customers. You should get the benefit of those investments.

Incentives, Promotions, Rebates. To generate increased product sales supplier may offer special incentives, promotions or rebates for sales of specific products to move out inventory or sales during specific periods to improve things like their cash position, inventory levels, financial reports, etc. As a buyer, if you don't ask for them many times you won't be offered them. Other sales practices, like which party if responsible to pay for demonstration products is also a form of discount if you get the supplier to include all those costs. In retail suppliers will pay for shelf space, they will offer special promotions sometimes at or below cost as part of a leader to get customers in to buy. You'll never know what incentives you can get unless you ask.

Performance. When the supplier performs well, they are rewarded with greater volumes and future business. When there are problems with the supplier's performance, they should pay to pick up the costs that they have created. If performance worsens, the supplier's responsibility to cover those costs should increase. E.g. If they are late, they pay for premium freight. If they continue to be late, they stock the material for you.

Inconvenience or added costs to buyer. Any time the supplier creates a requirement that adds costs or inconvenience to the buyer's operations; those added costs should be deducted from the price to be paid.

Convenience to supplier, solving a supplier's business problem or avoiding cost. When what we agree to helps solve a business problem for them or helps them avoid cost, we are reducing their cost infrastructure and shouldn't get the benefit of those savings.

"Add-ons" or services included in the price at no additional cost. Typical add-on's can include delivery, installation, service, warranty, maintenance, training etc. Where these have the most value is if they reduce your direct sales costs. If the entire benefit is passed on to the customer, it may represent additional value to them, but it isn't a reduced cost to you unless you typically included those costs in your selling price.

Receive better or more liberal terms and treatment than other customers. Not all customers are equal and not all of them will get equal treatment. Best pricing isn't the only issue to be concerned with. Better customers may pay the same price as you do, but they may get better or more liberal treatment on things like changes, returns, or may also get additional concessions for things like marketing and promotional programs, or other allowances.

CHAPTER 23. NEGOTIATING DELIVERY

Negotiating delivery terms is similar to understanding your Landed Cost Model. A landed cost model is a fancy description of equating the purchase being delivered to the point of destination. As most suppliers sales terms are FOB or Ex Works their factory, to compare the cost of purchases from different locations you must take into account the difference in costs to have the items delivered. A landed cost analysis will include as a minimum:

- The Price of the item.
- The actual cost of shipping the item from the origin point to the destination.
- The cost of insurance (as risk of loss passes at their factory on these terms).
- The cost of any duties, customs brokerage charges and other costs applicable.
- The cost of money (if payment is made at time of shipment as in letter of credits).
- It may also include other incidental costs incurred such as additional costs of packing, and packaging to protect the shipment.
- In addition there is the risk of loss or damage in transit

Every time goods are moved there are risks in making the shipment, and there are costs associated with the shipments. The risks are:

- The shipment may be lost (such as a package being lost in the distribution system, or the entire cargo is lost because of a disaster such as a plane crashing or ship sinking),
- The shipment may be stolen, or
- The shipment may be damaged (by either physical damage, or by failure to properly package, pack, or be damaged by the environment).
- The shipment may be prevented from being exported or imported because of failure to get the proper import or export licenses, or improper documentation preventing clearance.

How to manage the risk: The party that bears the risk of loss, damage, or theft, and the party who is responsible for export and import and all the other costs associate with the shipment are determined by the specific **delivery term** that is agreed and the **delivery point** which is established. A definition of delivery terms can be found in INCOTERMS that is published by the International Chamber of Commerce. Delivery terms range from Delivered, Duty Paid (DDP) where the supplier is responsible for all risks and costs to the buyer's location, to Ex-Works (EXW) where the buyer is responsible for all risks and costs from Supplier's location. The most common terms and there point for risk of loss transfers is:

Delivery term	Risk of loss point
DDP	Goods are at the disposal of buyer or designee, at the delivery point, on the method of transport used by supplier. (E.g. On board supplier's carrier at buyer's loading dock)
DDU	Goods are at the disposal of buyer or designee, at the delivery point on the method of transport used by supplier. (E.g. On Board the supplier's carrier at buyer's loading dock)
DEQ	Goods are at the disposal of buyer or designee, at the delivery point on the quay or wharf designated.
DES	Goods are at the disposal of buyer or designee, at the delivery point on the vessel at the designated delivery point. (E.g. Delivered to Federal Express, Narita Airport, Tokyo)
DAF	Goods are at the disposal of the buyer at the delivery point at the frontier.(E.g. Delivered to Port of San Francisco, prior to customs clearance)
CIP	Goods are at the disposal of the buyer at the delivery point, however supplier is responsible to procure transit insurance (Delivery is as a location usually different from supplier's facility)
CPT	Goods are delivered to the supplier's selected carrier at the agreed delivery point (which is usually different than supplier's facility).
CIF	Goods are delivered on the carrier at port of shipment, however supplier is responsible to procure insurance and pay for freight. (On-board the vessel or aircraft)
CFR	Goods are delivered to the carrier and have passed the ships rails (on-board the vessel or aircraft)
FOB	Goods are delivered on board the carrier designated by buyer (e.g. Delivered on the carrier at suppliers loading dock)
FAS	Goods are placed along side the carrier designated by buyer (e.g. delivered to Federal Express, at Kennedy Airport, New York)
FCA	Goods are delivered to the buyer or person designated by the buyer at the place designated by the buyer (e.g. Delivered to buyer's freight forwarder at their location)
EXW	Goods are at the disposal of the buyer at the delivery point (e.g. At the suppliers loading dock).

In every purchase you need to establish both the delivery term and deliver point such as: "DDP, buyer's facility located at: 5 Pine Street, Anytown, NY 12555". Both the delivery term and the delivery point are negotiable and some of the factors the buyer should consider in making this decision are:

- Is there substantial risk of loss or damage in transit? If there is, who could manage it more efficiently and cost effectively?
- Are there individual activities that the Supplier may be able to manage more cost effectively, such as inland transport prior to shipment?
- Does the buyer have the presence in the exporting country to effectively manage certain responsibilities?
- Will there be any financial advantages or impact to the depending on the location of transfer of title?
    i. Savings in duties paid because of the difference in paying duties based on supplier's internal transfer price versus buyer's purchase price.
    ii. Tax advantages to the supplier because where they earn their profits.

The delivery term also defines which party has the responsibility for preparing export documents, exporting, preparing import documents, and importing the goods. A list of responsibilities the is defined in the INCOTERMs, that are published by the International Chamber of Commerce, is listed below. Everyone that negotiates contracts should have a copy of INCOTERMs

Assume you want to buy a product from a supplier in Japan for delivery to your location in New York. To move the product from the supplier's plant in Japan to your plant in the U.S will includes all of the following costs:

> The cost to Load the product on a local carrier at Supplier Premises
> The cost of the domestic carrier
> The cost of preparing export documentation
> The cost of customs clearance for export
> The cost of any export charges
> The cost of loading the product at the carrier's terminal
> The cost of any unique transportation equipment and accessories required for the move
> The cost transit insurance
> The cost of the international freight carrier's charges
> The cost of unloading at terminal of import
> The cost of preparing necessary import documentation
> The cost of managing customs clearance
> The cost of any duties and other import charges
> The cost of the carrier at the receiving country
> The cost of unloading the shipment at buyer's premises
> The cost of any warehousing or demurrage charges incurred in route because of delays in things like clearing customs, or having the carrier pick up the goods as scheduled.

The specific delivery term used will define whether the buyer or supplier is responsible for each of the above costs. The delivery term also defines where the risk of loss also passes. Once the risk of loss passes to the buyer, the buyer assumes the cost of any loss or damage to the materials, subject to any possible insurance reimbursement provided for in the delivery term. Any delivery term that includes an "I" has the supplier paying for the cost of insurance to the defined delivery point. If the delivery term has the buyer assuming any risk of loss or damage in transit, the buyer should manage this risk by:

- Purchasing insurance to protect against the risk.
- Including specific packaging and packing requirements as part of the purchase specification. Most companies packaging and packing specifications are designed to reduce the possibility of damage in a cost effective manner. Insurance may provide the ability to recover the cost of the goods shipped. Packaging and packing tries to prevent damage in the first place so you get good product when you need it.
- If there are specific environmental risks (such as temperature or humidity levels that must be maintained), the buyer may include in their specifications that all shipping, and storage be in accordance with specified environments.
- The buyer will usually want to specify the carrier to avoid shipping with high-risk carriers.
- The buyer may want to specify shipping lanes to be used, to avoid shipment through high- risk ports or other areas where there is a history of substantial damage or pilferage. For example, there is still piracy in certain parts of the world on ocean shipment and a Buyer with high value cargo would want to avoid them.

If one of the standard delivery terms doesn't exactly meet your needs, you can always include the closest term to what you need, and then amend that to meet your requirements.

With all of the standard terms the responsibility to unload the product from the import country's carrier at the buyer's delivery point is buyer's responsibility. If you were buying something that you didn't have the ability to unload or if you wanted the item to be installed in a specific spot, you would need to add those requirements to the delivery term. For example, if you were buying a piece of capital equipment that you wanted to be installed by the supplier, the delivery term could be "DDP, buyer's facility located at: 5 Pine Street, Anytown, NY 12555 and supplier shall be responsible and bear all costs of unloading the product from the Carrier at destination and shall manage and pay for all rigging and installation costs to have the product installed in the location defined in the attached drawing". You could also buy the product Ex-works and still add responsibilities at destination with a delivery term like: "Ex-Works, supplier's facility in Tokyo, Japan, however supplier shall be responsible to coordinate delivery to buyer's facility and shall be responsible and bear all costs associated with unloading, rigging and installation of the product at the place defined in the attached drawing."

If your distribution costs are less than the supplier's, shouldn't you always buy ex-works? Or if the supplier's distribution costs are always cheaper than yours shouldn't you always buy the product delivered? While this may seem like the logical answer, it's not always the case. Delivery points impact where profits are made and that impacts the taxes to be paid. It also impacts the declared duty amount upon which duties are based. Delivery terms and delivery point also impacts cash flow. Those factors plus other risk factors should be taken into account in any decision on delivery terms and delivery points. For example, a supplier may be located in a high tax country and their strategy to minimize taxes is to sell their product delivered to your country through one of their affiliates. This will allow them to make a portion of their profit in your country where they will pay less tax. If they have to pay less tax they should be able to sell it to you for less. If they import the product, it will be at their transfer cost, which is less than your purchase price, so there may also be savings in duties paid. If you force a supplier to sell Ex-works you will also be giving up the financial advantage you have on payments. This financial advantage comes from the difference in when the payment term clock starts. When you buy on ex-works terms, the payment clock starts as soon as it is available at the supplier's dock, so while the clock has started, you will not have the goods until all the transit time, customs clearance time and delivery time has lapsed. If you buy based on a different term or at a point closer to your use, the payment clock doesn't start until the product is at that specific delivery point so you get an effective cash flow benefit based on the time the product is in transit to the point of delivery. The difference between the two can be substantial, especially for surface shipments.

In negotiating the delivery point you need to understand the impact to both you and the supplier of that delivery point from both a tax and duties perspective to make sure that it is the most advantageous for both parties. This is because where the title transfers under the delivery terms will determine where the supplier is making their profit from the sale. If you force them to have the sale occur in a high tax location, it will affect their profits, which can affect your price. If they are the importer of the product, you also need to take into account that the duties that they will pay will be based on the transfer price, not your purchase price which may also present an opportunity for savings. In negotiating the delivery term, you need to understand who is better able to manage the different aspects of delivery and what the costs will be. For example, the buyer may have much better international freight costs than the supplier, but the supplier may have much better inland freight costs in their country which might drive you to negotiating a delivery term such as FCA (Free Carrier at a named place), FAS (Free alongside ship at a named place) or FOB the port of shipment rather than Ex-works the supplier's plant.

The other aspect to take into account in negotiating delivery terms is the impact the delivery term has on other terms such as acceptance, payment, warranties, etc. Most of those terms are linked to when the buyer takes delivery of the product. For example, your payment terms may be 30 days after delivery; your acceptance rights may be 30 days from delivery; and your warranty may be 24 months from the date of delivery. For example, assume that you are purchasing computer monitors from a supplier in Taiwan. For something that bulky the most economical mode of shipment is ocean freight. Then assume that it takes 20 days for the shipment to arrive in the West Coast port, 2-3 days in customs, and another 5 days by motor carriers to get it to your site. If you purchase FOB Origin or Ex-works, all those time frames commence when you take deliver at the supplier's site. The impact of this will be that you will receive the material approximately 27 days after you took delivery. This means that from an acceptance or rejection of the goods standpoint you have all of 3 days to inspect or reject the material and if there is any further delay in transit or your inspection, your right of acceptance may have lapsed. If that happens it means your only rights for defective product are under whatever warranties you have. You have 3 days after receiving the material to make payment, and if there is any delay in transit, you could be making payment prior to even receiving the goods at your site. As to warranty, since the warranty period commenced when you took delivery, all the in-transit time has effectively reduced the warranty period and if it took you another 30 days before delivery to the customer, you would have warranty coverage for only 22 months, not 24.

If you will be buying products where you take delivery at any place other than your dock, you need to take the expected in-transit time into account when you negotiate other terms that are based off when the buyer takes delivery. If you don't the in-transit time will effectively reduce those other commitments and add cost.

CHAPTER 24 NEGOTIATING QUALITY, MANAGING QUALITY COST

There have been two things that had a major influence on my thinking on negotiating quality. The first was a quote that was attributed to the then president of Ricoh. The quote was simple but profound. In that he said that for a single problem the costs were:

Point at which the defect is caught	Cost
In design	$35.00
Before buying.	$177.00
Before manufacture.	$368.00
Before the product is shipped	$17,000.00
At the customer's location	$690,000.00

As time has passed and business models have changed, the cost of quality is probably even greater.

The second influence was a cartoon that appeared in Purchasing Magazine where the subject matter was about defects. It had a picture of the supplier's salesperson responding to a quality problem where there were a huge number of defects by offering to refund the purchase price. The buyer was noting that wasn't acceptable as he had tens of thousands of the parts installed in the field where the cost of the problem was far greater that the purchase price. Quality can be a significant cost in a supplier relationship

High quality suppliers	Lesser quality suppliers
Reduce inventory levels & the cost risk of carrying inventory	You must carry inventory to cover expected fall out or risk not meeting shipments
Eliminate incoming inspection	You must do inspection.
Reduce quality management costs	You invest time and resources to manage quality.
Allow you could ship products ctly to the end customer	You wouldn't do a direct shipment. That increases handling, transportation costs & of loss or damage.
Reduce the risk of obsolescence	Your risk of obsolescence is increased
Spare parts inventories are reduced	Spare parts inventories are increased, to account for potential fall out.
Reduce the impact to shipments	Can impact your delivery
Reduce customer satisfaction issues	Customer satisfaction issues impact how customers view you as a supplier
Your cost of quality is low	Your cost of quality can be huge depending upon the point where the defect is found

To help manage the cost of quality you need a number of things. The supplier and the product or service should be qualified. The contract must include the quality requirements, expectations and terms and controls to manage quality. On-going quality must be managed. As we've mentioned before, basic ways to manage performance and the resulting cost and risk and those are:

1. **Relationship.** Such as assigning a quality manager and or commodity manager to manage the supplier.
2. **Structural.** Structural tools would include things like required quality meetings, schedules, reports, escalation processes and audits to help drive quality performance.
3. **Control.** Control in the quality area is by provisions that control what the supplier must provide (such as specifications) how they must manage quality (Such as specific quality requirements) and control over the actions a supplier may take that could impact quality (such as changing the product or services, process, or subcontracting or assigning the work to a third party.
4. **Financial.** These are the terms that provide for the correction of the problem and the recover of costs associated with problems caused by the supplier's quality problems. For example the warranty against defects in material and workmanship should provide for a free repair or replacement of the defective product and the recover of costs associated with the return to and from the supplier. Epidemic defects type provision would allow for a greater recovery of costs in the event of an "epidemic" type problem.

Every good contract will have a mix of all these tools to drive quality performance, risk and cost. Let's take a quick look at specific terms that you may not think of as quality terms and look at how they are used to help manage the risk, cost and drive the supplier to manage quality.

The rights to inspection, tests, and accept or reject the product or Service. This stops the buyer's payment obligation so the buyer isn't financing the supplier's quality problem. Because it's not accepted, they warranty doesn't start until there is a replacement. If you didn't have the right to reject defective product you would have to pay and wait for the problem to be corrected and, it would reduce the effective period for your warranty. In the same acceptance provision you may also include the **right to recover any inspection, test and transportation charges** for defective material. The simple fact is if you assume those costs you are effectively paying twice for it and you are functioning and their inspector. You may also include **the right to reject entire lots** of products if they fail to meet a quality level. This avoids having to inspect an entire lot to sort out good versus bad.

The Warranty that the **product will be free of defects in material or workmanship** or the **service will have been performed with reasonable care and skill.** This warranty is to address quality problems that are found after the product or service has been accepted. The standard product or Service warranty and your quality cost will be impacted by a number of factors such as:

- The length of the warranty term you agree upon.
- When the warranty starts. Is it when the supplier ships it or when it begins to be used?
- What's included in the warranty? Does it include the cost of parts, but not labor?
- What the suppliers rights are if it can't be repaired, such reimbursing supplier for only the depreciated value.
- What's excluded from the warranty?
- Where does it have to be returned?
- Who pays for the cost to ship it to the supplier?
- How long does it take to get and RMA?
- How long it takes to correct it?
- Who pays to ship it back to buyer?
- How long of a warranty will remain in effect after repair or replacement.
- What actions will void the warranty
- What buyer's obligations are to maintain the warranty?

The less you get in terms of the warranty they provide, the more you have to assume or pay. The longer it takes to get a good one, the more it's costing you. The more inventories you have to stock because of problems the more it is costing you.

You may also have a warranty that **products will conform to the warranties, and specifications.** This ensures that the product quality will also comply with the specifications and warranties. So for example if a product violated an environmental warranty, even though it worked and met the specification, you could require replacement.

Products are free of defects in design. This protects against defects in the design of the product

Products are safe for use. This in conjunction with the General indemnification protects against quality defects that could cause personal injury or property damage.

Products are new. This warranty is to ensure that you get new product quality unless you specifically agree otherwise. If you used reconditioned parts in a product that you sell, you would need to advise the customers of that fact and that could impact your selling price.

Epidemic Defects provisions are intended to allow the buyer to recover incidental or consequential costs associated with the defect that would otherwise not be covered by the warranty. For example re-work costs, field costs, engineering costs to diagnose the problem are not covered under a normal warranty. Having an epidemic defect provision provides a major ROI incentive for suppliers to make investments to solve the problem.

General Indemnification. The general indemnification or hold harmless and indemnification are designed to protect buyer from personal injury claims that were caused by the supplier's defective product or negligence.

Insurance requirements in the contract provide additional financial protection over and above what may be protected by the supplier's assets

Limitation of Liability. What is in or excluded from the limitation of liability will have a major impact on you potential risk and cost of quality. For example, if all incidental and consequential costs were excluded you may not be able to recover things such as field costs, rework and problem identification in the event of an Epidemic Defect.

Termination of a Statement of Work or Purchase Order. Allows you to get rid of poor quality suppliers or force them to correct problems

Assignment. Restrictions on assignment without approval prevent the supplier from assigning the performance of the contract to a lesser quality supplier

Subcontracting. Restrictions or controls over the supplier's ability to subcontract all or major portions of the work can provide you with control to ensure you shouldn't get lesser quality.

Waiver a waiver clause it to require that each instance of the other party's noncompliance with any obligation or responsibility will not be deemed a waiver of subsequent instances. So if you waived Specification requirements once, it doesn't change the specification for future deliveries.

Bar Coded Label requirements. To manage the quality of inventory management

Packaging and Handling Requirements are to protect the quality of the purchase against damage in transit where we own the risk of loss or damage if you buy under Origin based delivery terms

Quality Documents that are made part of the contract to set requirements on how the supplier must manage their quality program

Purchase Specifications establish the quality of the product or service that you are purchasing

Control over changes to the product or process are **to** ensure that changes to the product or process that could impact quality, are not made without approval.

Handling of consigned materials These may include requirements around storage and handling, as improper storage can damage materials and improperly handling can damage items by things such as electro static discharge (ESD)

Quality Specifications may include general things like compliance with ISO Requirements, or they can include more detailed requirements such as:

- Guidelines and objectives provide for continuous improvement
- Rights to perform Quality Audits to verify compliance
- Document Control and Record keeping requirements
- Quality Problem Notification requirements
- Notice and approval requirements for any changes.
- How Nonconforming product will be managed and processes to isolate defective product to ensure it is not inadvertently shipped/used
- product Identification and Lot trace-ability requirements.
- Quality Reporting / Review Meetings to report and monitor correction of problems and status of continuous improvement
- supplier commitments for Shipped product Quality Levels (SPQL) and Reliability Levels.
- supplier commitments for continuous improvement

Contracts may also address things like cost of failing to meet the requirements such as re-work costs, re-qualification costs They could also address things like escalation processes in the event of a problem, or other commitments should the supplier not be meeting their commitments.

What are the costs of quality and reliability?

The cost of quality is really driven by the point at which the defect occurs. The cost attributable to quality problems is the one of the most difficult of all the total cost calculations to make. In other calculations you only have one or two variables whereas with quality problems there are multiple variables to be considered on a case-by-case basis.

- The cost of quality consists of the following elements:
- The increased cost for material, as a result of an increased safety stock necessary as a result of quality problems;
- the increased cost of inspection at incoming inspection;
- the cost of handling a failure, when the failure occurs at incoming (including administrative costs to return);
- the cost of handling a failure, when the failure occurs in process (including administrative costs to return) and scrap and rework costs.
- The cost of field defects includes all the other costs plus:

- o Cost to identify the defect,
- o Costs to purge both problem products and inventories in the field
- o Cost to replace the defective product with new
- o Cost to provide replacement products in the field
- o Cost of warranty management
- o The cost of scrap and re-work costs

Quality problems can also include product liability, customer relationship costs, and the cost to redesign products to eliminate the use of a quality product. let's look at these in greater detail:

QUALITY SAFETY STOCK. From a safety stock standpoint a bad item is the same as a late item. As such the calculation of safety stock cost can be calculated using the same formula as safety stock for late deliveries the amount of quality related safety stock would be in addition to any safety stock required because of delivery or quantity problems. In a worst case scenario the delivery could be late, when it arrives the quantity is less than ordered, and there are quality problems with the product that was delivered.

INCREASED INSPECTION COSTS. The second element in calculating the cost of quality is the increased cost of inspection required at incoming that was necessitated by the reduced level of quality. For example, if your program was to be managed without incoming inspection and the level of quality was so poor that it now required one hundred percent incoming inspection, the increased cost of quality is those incoming inspection costs.

COST OF FAILURES AT INCOMING INSPECTION. In addition to the added inspection cost you also have the cost of failures at incoming. This not the same as increased inspection costs and is not double counting. The rationale behind this is while the substandard quality level forced an inspection initially, the failure at incoming will require an additional inspection of the repaired or replaced material.

COST OF FAILURES IN PROCESS. With any reduced inspection you will have the risk of a failure of the material in process. The Administrative Costs associated with a failure in process are virtually the same as a failure at incoming. The difference rests in the cost of the failure rather than the cost of the inspection. The cost of a failure in process can be great for example: If a subassembly was imbedded in a larger product and did not fail until the finished product was turned on, the cost of that failure would be the cost to disassemble the unit to a level at which the failed unit could be replaced with a new one. The cost could also include the direct expense which results from the failure such as lost time in an assembly line production when the line has to stop because of a failure. In addition, if the problem was not deemed to be unique, it could also result in a purge of all potential affected items with resulting costs for all the re-work that would need to be done.

INCREASED INSPECTION. While you would expect that all factors considered, the greater the level of inspection the less failures you would achieve. While this is partially true it does not take into account infant mortality in components that will still allow for failure in process even after incoming inspection has occurred. In addition, it also doesn't take into account the adequacy of the test method to catch all potential defects or potential maverick lots.

RELIABILITY. Reliability costs include: costs associated with reliability problems which occur in the field such as spare parts and repairs inventories, cost of service calls, cost of replacement, processing returns of failed material, etc. The cost of reliability problems is difficult to compute for several reasons. First, most reliability failures occur in the field and you must rely upon the quality of the failure data that is received from the field. Second, because of the relative low cost of some items, it may be more economical to throw away the failed material rather than send it back through a repair loop. The elimination of the repair loop eliminates failure analysis. Third, there will be failures that occur without your knowledge, as not all material will come back through your channels for repair. Most reliability failures occur in the field and you must rely upon the quality of the failure data that is received from the field. Second, because of the relative low cost of some items involved it may be more economical to throw away the failed material rather than send it back through a repair loop. The elimination of the repair loop eliminates failure analysis. Third, there will be failures that occur without your knowledge, as not all material will come back through your channels for repair. There are two types of basic reliability failure costs. First, are the Infant mortality costs that occur either in incoming inspection, or testing of a higher-level system. The second type is when the statistical average of failures that occur in the field fails to meet or exceed the agreed to mean time between failures (MTBF) of the item.

There are two types of basic reliability failure costs. First, are the infant mortality costs that occur either in incoming inspection, or testing of a higher-level product or system. The second type is based upon the statistical average of failures that occur in the field when the product fails to meet the agreed to reliability commitment (mean time between failures (MTBF)). Infant mortality failures are reliability failures that occur in the manufacturing or test process. The cost of such failures is the same as an in process failure. The cost of a failure in the field is the most expensive of the quality/reliability cost factors. The cost includes:
- The base cost of a service call.
- The installation cost (After the technician arrives, how long does it take to have the part removed, the new part replaced and any testing performed).
- The administrative cost to return the item for repairs. This includes the cost of verifying the failure, issuing orders, packaging etc.

- Scrap cost for items that aren't repairable.
- The cost of repair of the failed item. Repair costs if the items that failed are usually only covered by a warranty of a duration that is far less than the agreed to MTBF.
- The cost of repair or re-work cost for the product the failed item was assembled on.
- The increased spare parts stock. Spare parts stocking levels are initially set based on projected failure rates but will be adjusted periodically to reflect the actual failure rates.
- Down time and losses that are encountered by the end user.
- The effect on service revenue profitability.
- The effect on future sales, since sales are based on total cost of ownership.

When you look at all these different costs, it's easy to see how the President of Ricoh identified the cost of a defect in the field as being multiple hundreds of dollars. Today the cost is much more. The simple fact is that standard warranty provisions only cover the repair, replacement, refund or credit for the specific part. Warranties do not cover any of the other costs associated with the defect. If all the supplier pays is for the cost to replace the failed part itself, the buyer is assuming all those other costs for a problem over which they have no control.

Many suppliers want to have it both ways if you let them. They don't want to be responsible for any costs associated with quality problems, and they want to be free to manage their products and production or work how they want to, without interference or control. In negotiations offer them a choice. If they want total control and flexibility, they must assume the risk and cost they create. If they don't want to assume the risk and cost, they must give up the flexibility and control to a point where you as the buyer can confidently assume those risks.

If you assume the risk, you need to create strict controls. This is done by:
- Qualifying the supplier to ensure they can perform and the risk is manageable.
- Requiring the supplier to adhere to strict quality standards and programs so that the supplier will consistently produce quality products. An example of this is International Organization for Standards (ISO) certification requirements. For specific items such as electronic components you can find standards such as Joint Electron Device Engineering Council (JEDEC), or Electronics Industry Alliance (EIA).

- Requiring that no changes be made to the products or processes without buyer's approval (or that you have sufficient notice to allow you to pursue alternative sources).
- Approval of changes should include not just form, fit, function but also anything that could impact reliability and serviceability.
- Always require advance notice of changes to the process. If you are assuming the major cost risk, require approval of changes to the process.
- Always require approval of changes to manufacturing locations or sufficient notice to allow other options or interim strategies to manage against start-up risks.
- Require approval of any subcontracting or changes in an approved list of material suppliers
- Establish clear specifications.
- Demand Quality Reporting
- Establish minimum acceptable quality levels.
- Have increased management requirements and costs for failing to meet agreed levels.
- Demand Continuous improvement.
- Demand Best Practices Quality Management Programs.
- Let them know that you reward suppliers who perform with more business and will penalize suppliers who don't perform with less or no business.

Warranty is not a solution for quality problems. Warranties only cover a small portion of the cost and may be even less because of warranty limitations or exclusions.

It is never a good practice to assume risks over which you have no control, so in addition to strict controls, you should negotiate an "epidemic defects" provision in the contract that provides the buyer the right to recovery consequential damages for field defects once the defects have reached a level that is of "epidemic" proportions. In negotiating an epidemic defects rate the important thing to remember is that until such time as that epidemic rate has been reached, the buyer is assuming the vast majority of the costs of the supplier's defects. Since the supplier has the ability to control the quality, they have the ability to control this risk. In negotiating epidemic defects, it is also advisable to separate safety defects from quality defects. The important thing that differentiates a safety defect from other defect is that a safety defect is a potential product liability issue for the supplier, so that it is in their best interest to have the product pulled from the field and the cost of field replacement of safety related defects should not be subject to any form of a epidemic rate.

When you put all of this into perspective, the greater the risk of a quality problem, the more diligent you need to be in terms of whom you select as your supplier, how you manage them, and what you allow them to do or not do. If you can't get full epidemic defects coverage, you should demand provisions in your contract that helps manage the supplier's quality and allows you to recover certain costs if they fail to live up to their commitments.

The first point of protection is supplier selection. A friend of mine has the saying that "you can't shine a sneaker". If the supplier doesn't have the processes, controls and discipline to manage production in a quality manner, you shouldn't use them.

All quality starts with the design. If you have a product that is poorly designed for manufacture, you may be able to take some steps in the process to improve the quality, but it will seldom be of the same quality as if the product was designed right from the beginning. product Quality begins at the design stage. products must be designed in a manner that allows for high quality, repeatable processes are used to manufacture of the item. This is what is called "design for manufacture". In evaluation a supplier, you can expect more quality issues and problems the more an item:

- Requires work by hand versus machine.
- Requires multiple steps versus one step
- Requires multiple processes versus a single process.
- Fails to take advantage of automation.

Designers that are good at the functional design or aesthetics may seldom be exposed to what's required to manufacture that design in high volume in a quality manner using the tools available. One of Procurement's roles is to involve suppliers in the early stages of design to review the manufacturability of the product in a quality manner. Designing in quality also requires that you look at the processes in terms of how the design and the required manufacturing practices will affect quality. Certain processes produce higher yields. The more the product design takes advantage of those higher yield processes, the better the quality. Another key activity in the design stage that affects quality is the selection of the suppliers who will provide materials and components. Before adding new suppliers of materials it is important to perform initial assessments of both the supplier and the materials.

A key way to manage this is by maintaining a qualified parts list from qualified suppliers as the source for designers to use in their designs. Treat all deviations from those qualified suppliers and parts lists with care and ensure that they are in fact qualified. Also include requirements that allow you to control any changes to subcontractors or material suppliers. If you have an unqualified supplier providing you product, what you are really doing is agreeing to accept a much higher risk in the cost of quality that may or may not be covered.

In evaluating a supplier there is one rule that you should live by: "don't expect that you will be able to change the supplier". If they don't have what you need or want, if at all possible don't use them! The reason is that in many cases to change will require a financial investment in new tools, process equipment etc. If a supplier can continue to supply you without needing to make the investment most of time they won't make that investment, and you have to live with the results. Change only comes from pain. If the supplier gets your business, they won't feel the pain to change their processes to improve quality until you take it away, and by that time you will have endured significant pain and cost on your own.

It is important that in every supplier relationship that you set the expectation that quality is a pre-condition to doing business and not a goal. People look upon goals as something nice to have, not something that is an absolute requirement. The first step is to move all responsibility for inspection from you to the supplier. The reasons are simple. First, if the commitment is to provide you with high quality product, the cost to ensure that should be borne by the suppliers. While there is an additional cost for the supplier to assume this responsibility, it is also to the supplier's advantage, as the sooner the supplier knows of the quality problem, the sooner they can correct the process problem that is causing the quality problem and reduced the total cost impact of the problem. If they wait until you receive the material, it increases the amount of the problem material in the supply chain by extending the time it takes to understand that there is a problem. It also significantly adds to the cost with all the extra movement of materials and addition of inventories required to deal with the quality problem, etc.

Force the supplier to monitor progress by measuring critical in-line parameters. Ensure that the supplier has the statistical capability to measure their process. Look at how they maintain and upgrade their employee and new employee knowledge and skills. Look for the quality tools and techniques such as statistical process control, measurement systems, analysis, quality planning, failure analysis, approval processes for materials and parts used, tooling and equipment requirements, calibration, self assessment programs, etc. The looser they are in the way they manage their business, the greater the likelihood problems will arise. To show how important you consider quality and get 110% of their attention, tie quality improvement to your future business. No improvement = less or no business.

To manage quality you must have robust supplier rating systems and ensure that the supplier is made aware of the problems. Use scorecards. Establish the different factors on the scorecard according to your priorities and the specific commodity attributes. In addition to product quality you also need to check and manage fulfillment quality as it can cause many of the same problems. The parts may be perfect, but if they are the wrong value, wrong part number, or the wrong suppliers, there is a quality problem with their fulfillment process that can require you to screen everything that is shipped. It they had 100% accuracy; the screening cost could be avoided.

Since many of the quality costs aren't covered by a supplier's warranty, how do you protect against those other costs? You need to either get the supplier to agree to assume those costs and risks, or if the buyer will be assuming the risks you need to make sure that you have the requirements in the contract that will allow you to manage those risks. Much of it gets down to whether you trust the supplier, believe what they say, and have confidence that they will proactively respond to any problems in a reasonable manner. If you don't, you need to verify that the supplier is managing their business in a sound, controlled manner that will consistently produce high quality products.

Since buyers bear a large percentage of the total quality cost in the relationship, the concept of verifying the supplier's program and doing on-going management is something that must used to manage the potential cost exposure of supplier quality problems. Companies who understand the real costs of quality are the same ones who push for their suppliers to have Six Sigma type programs to continually eliminate defects. In negotiating quality provisions, always take the position that your purchase price is paying for high quality performance and the party that has the greatest ability to manage the risk (which is the supplier) should have the responsibility for an ever-increasing share of the costs they create when they fail to manage it properly. If they won't agree, you need to make sure that you have sufficient control to allow you to assume the risk. If they aren't prepared to do either, you should probably take your business elsewhere.

Caution On Allowing Changes As Long As They Don't Impact Form, Fit, Function.

Form is the product's geography or dimensions. **Fit** is the connection location and type of connection for the material to connect. **Function** is defined as meeting the product specifications.

If you allow the supplier to make changes as long as it doesn't change the Form, Fit, or Function this means that as long as the product:
- It is the same dimensions / geography
- It has the same connection location and fit
- Meets the same product specifications

The supplier is free to make whatever changes they want without your approval. The problem with allowing changes as long as they don't impact the form fit and function of the product is two fold.

The first issue is that while the products may be of the same form, fit, or function, but they may no longer work in your application. For example, it's not uncommon for two suppliers to have parts of the same form, fit and function, and one works in your application and the other doesn't. The other problem is that such changes can also affect the quality of the product being purchased or the reliability of the product. A substitution of cheaper materials may meet all the requirements of form, fit and function, but it could also cause more quality problems, shorter reliability periods etc.

GLOSSARY OF PROCUREMENT AND CONTRACT TERMS IN NEGOTIATIONS

Many companies create their own terminology. For example in some companies I've worked at price reductions were called a variety of different things: "take downs", "positive PPV", cost reductions, etc. Walmart™ calls sales price reductions "Rollbacks". If you use internal terminology with suppliers make sure they understand exactly what you mean by it. If they use their own internal terminology in discussions, don't assume you know what they are talking about, ask them to explain what they mean. Here is a list of common terms you may need to understand doing procurement negotiations.

Acceptance. Agreeing verbally or in writing to the terms of a contract. . Acceptance is one requirement to show there was a contract. (contracts require an offer and an acceptance of that offer). Acceptance can also refer to receiving goods or services under the contract where you have the right to inspect it and either reject or accept it according to agreed criteria such as conformance to the specification or to an agreed acceptance and test process. The significance of acceptance is once accepted the items may no longer be returned for a refund and any defects must be managed under any applicable warranty provision. Acceptance may occur through an affirmative act, by the buyer's actions, or by allowing the right to accept to lapse.

Acceptance, test and rejection rights. Used in many types of contracts and will include the rights of acceptance, acceptance criteria, tests required and responsibilities in the event the item is not accepted such as the responsibility to correct the problems in a timely manner, responsibility for costs of additional test and acceptance etc. For purchase of volume quantities it may also include the right to accept or reject individual lots of the product when an individual sample of the lot fails to meet the acceptance criteria. Having the right to accept or reject by lot keeps the buyer from having to screen all products in the lot.

Access to premises, premises restrictions. Used when a supplier will be performing work on the buyer's site where the buyer wants to both control access to the premises or wants to place restriction on the supplier's use of the premises such as prohibiting certain types of work from being done or restricting the activity performed out of buyer's premises to only supporting the buyer.

Adjusted Basis. This is revaluing an asset to take into account depreciation, damage or other things that would reduce the assets value. For example if a Supplier was unable to cure an intellectual property infringement claim against a product they sold you, the remedy they may offer it to purchase the product back on an adjusted basis.

Advertising and publicity. Used in most contracts where the buyer (or supplier) does not want their names used in advertising or publicity materials of the other party because of the potential negative impact if could have on them, their Brand image or their relationship with other suppliers.

Affiliate. Similar to a subsidiary, except instead of using the measurement of the percent of ownership, its usually defined by having control over their actions. For example, a company (A) may have 3 wholly owned subsidiaries and those subsidiaries could each own one third (1/3) of another company. That other company would not be a subsidiary to any one of them as none on their own have more than 50% ownership. Company A could exercise control over what each of the three Subsidiaries do to a point where they can control the actions of that other company. Under the definition of affiliate based on control, that company would be an affiliate of Company A.

Agency. A concept at law that can make one party responsible for the acts or omissions of individuals that would be considered their Agent.

Agent. An agent is a person or entity that are authorized to act for another party. The person they act for is the principal. Agents can be created in several manners. You can contract with to appoint them as your agent. You can create apparent authority ratifying the agent's acts, or employment. Agents can bind the principal by contract or create liability if they cause injury while in the scope of the agency. For example if you hire a suppler and they injure someone during the scope of their work, they could be considered an agent of yours and you could be liable for their actions. The concept of agency is one of the reasons why buyers include indemnification and insurance provisions in contracts with suppliers (as they could potentially be liable for the supplier's actions).

Agreement. Most contracts will usually have a provision that describes all of the various documents that make up the understanding or "agreement" of the parties. The agreement will normally include the contract itself and all other documents that are listed in or incorporated by reference into that contract.

Allocation of supply / constrained supply. Occurs in periods of excess demand where the supplier provides only a portion of the requested supply due to the need to also support other customers. In most allocation of supply provisions the buyer will want to be assured of a pro-rata share of the available supply based on past history, forecasts or orders. Without a commitment to allocate supply a supplier's natural tendency during periods of excess demand is to allocate supply to customers or channels that provide them the highest profit or return.

Amendments. As change will always occur, every contract needs to define the process by which it may be changed or "amended". Terms will normally describe the requirements for amending the contract, such as who must sign any amendments and it may include authorized methods to amend certain portions of the contract. Under contract law principles the latest writing in time between the parties will have precedence so an amendment may be amending the contract or it could be amending prior amendments, so the drafting of any amendments needs to clearly identify exactly what is being amended and if it applies to a limited scope it should also describe the scope that it applies to, otherwise an amendment that was intended for a single situation could amend the entire contract.

Amortization. In procurement this describes a situation where costs not initially paid for by the Buyer are paid off over time as part of the purchase price to liquidate that cost.

Annuity. An annuity is a stream of income that comes from an investment. In procurement an annuity stream would be all the sales the Supplier would receive after the initial sale such as service, maintenance, spare parts, repairs.

Appendices. This describes a document or documents that are "appended to the contract" that should also be incorporated into the contract by reference.
Applicable law and jurisdiction. If a dispute arose between the parties and it went to court, "applicable law" would determine which locations law would be applied in resolving the dispute. As any court could potentially hear the case and still use the agreed "applicable law" to come to their decision, buyer's will also usually want to control where such cases will be heard (the "Jurisdiction"). For example if you had a clause that said that the applicable law was New York, and the Jurisdiction was the Federal Court in Manhattan, the suit could only be heard by that court and when they heard it, they would apply the law of New York State in making their decisions.

Approved vendor list (AVL). This is used when the buyer wants to manage the quality of the material suppliers and subcontractors that a supplier may use to perform the work and limits them to only those suppliers that are included on the buyer approved list.

Annual Percentage Rate. An annual percentage rate is the effective rate being charged. For example there may be a daily rate of .03 percent. The APR is that daily rate time 365 or and APR of 10.95%.

Arbitration. A dispute resolution process that must be mutually agreed to by the parties to bring in an independent third party or parties to help resolve the dispute. Commitments to agree to arbitration may be binding or non-binding on the parties. Many buyers do not like arbitration provisions as they feel that it allows a supplier to avoid being forced to come to a reasonable resolution of the dispute in lieu of having to go through the cost of litigation.

Arm's Length Transaction. This is most frequently used in procurement to describe the relationship a supplier will want to have with their subsidiary where each acts on their own interests. A closer relationship where the supplier is involved in the activity directly can create legal or tax impacts. For example, to maintain an arm's length transaction on product sales the supplier sells the product to the subsidiary at what's called "transfer price" and the subsidiary makes the local sale according to their own terms.

As-is. When a product is sold to you on an as-is basis it is being sold without any representations or warranties as to the product. In simple terms it means what you purchased is all that you will ever get.

Assignment. An Assignment is an act where a third party is transferred rights or responsibilities that were previously the responsibility of one of the parties of the contract. If you sold a Business to a 3rd party, and they needed to continue to make purchases, you would want to assign your contract to that 3rd party. If you contracted with a supplier to perform work, you may not want them to assign that to a 3rd party as it may impact the performance, value received etc. Most assignment provisions include the buyer and supplier's assignment rights. For example, the contract could prohibit assignment by both parties, unless the Business or Portion of the Business that was providing or using the item is sold to a third party. Under an assignment the assigning party remains secondarily liable under the contract if the assignee (the part the contract was assigned to) fails to perform. The exception to this is when the parties have agreed to an assignment and novation.

Assignment and novation. A novation is a form of release of a contracting party from their obligations by agreeing to only look to the new party that the contract was assigned for all rights and remedies, thereby discharging the original party's contract obligations. Whether a buyer would want to agree to an assignment and novation would be dependent upon the circumstances. For example if a supplier was spinning off or selling part of a business to a much smaller entity, that would impact your ability to recover damages in the event of a problem and you probably would not want it to be an assignment and novation as you would want the original supplier to still be secondarily liable to you for performance under the contract. A novation discharges the assigning party's obligations under the agreement.

Assignment (partial). A partial assignment is when the original parties agree to in effect create two agreements. The original contract is retained in part, and the new agreement may cover part or all of terms of the prior contract.

Audit rights and costs. Any time you have a contract that is based on cost or that includes things like reimbursable items, you should have the right to perform an audit to ensure that what you are being charged as costs or reimbursable expenses can be substantiated. Most audit provision will also include language that makes the supplier responsible for some it not all of the cost of the Audit based upon the results of the Audit where the buyer assumes all costs in the event there are no problems found, the supplier assumes all costs in the event the problems found exceed an agreed threshold and frequently a sharing of the expense in between. The goal is to encourage the right behavior, by their being liable for the cost if they fail to behave properly.

Authorized channel. A third party that has a contract with a supplier to re-sell the supplier's products. As not all suppliers may be willing to sell to a third party that you may be doing business with on an "outsourced" arrangement, the supplier may need to be authorized to purchase from supplier "Authorized Channels" such as distributors. You may require the use of authorized channels to simply protect against purchases in the Broker market that can be fraught with problems, counterfeit products, etc.

Authority. A right with the power to act. There are different types of authority. "Apparent authority" is when a principal gives an agent various signs of authority to make others believe he or she has authority, such as an independent sales representative that accepts orders for a company which the company ships against. "Express authority" or "limited authority," where the scope of the exactly authority granted is spelled out, "Implied authority," which flows from the position one holds. For example an Officer of a Company has implied authority to bind the company. "General authority," is a broad power to act for another.

Back door selling. Practice of supplier sales people trying to sell direct to the user instead of through Procurement

Bailment. Placing property in the custody and control of another party (usually by an agreement in which the holder (the "bailee") is responsible for the safekeeping and return of the property. The "bailor" (owner of the goods) leaves the "bailment" (goods) with the "bailee" (custodian). The transaction is a "bailment."

Bankruptcy. Bankruptcy statutes permit persons and businesses that are insolvent or potentially insolvent, to place their financial affairs under the control of the bankruptcy court. Under US Bankruptcy law there are various forms of Bankruptcy. A Chapter 11 bankruptcy allows a business to reorganize and refinance to be able to prevent final insolvency. Chapter 13 is similar to Chapter 11, but is for individuals to work out payment schedules. If reorganization isn't possible, a Chapter 7 bankruptcy the trustee appointed by the court, dispose of all the assets and pay the debts in order of precedence. The first priority is taxes, then secured creditors. Any remaining amount would be divided between unsecured creditors and the court declares the debtor bankrupt and discharges the unpaid debts. For a procurement person one of the key things to know is that once a company has gone into Bankruptcy, the trustee does not have to honor prior agreements that existed between the Bankrupt company and its customers or suppliers

Benchmark. A process where products, activities, or costs or terms are analyzed against companies who are best in class or amongst competitors

Benefits. The value provided to the end customer from the use of features included in the supplier's product.

Best pricing clause. A best pricing clause requires the supplier to extend to you the best price that they extend to other customers. suppliers usually want to avoid such commitments or make them subject to certain qualifiers such as "under the same quantities and same terms" which allows them to price differently. For a Best Pricing Clause to be of value you need to have audit rights, otherwise you are relying on good faith for them to notify or change your price when it is not the best price.

Bill of material (BOM). The name given to the listing of components, materials or subassemblies that makes up a higher-level assembly, subsystem or system. For example a BOM for a circuit card would include the board that the materials are placed on and all the materials incorporated in that circuit card.

Bill of materials cost. Used primarily in manufacturing. For example if you hired a contract manufacturer to produce a product, you would negotiate to cost of all the materials listed on the bill of materials, the cost of the value added the contract Manufacturer provides, their material acquisition costs and the contributions to their overhead and profit.

Bonds – A bond is a financial guarantee provided by a third party (usually an insurance company) that promises certain performance.
- Payment bonds are used to ensure that a supplier pays all its subcontractors and materials suppliers to prevent liens being placed against the item purchases. Frequently used in purchases of construction or repairs where the laws may provide Subcontractors or Materials suppliers the right to place "mechanics" or "material man's" liens against the work to ensure they are paid for their services.
- Performance bonds are used to protect against the additional costs of completing the work in the event the supplier fails to complete the work. More commonly used in purchases of construction or repairs where the cost of completing partially completed work could be substantial.

- Fidelity bonds are used to protect against theft by individuals. Fidelity bonds are used when an individual or supplier may be entrusted with access to certain buyer or buyer customer's areas. Fidelity Bonds are used in the purchases of services where the supplier has access to things of value held by the buyer or its customers.

Boycott. An organized effort to avoid purchases from or business with a business or business of a particular country.

Brand. A brand is promise of value to a specific set of customers. With that Brand, the customer should be able to expect certain attributes of the product similar with other products of the same brand. For example Tide™ laundry detergent is a brand of Proctor & Gamble.

Breach. The failure by a party to the contract to meet a firm obligation in that contract, without a legitimate legal excuse. This may include not completing a job, not paying in full or on time, failure to deliver all the goods, substituting inferior or significantly different goods, being late without excuse. Any act that shows the party will not complete the work is an "anticipatory breach"), A *Minor Breach* is an insignificant divergence from the terms of the contract. This would not be cause to terminate the contract, only a cause to collect damages. A relevant and significant breach by the other party is a valid excuse by the non-breaching party not to perform and terminate the contract. Examples of material breaches would be a breach of warranties, a breach of material representations or a breach of anything that is defined by the contract as material. For example, if any contract said, "time is of the essence of the contract", the failure to delivery a product or service on time would be a material breach.

Broker. A third party reseller of a supplier's product that typically is not part of the supplier's authorized channels. Brokers procure excess material from another company and resell it in the market.

Buyer instructions. The risk in the buyer providing instructions on what to do or how to do something is that in doing so, the buyer becomes responsible if there is a problem that results from those instructions. As such, contracts may include provisions that define who within the buyer's company is authorized to provide instructions or it may include language that tries to avoid the shift in liability such as buyer may make "suggestions", and upon the supplier's accepting or implementing those suggestions supplier is taking those as their own and remains responsible. For example, buyer may have minimum safety standards or guidelines for operating on buyer's premises, but those standards will usually also include language that makes the responsibility for management of the safety of their operations and their employees the supplier's responsibility.

Buyer responsibilities /deliverables. In the performance of many purchase activities the buyer may have certain responsibilities such as providing reviews and approvals or providing certain deliverables such as information, materials, etc. Any time there is a buyer responsibility or deliverable there is also a potential liability to the buyer should the buyer fail to perform the responsibility or provide the deliverable. So any time you have a commitment in which the buyer's has responsibilities, you need to manage that potential liability by managing or capping the potential liability. For example, if buyer failed to perform certain reviews or approvals on time, you might have language that provides the supplier with a day for day extension of the schedule as the sole remedy for such delay, or you could include language that limits buyer's potential liability for such failures.

Buyer's market. A time when there is excess supply versus demand.

Cancellation. A negotiated right for the buyer to cancel individual purchase orders subject to the agreed upon cancellation terms where buyer may be liable to pay for certain costs associated with the cancellation depending upon the point at which the cancellation occurs.

Carrier selection and use. The delivery term that you agree upon will determine a number of things. It determines who bears what expenses in the shipment of the product from the supplier to the buyer. It also determines at what point title and risk of loss to the item transfer from the supplier to the buyer. For example under Ex-Works the title and risk of loss transfers at the supplier's dock. If the buyer is going to be responsible for the risk of loss, the selection of the carrier that will be used and the supplier's use of that Carrier can be an important factor in terms of the management of the risk as not all carriers are equal and some have higher incidence of loss by damage or theft. To manage against the risk of loss, some delivery terms may require the supplier to provide for both the contract of carriage and insurance. This is used when the supplier selects the carrier but is also responsible to providing insurance against the risk of loss or damage to the items while in transit. For example CIP delivery term has the supplier provide Carriage and Insurance Paid to the specified point.

Carve out. The words carve out mean to exclude a particular issue or point from responsibility or from the clause. For example: Except for _____ supplier shall be responsible. The except for language is what's called a "carve out". Probably the most important area where carve outs may be used is in the limitation of liability provision where there may be limits on the types of damages that may be claimed and their may be caps on the amount of liability.

For example if you had language like this:

> Neither party shall be liable for incidental, consequential, special damages or loss of revenue or profits; supplier's total liability under this contract shall not exceed _____. buyer's total liability under this contract shall not exceed.

The net result would be that you would be limited to only direct damages and the amount of direct damages would be capped at the stated amount. With a carve out it look like this:

> Except for Epidemic Defects, General Indemnification and Intellectual Property Indemnification, neither party shall be liable for incidental, consequential, special damages or loss of revenue or profits,

> Except for Epidemic Defects, General Indemnification and Intellectual Property Indemnification

> "Supplier's total liability under this contract shall not exceed _____. Buyer's total liability under this contract shall not exceed.

The net result would be that with the carve outs for the three provisions identified, you would be able to claim all types of damages instead of being limited to only direct damages and the damages would not be subject to the dollar cap on liability.

Caveat emptor. This is the Latin phrase for "let the buyer beware".

Changes. Virtually every contract needs a variety of provisions that address changes that may occur, such as: product or Service Changes by supplier; Engineering Change" or "EC" that may affect quality or operation; Engineering Change Processes and approvals; Subcontractor changes; buyer's right to make changes to product, Services, or Deliverables; Cost management of changes; remedies in the event of Unauthorized Changes; Changes Authorized By The contract; Price Changes; Cost changes due to change in the scope of the work or services for both added or reduced work. For the buyer you want change provisions that prevent changes to the product or service or who performs the work that could effect its quality, performance, value, or ability to operate as needed and you want to manage the cost impact of changes so you pay a reasonable cost for any increased work you requires and you get reasonable reductions for any reduced work.

Change of Control. A change of control occurs when one of the parties to the contract are completely acquired by another party, It is not an assignment as long as the original entity remains in tact as part of the new organization. If the controlling party wanted to have the contract moved to a different entity in their organization that would be an assignment. If it is very important who you deal with, you may want to have a change of control provision that provides you certain remedies in the event of a change of control such as having the right to terminate the contract so you aren't forced to do business with someone you don't want such as a competitor.

Channels. Most companies' sell through a variety of different markets and each market will have different sales strategies. Who they sell to are their sales "channels" Examples of sales channels are direct sales to end customers, distribution, re-sellers, dealers, original equipment manufacturers (OEM), value added resellers (VARs), etc. In their sales strategy each distinct channel may be treated differently in terms of the pricing, discounts & allowances or terms they receive. There is also usually further stratification where suppliers have "tiers" within an individual channel that are based upon volume of the customer's purchases and their importance to the supplier. Tiers within the same channel will receive different pricing, discounts and terms. For example, a supplier could have an OEM channel that has terms pricing and discounts that are different that all the other channels and within that they may also have multiple tiers where different OEM's get different terms, pricing and discounts depending upon the tier the are put in by the supplier.

CM or contract manufacturer. A third party that may produce products for one of the parties to the contract. Similar to an outsource supplier

Code means computer programming code, including both **object code** (computer programming code substantially in binary form that is directly executable by a computer after processing, but without compilation or assembly) and **source code** binary form that is directly executable by a computer after processing, but without compilation or assembly) and "source code" (computer programming code that may be displayed in a form readable and understandable by a programmer of ordinary skill, excluding object code).

Collusion. The situation when multiple businesses enter into an illegal agreement to defraud or deceive the buyer. For example an agreement by supplier to fix a price would be a form of collusion.

Company guarantee/ parent guarantee. In the legal structure of companies there may be a parent or holding company and there are usually subsidiaries and affiliates. Each Subsidiary or affiliate is an independent legal entity that may be owned by the parent or holding company. If you do business with a subsidiary or affiliate you are not doing business with the supplier itself and unless there is a specific commitment by the supplier, the supplier is not responsible for the liabilities of the Subsidiary or Affiliate. If the Subsidiary or Affiliate does not have the assets or resources on their own to stand behind all the contract obligations, you may require a "Company or Parent Guarantee that would be signed by the supplier that makes the supplier financially liable for the Subsidiary or Affiliate allowing you to do business through the Subsidiary or Affiliate, while having the financial resources of the supplier standing behind the performance of the Subsidiary or Affiliate.

Communications / notices. In every contract there will be a number of notices that may be required. For example, to terminate a contract for cause, you would normally be required to provide a notice of the breach where the supplier is requested to cure the breach (a "cure notice") and if the supplier failed to cure the breach within the agreed cure period you would provide them with a "termination notice". Other notices may be required for things like end of life of a product or service, or notice may be required of certain changes that the supplier may be allowed to do without approval. Communications provisions provide instructions on when there are required communications or notices, where those notices must be send, who they are to be sent to, the allowable methods by which they may be provided and when they are effective as many notices are time sensitive, requiring performance or a response within a specific period after the receipt of the notice.

Competitor of buyer. Competitive concerns can arise in a number of areas. For example if you have products or designs that are highly sensitive or unannounced you may want to place restriction on access to that at a supplier's location by competitors such as requiring the activity to be performed in a place and by people that would not be dealing with or be accessible to a competitor. Assignment provisions could also be constructed in a manner that either prevents the assignment of your contract to a competitor or allows you the right to terminate the contract without liability if a competitor of buyer acquires the supplier.

Competitiveness. A competitiveness type of provision is usually needed when you are making a long-term commitment to purchase product or are locking yourself into a specific product and want to ensure that the price or technology of the product or service remains competitive. To be most effective it should include a pre-agreed form of benchmarking that the parties agree establishes the competitive benchmark. If change to another supplier would be difficult or costly, a competitiveness provision must force the supplier to adjust their pricing to meet the competitive benchmark. If a change in suppliers is relatively easy, and low cost, the competitiveness type of provision may be focused.

Comprehensive and general liability. A type of insurance that covers potential liability for personal injury and property damage claims.

Common Law. The traditional unwritten law of England based on custom and usage that follows precedent that was set in prior cases. It did not include the so-called law of equity (chancery), which came from the royal power to order or prohibit specific action.

Condition precedent. An act that must occur for there to be a commitment. A simple example would be a contract that says if the New York Yankees win the American League championship in 2010; I will sell you Championship hats for $8.00 each in minimum quantities of 1,000 hats. The winning of the American League championship would be the condition precedent to the commitment to sell the hats. suppliers may try to use conditions precedent as ways of eliminating their obligations. For example a supplier could structure their obligation to provide Intellectual Property Indemnification based on receiving prompt notice of the claim from the buyer. The providing of prompt notice is the condition precedent to the obligation. If the buyer failed to provide the prompt notice, it failed to meet the condition precedent to the supplier providing the indemnification.

Confidentiality/ exchange of information. Confidential information is information that a company wishes to keep secret because it provides the company with a competitive advantage in the marketplace. Proprietary Information is used to indicate ownership. All information that is proprietary is not necessarily confidential. There are four basic ways a company can protect their proprietary rights: Patents protects an idea and provide a right to exclude others from making/using/selling for a period from filing date. Trade Secret protects an idea in perpetuity but is susceptible to reverse engineering or other introduction to public domain. Copyright protects a particular expression of an idea from copying. Trademark identifies the source of a good or service to eliminate consumer confusion. Most non-disclosure agreements involve the sharing of trade secrets. Trade secret information is information or technology that has been kept secret (or is not widely known in the industry) and that provides special or commercial value or advantage to that company. A trade secret can be any type of information and three conditions are usually required: 1) the information is not generally known or readily ascertainable, 2) the information is valuable to its owner (or would be valuable to a competitor), and 3) the company must demonstrate that it intended to keep the information secret. One of the ways companies demonstrate the intent to keep trade secret information secret is by requiring confidentiality or non-disclosure agreements on their information. suppliers will want to protect are things such a specifications on unannounced products, business plans, product road maps, cost information, technical information about their products or processes, etc. buyers may want to protect many of the same types of things. There are inherent risks in receiving confidential information that include being liable should the information be disclosed to another party, but the biggest risk is the potential that a supplier's confidential information will find its way into the buyer's product or services which would give rise to potential claims for misappropriation of trade secrets. To protect against that most companies want to restrict the flow of information that they receive and would include language that says that information that is provided is non-confidential unless it is provided under a separate confidentiality or non-disclosure agreement and place controls on what may be received, who must approve it and how it must be managed so as to prevent that information from being incorporated into the buyer's products or services.

Conflict of interest. A situation in which someone in a position of trust, has competing professional or personal interests.

Conforming orders. Purchase Orders that conform to all the requirements of the contract.

Conforming invoice. An invoice that meets all the invoicing requirements set forth in the contract. For example, the contract may require that the invoice include the P/O Number; part number; quantity ordered, price; ship to address; invoicing address; method of shipment and name of carrier; requested delivery date. If all these items were not on an invoice, it would not be a conforming invoice.

Consents and approvals. In many contracts the buyer may want to require their consent or approval of anything from the personnel assigned, subcontractors used, changes to what is being provided or agreeing that certain stages or the work or deliverables are acceptable so that the next stage may begin. Consents and approvals are in effect buyer deliverables and any time there is a buyer responsibility or deliverable there is also a potential liability to the buyer should the buyer fail to perform the responsibility or provide the deliverable which in this case would be the providing of the required consent or approval. So any time you have a commitment in which the buyer's has responsibilities, you need to manage that potential liability by managing or capping the potential liability. For example, if buyer failed to provide the consents or approvals on time, you might have language that provides the supplier with a day for day extension of the schedule as the sole remedy for such delay, or you could include language that limits buyer's potential liability for such failures.

Consequential Damages. Damages that are not directly related to a breach but which are a consequence of the breach.

Consideration. A vital element in the law of contracts, consideration is a benefit that must be bargained for between the parties, and is the essential reason for a party entering into a contract. Consideration must be of value (at least to the parties), and is exchanged for the performance or promise of performance by the other party (performance itself is consideration).

Consignment. Consignment is similar to a bailment where goods are provided to another party except with a consignment the goods will be used or sold by that party according to the terms of the consignment. Consignment terms usually address the handling of the consigned materials, the responsibilities for loss or damage, safeguarding and insurance on the items, how the items will be used and the return or accounting for any unused/unsold Consigned Materials.

Continuous improvement. Requirements in contracts for continuous improvement are intended to help reduced buyer's cost of ownership by improvement by the supplier to its products or services, their quality, their administrative processes. Some continuous improvement requirements may further be linked to committed reductions to the cost of the products or services.

Contract term. The period during which the contract is legally in effect it begins on the "effective date" of the contract and it ends when obligations have been "discharged".

Contributory negligence. This is a negligent action or failure to act that may have partially caused an injury. If both the Buyer and Supplier agreed to contributory negligence in the event of an injury to a third party, both would share in the damages caused according to their individual percentage of responsibility.

Conversion. This means the treating of someone else's property as their own. In procurement there could be a conversion or theft if the Buyer had property that was bailed to, consigned to or loaned to the supplier or a third party and they used or sold that property in violation of the agreement that created the bailment, consignment or loan of the property.

Cost. For a list of common cost accounting terms that you may encounter in a negotiation see Chapter 21.1.

Cost of money. Could be either the financing cost for you to borrow the money the value you place on that money. Cost of money can be the cost of certain payment terms and is used in calculation of cost of inventory, cost of quality and cost of reliability as all of those require an investment for inventory. Cost of money is also used in determining costs on a net present value or discounted cash flow basis

Cost of Inventory. The cost of money for that inventory and the specific costs associated with that inventory such as warehouse costs, insurance, and risk of loss, damage or obsolescence.

Cost of Quality. The combination of the actual cost incurred in managing the quality problem at incoming, in process, or in the field. It includes costs such as the increased cost of inspection, returns, re-work, field problems and the cost of inventory that those problems create. Cost of reliability is similar to the cost of quality except if deals primarily with the cost of failures that occur in the field strictly from failure of product. Warranties can reduce the cost of reliability.

Cost model. An analytical model used to determine what an item being purchased should cost.

Counterparts. Where the different parties' signatures appear on separate copies of the contract it is said to have been signed in "counterparts". For an agreement to be signed in Counterparts, that parties must agree to that in the contract that an agreement signed in counterparts will be enforceable. An example could be when you need to have an Agreement signed by a supplier and multiple of its subsidiaries. If you had language that authorized signing in counterparts you could send separate copies to each of the supplier entities to sign rather than having a serial signing process where all have to sign the same document.

Country of origin. Used in export/import documents and governmental submissions. Country of origin will affect its admissibility, the rate of duty, its entitlement to special duty or trade preference programs. Generally the country of origin is the country in which the product had its last substantial transformation. For example a circuit card with components from various different countries would normally have a country of origin of where the circuit card was assembled.

Cover or the right of cover. A contractual or common law right that allows the buyer to re-procure the materials based on supplier's breach of an obligation and charge the supplier the incremental cost paid to purchase those replacement products.

Creditworthiness. This is determination of whether the business is reliable enough to be given or lent money or be provided with extended payment terms that is based on the credit history, credit score or review of the party's balance sheet. If a supplier is concerned about the creditworthiness of the buyer they may require things such as a letter of credit to ensure they are paid for the shipment or require advance payment.

Cure. Cure means correcting the problem. The right cure means the right to correct a claimed breach. For example, in a termination, the buyer will provide a notice to the supplier to correct the breach by a specific period of time agreed. The correction of that breach is a "cure". If the supplier failed to cure the breach within that allowable period, buyer may then terminate the contract for cause.

Currency. The applicable currency for a contract will be what the parties agreed will be the country's currency that prices are based upon or the required currency for payment.

Currency Fluctuation. A situation where the change in currency exchange rates between countries could affect pricing.

Currency fluctuation bandwidth. Agreement between the parties where as long as the currency exchange stays within a particular range or band, the price will not change.

Customer. Most frequently used to describe the ultimate end user of the purchase when the product or service being purchased is re-sold.

Customer satisfaction. Most frequently used in Service type contracts where the measure of the supplier's quality or performance is based upon certain criteria used to determine customer satisfaction with the service. For example if you were purchasing call-handling services, one of the customer satisfaction measures could be average response time.

Damages. The losses sustained by a party resulting from the breach by the other party from meeting their obligations. Damages may be direct, incidental, consequential, special, or liquidated.

Damage types:

- **Actual damages**: losses sustained as a direct result of the injury.
- **Direct damages**: Losses that are an immediate, natural and foreseeable result of the wrongful act. Damages that are sustained from the direct or proximate cause of the breach. For example, if a supplier failed to ship on time, the direct damage would be the cost of cover that is the incremental cost to procure it from an alternative source.
- **General damages**: Includes direct damages and damages for losses whose monetary value would be difficult to assign.
- **Consequential or special damages:** indirect loss or injury. Losses sustained not as a natural result of the injury but because of the circumstances, e.g. damages relating to the business that are easily calculable in monetary terms. If the damages were reasonably foreseeable at the time of contract that the injury would probably result if the contract were broken.
- **Incidental damages**: Losses incurred in handing and caring for goods, reasonable expenses for cover, all other reasonable damages from the breach that don't fit any other category.
- **Expectation damages**: Damages that are designed to put the injured party in the position they would have been in had the contract been completed (such as making certain profits).
- **Liquidated damages**: An amount agreed upon by the parties to the contract as adequately compensating for the loss. Liquidated damages must reasonably proximate what the damages would have been.
- **Punitive or Exemplary damages**: damages for serious or malicious wrongdoing that is intended to punish or deter the party from doing it

again or deter others from behaving similarly. In many jurisdictions punitive damages are not allowed.

Date Numbering Conventions. In different countries there are different date numbering conventions. For example in the US a date is expressed as month/day/year. In England the date is expressed as day/month/year.6/12/2007 would mean June 12th 2007 in the US or December 6, 2007 in England. To avoid problems, spell out the Month in any contract.

Day. You need to define what you mean by Day in your contract so the parties will know whether it is a calendar day or business day. For example 49 calendar days is 7 weeks. 49 business days, not counting any holidays is 9 weeks and 4 days. If you use business days, you also need to define which party's Business Days applies as they most likely will be different if you are dealing with different countries that have different holidays. For services it may also require defining the hours that constitute a day for provision of service. For example a commitment to respond in 4 hours versus 4 business hours can be substantially different in terms of when the service must be performed.

Delivered duty paid (DDP). A delivery term where the supplier is responsible for all actions, costs, duties and risks that are incurred in the delivery of the product to the DDP point.

Defect. The failure product or service to meet the specification is a called a defect.

Definitions. Contracts use definitions for basically two main purposes. One is to abbreviate a name or term and the other is to establish a special meaning for that word under the contract. For example, instead of having to say Acme Industrial and Holding Company Limited every time you refer to them you could define "ACME" to mean "Acme Industrial and Holding Company Limited". If you wanted to have any reference to Days mean calendar days, you would define "Days" as calendar days.

Defined term. A term that is defined in the definitions section of the contract or within the contract when first used that creates a single meaning any time that term is used. Defined terms are capitalized to show that the defined term is being used and only has that meaning.

Delivery (hardware, equipment. packaged software). In the negotiation of delivery there are a number of items that traditionally get negotiated. The lead-time for the delivery, the specific delivery term, the delivery point, what constitutes on time delivery and what remedies will be available if the supplier fails to delivery on time.

Delivery lead-time is the agreed time between when buyer's order is received by supplier until delivery to the buyer in accordance with the agreed delivery term.

Deliver - on time delivery. Usually describes what is required for delivery, which may be fixed at a specific date or lead-time where delivery to that is absolute or may be subject to a pre agreed delivery window that may allow slight early or late deliveries. The failure to deliver on time is cause for any agreed remedies for late delivery.

Delivery point. Describes the place at which the product will be delivered to the buyer in accordance with the agreed delivery term. For example, if you purchased an item Ex-Works supplier's dock in Shanghai, China, the delivery term is ex-works, and the delivery point is the supplier's dock in Shanghai.

Delivery remedies. Depending upon what you are buying, its impact to you, and your ability to support your needs by alternative means you may negotiate the remedies that the supplier is obligated to provide for their failure to deliver on time. Typical delivery remedies may range from:

- Right To Cancel Orders Without Liability When Delivery Is Late;
- Paying premium costs associated with expedited delivery;
- Reimbursing the buyer for any cost of "Cover";
- Damages;
- Liquidated damages.

Delivery terms. The delivery term establishes both buyer's and supplier's obligations related to the delivery. The delivery terms also establish the point where "delivery" occurs which also triggers things that are linked to delivery such as when warranties commence or what the obligation to make payments is measured against. A book that explains many of the common delivery terms is published by the International Chamber of Commerce and is called INCOTERMS. The specific delivery term selected determines:

- What the supplier's responsibilities are for providing the goods and commercial invoice.
- Who is responsible to load or unload the product from the carrier.
- Who is responsible to obtain any necessary export licenses.
- The point at which the risk of loss for damage or loss in transit changes from supplier to buyer.
- Who is responsible to contract for the carriage?
- Who is responsible to carry insurance while in transit?
- Where the delivery to the buyer occurs?
- What constitutes delivery?

- Who is responsible for managing the import of the item?
- Who pays for any import duties?

INCOTERM's are listed in Chapter 23 Delivery and while these are standard terms, the buyer and supplier can agree to modify them to suit their needs.

Delivery – other terms. If delivery will be to a third party any contract may include different delivery terms that allow things like drop shipments to the customer or responsibilities for maintaining customer information as confidential when shipments are made directly to customers.

Demand. Demand is one of the elements of cost. Rate times demand makes up your cost. Demand can be for direct costs, such as the volume of the products you order. There can be indirect demand that adds to your costs such as when a supplier has a quality problem that creates a demand for all those other costs associated with managing quality.

Deliverables (development, software, services). In developed works types of contracts deliverables means items that supplier prepares for or provides to buyer. Deliverables include developed works, and rights to pre-existing materials, and tools. In licensed works types of contracts it means items that supplier prepares for or provides to buyer and includes licensed works. In services deliverables would include a detailed description of the services the supplier will provide to the buyer including any acceptance or completion criteria, requirements for testing, maintenance and support for the Deliverables.

Demurrage. Used to indicate a surcharge for delays in delivering a product. For example a freight company may charge demurrage if they have a product to be delivered, which you have requested not be delivered. It covers their cost of holding the item. For example if you had a trailer load of product, the demurrage charge could be the cost per day for they're not being able to use the trailer.

Direct cost. Direct costs are costs that can be directly attributed to the product or service being purchased.

Discharge. A contract is discharged by performing one's duties or by being excused from performing. Discharge may occur by:
- Performance.
- Conditions that excuse performance, such as force majeure.
- Impossibility of performance.
- Impracticality of performance.
- Frustration of the contract by the other party, such as their failure to meet their commitments.
- Illegality, if performing would require to do something illegal.
- By rescission of the contract by the other party.

- By novation where the other party agrees to look to a 3rd party for performance.
- By lapse of the term.

Discounted cash flow. Discounted cash flow is the reverse of a net present value analysis. Net present value analyzes the value of a commitment in time in today's dollars. Discounted cash flow analyzes the cost in today's dollars to meet a commitment in the future. For example how much would you have to invest today at the current interest rate to have a certain amount in the future?

Discounts and allowances. Used to describe reductions in the selling price. Most suppliers have tiered pricing that is established based upon the sales channel, type of customer, volume of sales, and other factors in which they determine the relative importance of the customer. For example for Original Equipment Manufacturers (OEM's) they may have three tiers where the largest customers are provided the greatest level of discounts and allowances, the next tier get less and the lowest tier gets the least for that channel. See the chapter the various types of discounts.

Dispute resolution. Most contracts provide one or more methods of dispute resolution. For example there can be informal dispute resolution processes where issues are escalated to higher levels in each company in hopes of resolving the problem. The parties could agree to either binding or non-binding arbitration by and independent third party or parties. Formal dispute resolution would be through the courts and in preparation for those types of disputes, most contracts will provide for the governing law and jurisdiction. In most cases the parties to a contract can agree to both the governing law that will be used to interpret the contract in the dispute and the jurisdiction where the case will be heard. buyers will want applicable law and jurisdictions that are either where they are located or which would be most favorable to them. Another term that may be found in contracts regarding disputes is a "continued performance" clause that requires the parties to continue to perform while the dispute is being resolved so that one side cannot force the other side to agree under the threat of stopping work.

Distribution. Distribution can be used to describe the physical / electronic functions and activities that manages the warehousing and delivery of product to the various channels or directly to customers or when used to describe a company it means a sales channel of the supplier that purchases products and resells them to buyers or with value added services.

Dock. When used in conjunction with the supplier it means the supplier's shipping dock location. When used with the buyer it means the buyer's receiving dock location. For example shipment will be DDP, buyer's dock.

Documentation. The requirements for documentation will vary based on the type of purchases for example if you were purchasing a piece of equipment it could include operating manuals, maintenance manuals, service manuals, if you were having something constructed it could mean things like all of the above for any equipment includes and as-built/as constructed drawings. If you were having work done on a time and materials basis it could include records that substantiate all the charges. If you were buying a part used in manufacturing it could include the all information related to the part or its manufacture including quality documentation. For services documentation could include all the items that may be required to perform the service such as training manuals, service manuals, illustrated parts breakdowns, For software it may include all product code, publications, and documentation. For any documentation that you require you need to identify things such as the required format or media, number of copies, when those must be delivered and the suppliers obligations to update that documentation over time as changes up updates occur. If you needed to re-distribute the documentation in conjunction with the re-sale of the product that the document is associated with, since most document is copyrighted materials you would also need the supplier to provide you with a license grant on that documentation allowing to do such things as use, modify, translate, and the right to make derivative works of such documentation and whether the supplier's original copyright notice must be maintained.

Duties. A form of tax imposed by a country on shipments of products into that country. Duty rates will vary based on the import country, the exporting company and the type of goods being imported.

EDI. Electronic data interchange are standards for information to be exchanged electronically. The standards emulate common documents that would be used for tasks. Common EDI Standards include:
1. Invoice (810/INVOIC)
2. Remittance Advice (820/REMADV)
3. Planning Schedule (830/DELFOR)
4. Forecast Response (830/DELFOR)
5. Purchase Order (850/ORDERS)
6. PO Acknowledgment (855/ORDRSP)
7. Advance Ship Notice (856/DESADV)
8. PO Change (860/ORDCHG)
9. Pull Notification (862/DELJIT)
10. Product Transfer & Resale Report (867)
11. Functional Acknowledgment (997/CONTRL)
12. Inventory Inquiry/Advice (846/INVRPT)

Effective date. While a contract may be fully executed by the parties on one date, the parties are free to establish the date on which the terms of that contract will be effective. For example: it could be effective when executed by both parties; it could be made to retroactive to apply to a date prior to the date it was executed; and it could be effective a date in the future after the contract is signed. The date agreed by the parties for the contract to become effective is the effective date.

Effectivity date. This describes when a particular change will take effect. For example for price changes that are negotiated, is effective date some time in the future, immediate, or does it retroactively apply to any open orders that haven't been billed.

Electronic Funds Transfer (EFT) Allows the buyer or supplier to initiate credit entries to the others Bank account in connection with EDI transactions where payments made to the Bank account on that party's behalf satisfies payment obligations. For example the buyer would have an EFT agreement with the supplier where all payments will be electronically transmitted to the supplier's account at a specific bank and the reverse could be true for any refunds or payments the supplier would make to the buyer.

Emergency Orders. Emergency Orders describe situations where they parties have agreed to provide a significantly reduced lead-time for certain circumstances. For example the buyer and supplier could agree to have the supplier to use best efforts to respond to emergency orders from its existing stock or work in process. For a supplier to guarantee delivery of an emergency order there normally needs to be a commitment by the buyer to pay any incremental costs of expedited processing to meet the reduced lead time or supplier must carry finished or near finished inventory to meet the emergency order needs which usually involves addressing additional costs of carrying the inventory and responsibility for the inventory in the event it isn't ordered or becomes obsolete. The most common users of emergency orders are for spare parts or repairs for services when the buyer's inventory has been exhausted.

Encumbrance. An obligation, right, or interest that limits complete title to owning real property. For example a supplier of a major piece of capital equipment may, if the contract allowed it, retain a security interest in the product until they are paid. A lien against a title when you get a loan on a car purchase from a bank would also be an encumbrance.

Engineering Change (EC). A process that adds, deletes or changes a product or element where the specification is under formal change control.

Enjoin. A court order to perform or cease performing a certain act. For example, if you purchased a product that infringed upon another companies intellectual property a court could enjoin a supplier from continuing to sell that infringing product or it could also enjoin purchasers of that product from using the product.

End-of-life (EOL). Generally, that point in time when the production of a product offering ceases and the product is officially withdrawn from the marketplace. In dealing with end of life, you normally would get commitments on how long the product will be available or requirements for extended notice of the intent to end of life a product and the right to make last time buys. End of life activities by suppliers can impact buyer's ability to continue to produce their products or buyer's ability to service products contains it that has been sold. So normally buyers will want extended end or life notice periods to determine the potential impact, qualify alternatives or determine the appropriate end of life buy quantities needs to support ongoing needs.

End-of-life plan. A plan that is developed to ensure the orderly transition from the product that will going end-of-life. An EOL plan could include qualification of replacement product and/or purchase of a quantity of the existing product to cover on-going use until no longer needed or a replacement product is qualified (end of life buy).

End of service / end of support. The point at which a company will no longer provide service or support on a product, which means the customers may need to either migrate to a different product or version or be responsible for their own service or support.

Engineering change (EC). A process that adds, deletes or changes a product or element where the specification is under formal change control.

Enhancements (software) Used in software to describe changes or additions, other than error corrections, to code and related documentation. Basic enhancements are all enhancements to the code, other than error corrections, including those that support new releases of operating systems and devices. Major enhancements provide substantial additional value and are offered to customers for an additional charge. If you are purchasing major enhancements you may negotiate an additional warranty period and period for error correction associate with those enhancements

Entire agreement clause (also know as a merger clause). Most contracts have what is called a "merger" clause in which the parties agree that the contract represents the entire understanding between the parties on the subject matter, so that all documents, conversations, etc. that occurred prior to the contract are considered to be merged into the contract. As a buyer this means that any representations, promises or documents that may have been made prior to the contract need to be made part of the contract if you want them to apply. With an entire agreement or merger clause only what included in the contract will be looked at unless the contract has conflicting terms or is unclear.

Environmental. Many contracts will address environmental issues either through specifying specific environmental requirements that must be met by the supplier and/or by the inclusion of specific environmental warranties. For example, there can be environmental requirements on what materials are used in the process to make the product, the product itself, or the packaging or crating that is used.

Epidemic defects. Normally used to describe situations where the number of defects have exceeded a quantity threshold that rather than have the supplier only provide the replacement product for the defective materials, the supplier is obligated to assume a much higher percentage of the actual cost that the buyer sustains as a result of those defects. Epidemic defect provisions are usually included for the buyer to recover additional remedies for the defect.

Equity. Equity describes rights and procedures designed to provide fairness. In equity, Courts do the fair thing by court orders such as taking possession of assets, imposing a lien, or issuing an injunction ordering another party person to do something or stop doing it to prevent irreparable damage.

Error. A defect in software is called an error. Software warranties provide for error correction.

Escrow (software, hardware) is the process by which certain materials hare held by a third party (an escrow agent) for the purpose of providing protection to the buyer in the event supplier fails to perform, or becomes bankrupt, etc. In an escrow situation you normally address with the custodian or agent will be, fees for the escrow service, responsibilities of supplier for the initial deposit, updates, rights of the buyer to inspect, requirements in the event of loss or damage to escrowed materials. The escrow will describe what events trigger the delivery of the escrowed materials. It will also include the description of "escrowed materials", responsibilities of custodian escrow use, and the treatment of escrowed materials by buyer once they are disclosed to the buyer.

Estoppel. A bar or impediment (obstruction) which precludes a person from asserting a fact or a right or prevents one from denying a fact due to a person's actions, conduct, statements, admissions, failure to act or judgment against the person in an identical legal case. Estoppel includes:

> Being barred by false representation or concealment (equitable estoppel),
> Failure to take legal action until the other party is prejudiced by the delay (estoppel by laches), and
> A court ruling against the party on the same matter in a different case (collateral estoppel).

Evergreen contracts / Self-extending contracts. An evergreen contract is one that remains open until a specific even occurs, such as one of the parties providing notice of the intention to terminate the contract. In many jurisdictions, an evergreen contract may not be enforceable, so parties may use self-extending contracts. A self-extending contract has a specific term, which may be extended in agreed terms based on an action or inaction of one of the parties. For example, the contract could be that the contract will self extend in one year increments if no one provides a notice of intention for it not to self extend within some agreed period.

Exclusion. An items or list of items that are not covered under a specific commit. For example there can be warranty exclusions, exclusions under insurances or negotiated exclusions to specific commitments.

Executed contract. A contract that has been fully executed (signed) by the parties.

Executory contract. A contract in which all or part of the required performance has not been done.

Exhibit. An exhibit is document or object that is referred to and incorporated into the main contract that provides clarity.

Ex-works. A delivery term where the buyer takes the product at the supplier's dock and is responsible for all costs and risks to get the product from supplier's dock to buyer's dock

Features and benefits. Used in selling products. Most companies try to create products that have unique features to differentiate themselves from the competition. Benefits are the benefits that customer will achieve from those unique features. If a unique feature provides the buyer with benefit they may have no competition if other suppliers don't have the same features or, they may be able to charge a premium for the additional value of that benefit.

Failures in time (FIT Rate). A statistic measure for a component of how many failures the component will have per one billion operating hours. The lower the FIT Rate for a component is, the better the component.

FOB (free on board). A delivery term that is slightly different than ex-works in that the supplier and not the buyer has the responsibility to load the product on the buyer's carrier

Force majeure. An act of god, or an act beyond the control of the party. Force majeure provides an excusable delay from performing. In negotiating a force majeure provision buyer need to establish what is included in those events (such as are labor actions included) and what the supplier's responsibilities are to recover from the force majeure. In addition buyer's may want to establish what rights the buyer may have to terminate the purchase if the force majeure event is extended or would frustrate the purpose of the purchase. For example the purchase is for a specific event and the supplier will not be able to recover until after the event has occurred.

Form, fit and function. Used to describe a product that is similar, but not exact to another. It's of the same form or dimensions. It's of the same fit, as in connections; it's of the same function meaning it does the same thing. The problem is you can have an item of the same form, fit and function which doesn't work the same in an application as the two items respond slightly different, and firm fit and function does not also mean that it's the same quality, or same reliability.

Fiduciary. A person or business that has been given the authority to act for another. For example an agent is a fiduciary who has the fiduciary responsibility to the principal to act within the scope of their agency.

Field replaceable unit (FRU). The lowest level assembly or product that can reasonably replace in the field by a service technician to repair or replace defective product.

Finally awarded. A term that supplier's may try to insert in contracts where their obligation to buyer is to pay the buyer only after the damages or costs have been finally awarded. For something to be finally awarded the supplier must have exhausted all appeals which could take many years making a commitment to pay based on damages or costs finally awarded a bad deal on a net present value perspective.

Fraud. Fraud means the intentional use of deceit, a trick or some dishonest means to deprive another of its money, property or a legal right. A party who has lost something due to fraud is entitled to file a lawsuit for damages against the party acting fraudulently, and the damages may include punitive damages as a punishment.

Funny money. A term coined by Dr. Karrass that describes a practice intended to make the impact or cost seem much less. For example, a company selling a product "for only $19.95 a month" when there are six months to pay the full amount the seller wants you to think about the $19.95 and not the $119.70 that the item is really costing. For only $.50 more makes the cost seem small unless you are buying a million where the real cost is $500,000.

Gate Keeper. Someone who prevents the sales person from dealing direct with the internal user. That is usually the procurement function.

General Indemnification. A provision where the supplier agrees protects the buyer against 3rd party claim for personal injury or property damage caused by the supplier, their Subcontractors or their personnel.

Good faith. The intent to act honestly and without any intent to take an unfair advantage of the other party. Lack of good faith is very difficult to prove.

Grace period. A period of time before the failure to perform is subject to agreed remedies. For example the parties to a contract could negotiate a grace period on payments before any late payment charges are assessed.

Grey market. Grey market products are legally purchased through a legitimate channel, and are subsequently resold through another channel or in another location that wasn't originally intended or authorized. This occurs usually when there is a cost advantage of buying in one geographic location and re-selling it in another where the supplier's pricing structure is higher. It can also occur where one company buys more than their needs to get a better cost, and sells the excess to a third party for their resale.

Guarantee. A formal promise in writing that certain conditions will be met. For example a supplier of consumer products could provide a guarantee against defect in material an workmanship where they directly agree to repair or replace it. Guarantees usually apply to consumers and flow with the product. Warranties are in contracts and are generally not assignable to third parties.

Hedge. An investment to protect against market fluctuations. In procurement the most common use would be with respect to managing currency exchange exposures. For example purchasing foreign currency for the future at what's called a forward rate is a way to hedge against currency exchange risks. If a company also generate local sales and revenues in that other country those revenues would be considered a natural hedge against the exchange risk.

Hold harmless. Hold harmless means to agree that the other party is not at fault. Used in conjunction with a General Indemnification where you ask a supplier to defend, hold harmless, and indemnify you against 3rd party claims for personal injury or property damage. The would make the supplier responsible to defend against the claim, including paying the legal costs associated with the defense, and pay for any cost or damages awarded which is the indemnification. The hold harmless piece means that they cannot turn around and sue the buyer for any negligence the buyer may have had that contributed to the injury or damage.

Holding company. Usually a Subsidiary or Affiliate of the Parent Company that owns other companies that the supplier has owns or controls. For example, a company could have an Off-Shore Holding company located in a tax haven that owns a number of supplier entities where the profits of those revert back to the Holding Company as part of tax management program.

Incidental damages. Damages which are not directly caused by the act but which are incidental to it. For example, if a component placed on a circuit card failed, the direct cost would be the cost of replacing the component, Incidental costs would be the cost of re-work to take the failed component off the card and replace it with a good one or the cost of having to send a Service technician to a customer site to remove and replace the affected item.

Incorporation by reference. A legal concept that allows incorporation of other documents into the contracts by referring to something that adequately defines that other document and makes them part of the contract without specifically having to write out all that is contained in that document. For example, "supplier's proposal dated ___ is hereby incorporated by reference into this contract". Would include all that is contained in that proposal as part of the contract.

Incoterms. Delivery terms published by the International Chamber of Commerce.

Indemnity. This means to effectively stand in the other party's shoes and be responsible for any costs or damages awarded under a claim. For example for personal injury the General Indemnification requires the supplier to defend, indemnify and hold harmless the buyer from the claim which in simple terms means the supplier will pay for the cost of the defense, and will pay for any costs or damages awarded and cannot sue the buyer to recover any of those costs as they have agreed that the buyer is harmless.

Indirect costs. In negotiating cost and indirect cost is one that cannot be directly attributed to the manufacture or the product or performing the service purchased. For example SG&A expenses are indirect costs. Any costs that are allocated are indirect costs.

Infringement. Using a 3rd party's intellectual property without their authorization. For example, if a company has a patent on a specific concept and buy a product that has a design that includes that process and that design did not have a license from the owner of the patent, that design would be infringing the rights of that 3rd party's ownership of that patent.

Injunction. A writ (order) issued by a court ordering someone to do something or prohibiting some act after a court hearing. The procedure is for someone who has been or is in danger of being harmed, or needs some help (relief).

Insurance. In a contract setting the buyer may include insurance requirements that the supplier must maintain under the contract as a financial means to protect against various risks. Comprehensive General Liability is to cover against 3rd party claims for personal injury or property damage cause by the supplier of supplier Personnel's negligent or intentional acts, Auto Liability is to cover against 3rd party claims for personal injury or property damage cause by the supplier of supplier Personnel's negligent or intentional acts caused in the operation of a motor vehicle. Workers compensation or Employer's Liability Insurance is to protect the against personal injury claims by supplier's personnel for injuries sustained while performing the work. Specific commodities may also require insurance against Errors and omissions in the design or insurance to cover completed operations) Key issues in Insurance are: The financial stability of insurance company as that impacts whether the buyer may recover under the insurance; waiver of subrogation rights, to prevent the insurer from suing the buyer for the damages they paid out; notices of changes, cancellations so the buyer will know if the supplier is doing anything that may impact the coverage; naming the buyer as an additional insured so that the buyer will continue to have protection even if the supplier's policy were terminated for fraud.

Intellectual property. Intellectual property includes patents, trade secrets, registered and unregistered designs, mask work rights, copyrights, moral rights, and other protections under law to that are to protect rights inventions, designs or information.

Intellectual property indemnification. This means to effectively stand in the other party's shoes and be responsible for any costs or damages awarded under a claim for infringement of a 3rd party's intellectual property. Most IP Infringement provisions also identify specific remedies the supplier must provide in the event of and infringement.

Inter-company transfer. Intercompany transfer describes the process of transferring and accounting for the transfer of assets between different supplier legal organizations. In inter-company transfers, the product is transferred (sold) at the product's transfer price.

In-Transit. The period of time from when a product leaves a supplier's dock until it arrives at the buyer's dock.

Inventory cost. The cost of holding something in inventory which includes a combination of the cost or value of money and the cost associated with holding it such as space, utilities, insurance, and risk of loss or damage, obsolescence.

Joint and several liability. When multiple entities of the same company sign a contract their signature alone would make them severally liable for their own actions and debts, but not the actions and debts of the other entity. If you want each of them to be both responsible for their own and for the other entity they would need to sign the contract agreeing that they would be "jointly and severally liable" for the acts and liabilities of the other entity. For example, if a subsidiary and the parent company signed as being jointly and severally liable, both are agreeing to be liable and responsible for the acts and liability of the other so the Parent would be liable for the Subsidiary, similar to as if they provided a Parent Guarantee.

Joint Drafting. As the rules of contract construction would have any ambiguities be ruled against the drafter of the contract, if there was significant negotiation of the terms that involved joint drafting, the parties may include a provision that the contract was jointly drafted, so ambiguities would not be interpreted against one party.

Landed cost. Landed cost includes the price plus all distribution cost, duties, and other fees required to get the product to the point of use.

Legitimacy tactic. A tactic used to provide credibility to the party's position. Simple examples of a legitimacy tactics are price lists, pre-printed or industry standard terms, standard discounts, etc. Legitimacy could also be simply showing opinions of an expert or acceptance by other parties that would provide credibility.

Leverage. A term use to describe an apparent power or advantage one party has over the other in the negotiation. Whether that advantage actually exists depends upon the circumstances and whether the party will be impacted as a result. For example, if you have multiple suppliers all competing for the same business you have competitive leverage. If the supplier doesn't care whether they get your business or not, you don't.

Liability Theories:

- Contractual - what the supplier is obligated to do under the terms of the contract.
- Negligence – Liability that is created by the failure of the supplier or supplier's employees or agents to act reasonably, which injures the buyer's property, buyer's employees or the property or person of third parties. It can also include buyer's reliance on the supplier's expertise to provide conforming goods or to satisfy a duty owed to buyer.
- Warranty - The assurance by supplier to buyer of the existence of a fact upon the buyer may rely without having to verify the fact.
- Misrepresentation - A false or misleading statement made. For example a statement that a solution will work when it in fact won't.
- Strict – the act itself would represent negligence such as the design of an inherently dangerous product.

LIBOR. London Interbank Offered Rate is one of a number of interest rates that contracting parties could use as a standard for interest rates when a provision is subject to interest being charged.

License. For certain items that you procure such as software, you are not purchasing the software. What you are doing is purchasing the right to use the software according to specific terms that are agreed by the parties. The right to use the item is created through a license grant that identifies the specific rights that you have to use the item. While software licenses are the most common form of licensing, there are a number of other types of licenses that could be negotiated. For example, if a supplier agreed that you could have a third party manufacture their product for you, or you could manufacturer it, you would have a manufacturing license to make or have made the product. If you needed to get access to certain materials to do self maintenance on a product, a separate license could be agreed that provides those rights and access to proprietary supplier materials, subject to certain fees or restrictions set forth in the license.

Lien. A legal cloud on the title of an item. For example, in construction of services many jurisdictions provide contractors and subcontractors with the right to file a "mechanics lien" against the item they worked on as a tool to ensure that they are paid. Any subsequent sale of the item would be subject to that lien until such time as there is a release of that lien. To manage against liens the buyer may require a warranty that there are no liens or as part of their payment process the buyer could require a waiver and release of liens from the supplier for all subcontractors and material suppliers.

Life cycle cost includes the purchase price plus all the costs associated with the product during the term of its useful life that could include maintenance, repairs, spare parts, or in the case of equipment could include operator costs, energy costs, operating and maintenance costs or consumable supplies.

Limitation of action is a contract provision in which the parties agree that any claims must be brought within a certain period after they are first identified as a way to prevent against claims or cost arising well after the work has been performed.

Linking. A negotiating tactic where two issues are linked together for resolution. If you want X, you must give me Y is an example of linking issues.

Limitation of liability. An agreement between the parties to either limits the types of damages that may be claimed and/or the total amount of damages that may be paid. It may further limit the types of damages that may be claimed. Limitations of liability may include exclusions or carve outs from the limitation. For any financial limits it would describe the basis for that limitation that could be on a per product basis, per incident, per year or for the term of the contract.

Long-term support. Long term support refers to either spare parts or repairs for a product that is no longer covered by the warranty or the ability to purchase support when not purchasing maintenance agreements. An example of long term support would be to have pre-agreed upon the cost of out of warranty repairs.

Lots. Usually involved in acceptance or rejection of product. For example if a product has a shipped product quality level (SPQL) level agreed and a statistical sampling of a reasonable quantity of the product could be made shows that there were enough defective products to exceed the agreed level, the buyer could have the right to reject all of the items received (the lot), and return them to the supplier to screen out the good from the bad. Without the right of rejection by lot the buyer would need to screen all of them and could only return those that are defective.

Manufacturers' representative. A third party under contract with the supplier that acts as an independent commissioned salesperson to sell product to the buyer. As an independent 3rd party, they have no authority to commit or bind the supplier unless the supplier also makes them a form of agent.

Manufacturing overhead. Costs that cannot be directly attributed to the product but are then assigned to the product before the addition of general overhead and profit. Usually an allocation spread across all products as a percentage rate.

Market Requirements. Requirements provided by marketing organizations that represent their interpretation of customer wants and needs that represent potential markets.

Market Segment. Potential purchasers within a market who have common wants, needs, and similar buying behaviors. A segment may be divided various characteristics: Industry, Geography, and Brand, Buying behaviors.

Material. In procurement contracts it would be used to describe things that are significant or relevant. For example the agreement may describe specific breaches that constitute a material breach. A buyer may want not want to be liable for failing to meet certain dates for their performance unless that failure had a materially adverse impact on the supplier. In that case the impact to the supplier had to be significant, relevant, and adverse (negative).

Materials Acquisition. A process that provides commodity planning and management of purchases.

Materials Acquisition Rate. The percentage of cost that's attributable to providing materials acquisition.

Materials liability is normally discussed in cancellation provision where your liability should be based upon how custom or unique the product is to you and what the supplier could reasonably do to mitigate the liability. For example you should have limited liability on standard products or services and would normally have much greater liability for custom products or services, which would depend upon the point at which it becomes custom.

Mean time between failures (MTBF). The statistical average length of time a product will operate without failing which is usually expressed in a number of hours or operative environment. For example, a product with a 100,000-hour MTBF should fail on average in slightly over 11 years.

Mean time to repair (MTTR). The average time it takes to perform a repair of a product. In statistics the "mean" is the average.

Mechanics Lien. Certain jurisdictions may have laws designed to protect suppliers that provide work on real property to prevent the sale of the property before the supplier is paid. For example if a contractor failed to pay a air conditioning subcontractor, that air conditioning subcontractor could file a lien against the premises where the work was done so they either the owner or the contractor needs to pay them before the building could be sold and possibly before any financing or re-financing can occur.

Merchantable quality. A product of merchantable quality simply means that the product must be of quality and value to make it fit for sale under normal circumstances. When a product is sold as-is the party making the sale is not making a representation that the product is of merchantable quality.

Merger. The combination of two or more businesses or entities into one.

Merger Clause. There may be prior contracts between the parties and prior correspondence in advance of the contract. A merger type of clause "merges" all of those prior contracts or understandings into the terms of the contract so the only document that states the parties' commitments and obligations is what is included in the contract.

Minimum order quantity. An ordering requirement by the supplier that may be based on simply dollars required to make the order worth processing or based on some other requirement such as a packaging based requirement that the order be based on the quantity placed on a reel, tube or package they usually use.

Misappropriation of trade secrets. A type of claim made that information that consisted of trade secrets of the party has been wrongfully taken and used by another party. Misappropriation of trade secret claims are more likely to rise when one party like the buyer has received confidential information from the supplier that is not know, and either deliberately or inadvertently used some or all of that information in their own product. Misappropriation claims are why most companies want to significantly limit and control the flow of confidential information they receive as each receipt presents a possible risk.

Misrepresentation. The misstatement of facts to obtain money, goods or benefits of another to that they are not entitled to have. Misrepresentation may also called "false pretenses."

Mitigate. The requirement that someone injured by another's negligence or breach of contract must take reasonable steps to reduce the damages, injury or cost, and to prevent them from getting worse. If you require a supplier to mitigate costs associated with a cancellation or termination, they would be required to take actions to try to keep those costs to a minimum by canceling their orders, rescheduling work, selling the product to other parties, etc. In most cases supplier's would want any standard for mitigating cost to be "commercially reasonable" which effectively means that if it would cost them money to do it they don't have to unless you paid for those additional costs.

Mobilization period. The period from the award of the contract until work actually commences.

Most favored customer. A most favored customer provision requires the supplier to extend the buyer the same prices and terms as their most favored customer or the best of the best. Most are either not agreed to by suppliers, or if they are agreed they are significantly modified to make it most favored for customers purchasing like product, under like volumes and under like terms. Having a most favored customer contract without having the right to audit makes it useless.

MSRP. Manufacturers suggested retail price is also referred to as list price.

NDF (no defect found). The situation where a product has been returned to the supplier as defective and after the supplier's examination or testing or the product, no defect can be found and the product meets the specification.

Negligence. Negligence is a failure to reasonable actions or failure to take reasonable steps that results in loss or injury to a third party. For example under the theory of strict liability an itself would represent negligence. For example the design of an inherently dangerous product would be negligence that would lead to strict liability.

Net present value. A financial evaluation of the value of a future payment of commitment in today's dollars taking into account the impact of the compounding affect of interest on the value of future commitments.

Notices. In contracts there are numerous different types on individual notifications that one party is required to provide the other party. For example, if you intended to terminate a contract for cause, you would provide the other party a "cure notice" in which you notify them of your intention to terminate if that party fails to correct (cure) the problem by a certain date. If they failed to cure, you would then send a "termination notice" advising them that the contract was terminated because of their failure to cure.

NRE. Non-Recurring Expenses. A one-time charge associated with the purchase of an item. For example a design fee would be a non-recurring expense.

Obligation. This means the legal duty to perform an act. For example if you received conforming goods, you would be obligated to make payment for the goods.

Option. A contractual right that may be exercised in the future. For example a buyer may have a option to purchase additional products or services in the future or they may have the option to extend the term of the agreement for an additional term.

Original equipment manufacturer (OEM). OEM describes manufacturers that purchase products where that product is then included in their product. OEM's do not directly compete with the sales of the supplier's product as they are selling a higher-level assembly or product that contains the supplier's product.

Order of precedence. A term that creates the order of priority between all the different documents that may make up the contract in the event of a conflict between the documents. For example if Document A says 1, 2, & 3 must be done and Document B says X, Y, and Z must be done, if document A is higher in the order of precedence, the interpretation would be that 1, 2, 3, X, Y and Z must be done, but it there is a conflict between what's called for between the two, what's required by A will have priority. Priority applies only to conflicting items, if an item is additional or complimentary, the order of precedence will not apply.

Ordinary Course of Business. This refers to normal or routine activities of a business and would not include any unique or special circumstances.

Out-of-pocket expenses. An amount paid to a third party. For example if a supplier wanted to reimburse the buyer's out of pocket expenses the buyer would not be paid for any internal costs, they would only be paid for what they paid others.

Outsourcing. Purchasing a product or service from a supplier where that product or service was previously manufactured, performed, or controlled internally.

Parent guarantee. Used when there are purchases being made from supplier subsidiaries or affiliates where the parent company agrees to be financially responsible for the obligations of those subsidiaries or affiliates so you have their resources and assets standing behind the commitment.

Payment terms. The agreed upon terms for payments between the parties. They can include things like net terms (Net 30, 45 or 60), In addition the payments terms could include requirements for payment vehicles such as letters of credit, agreed discounts, payment schedules, retainage requirements, invoicing requirement, set off rights, processes for managing disputed charges, reimbursable expenses and guidelines for reimbursable expenses, audit rights on payments. or customer related payment terms such as "pay when paid" so the supplier gets paid when the buyer gets paid by their customer. In addition payment terms may also address when payments aren't required such as: non-conforming goods, products or services; non-conforming invoices; excluded uses such as training or education; backup and archival purposes; alternate work station for licensed works; and items that become available generally to third parties without a payment obligation.

Penalties. A penalty would be any amount in excess of actual damages that would be charged for non-performance. In many jurisdictions law does not allow penalties for non-performance.

Performance cost. The term I use to describe costs associated with problems with the supplier's performance in terms of on-time delivery, quality, warranty, administrative processes etc.

Period of availability. The period during which the product or service will be sold. May also be used to establish a firm commitment to have products available for a specific term. These commitments have limited value unless you also lock in pricing during the entire term of the period of availability. Otherwise the supplier could price it so its cost prohibitive negating their commitment of availability.

Pledge. To give or promise something as repayment of a debt. For example a supplier wanting to borrow money from a bank may want to pledge the receivables they have with the buyer as security against the loan. In most cases this would require an assignment of the receivables and whether a supplier could do that would be dependent upon the assignment provision in the contract.

Point of no return. The point in the procurement process at which you have gone so far with one supplier that you have no other options or your other options aren't acceptable because of the impact they would have on things like schedule, or cost.

Prequalification. The process employed by buyers to determine that the supplier is qualified to provide the product or service for the buyer. Typical prequalification includes things like financial qualification, verification of performance, capacity, quality, and service capabilities.

Price curve. A term used to describe the traditional change in price over the product life where it starts high, is reduced as others enter into the market, reduces to its lowest level when there is maximum competition and then may increase as some suppliers exit the market creating an imbalance of demand versus supply.

Prime rate. An interest rate that banks charge to their most creditworthy customers. If establish an interest rate the parties specify both the rate and source. For example it could be the LIBOR rate published in the Financial Times or the prime rate as published in the Wall Street Journal or another rate and source.

Priority (financial priority). In the event of a bankruptcy, the law will follow a defined financial priority for the distribution of any assets. For example if you owned and could identify property loaned, bailed or consigned to a supplier you would have the right to recover it. If you had a security interest in the property you would have the right to recover it. If you were an unsecured creditor you would have to wait in line according to the financial priority to get down to your class of creditors before getting any payment.

Privity of contract. Under contract law there must be privity of contract to enforce the contract against the other party. Privity of contract extends to the parties that sign the contract and any parties named in the contract as third party beneficiaries. For example, if you have a contract and the supplier agrees that they will agree to the same terms that is in your contract to third party (such as an outsourced supplier), that creates a separate contract between the supplier and the third party and you would not be able to enforce the terms of that contract on the supplier for those third party purchases as you are not a party to that contract and you do not have privity of contract for those purchases. If that contract named you as a third party beneficiary to that contract, you would have legal rights under that contract.

Product life cycle. Describes the period from a products introduction to its phase out

Product specifications. The technical description of the products capabilities, requirements or objectives, a detailed description of how objectives will be met. It may include user requirements, product descriptions, configurations, detailed hardware, software descriptions and considerations, performance characteristics, etc.

Prospecting. A term used in selling where the sales person is trying to generate or find interest in the product usually through end user contacts. For example, providing samples of a product is a prospecting activity.

Public domain. In procurement public domain could come into play in two situations. If you entered into confidentiality agreements and the other party make the information available to the general public or public domain without any confidentiality requirements, if your confidentiality agreement was written properly that should excuse you of any further obligations on that material. In the second instance, copyright law only protects the authors for a limited period and once that period has lapsed the information is considered in the public domain and may be used by anyone.

Ramp-up. The period in time during manufacturing when it moves toward full volume production.

Ratify. To approve a prior action that did not have the requisite authority or approval. For example if a contract was signed by a party without the requisite authority, to make it an enforceable contract you would need a writing by a party that has the requisite authority where they agree to ratify that prior action.

Rebate means a discount to return of a portion of what was paid. For example a supplier could commit to a price rebate if you purchased a specific volume of products or services by a specific date.

Reciprocity. A mutual exchange of privileges between businesses or individuals. Also used to describe the practice of linking buying and selling e.g. If You Buy my products I will buy your products.

Remedy. Remedies are actions the buyer may take or require if the supplier fails to meet a duty to the buyer. For example, the buyer may look for "all remedies available at law" where the law may provide for specific remedies. The may look for remedies "at equity" which looks to the courts to provide an equitable remedy for a situation. There may also be specific remedies that may be pre-agreed. For example, many on time delivery clauses allow the buyer certain options in the event of late deliveries such as cancel the order, require expedited shipment at the supplier's expense or have all remedies available at law or equity.

Replevin. The right to sue to recover properly improperly taken or withheld by another party. For example if you consigned material to a party and they refused to return it you would seek an order of replevin where with appropriate legal authorities you could enter the premises and take back the property you own.

Representation. An affirmative statement made by one party, upon which the other party can rely. If a material representation proves to be untrue, the party receiving the representation may terminate the contract.

Reschedule. A pre-negotiated right to take open orders and reschedule their delivery, usually to a later delivery date. Rights to reschedule will vary depending upon whether the product is standard and may be sold to other customers where the impact is minimal or custom where the impact could be much greater depending upon the point in time when the reschedule occurs and the degree of which the product is custom at that time.

Rescind. When both parties to any agreement mutually agree to end the agreement, the agreement is rescinded as opposed to terminate or expired.

Restocking charge. Charges some suppliers or distributors try to include in their contracts to cover their costs associate with accepting the return of good product back into their inventory.

Rework. Usually used in conjunction with manufacturing defects where a defect in a component would require that the component be removed from the product and be replaced with a good component. The removing, replacing and testing of the replaced item is rework.

Return material authorization (RMA). The authorization provided by the supplier to return defective product to the supplier. Used as part of the warranty redemption process.

Return on investment (ROI). In negotiations you may use ROI to decide whether you will agree to certain options or you can use it to discuss how long it is taking for the supplier's product to provide you with the needed ROI to try to negotiate a reduced price or extended payment terms so the ROI improves.

Right of first refusal. A contract right of either the buyer to make a future purchase or the supplier to make a future sale by matching the best offer of a third party.

Sales, general and administrative (SG&A). This is a charge imposed on all products to cover expenses that are not directly related to the cost of the product itself. It covers expenses such as marketing, brand advertising, and corporate services. It is typically assigned as a percentage of the product cost.

Sales chain. All the channels a product must past through before it is sold to a buyer. For example, the supplier will sell the product to a supplier subsidiary. The supplier subsidiary may sell the product to a distributor who the buyer purchases from. These three entities would be the sales chain.

SEC. The Security and Exchange Commission. Its connection to procurement is that the SEC has issued revenue accounting rules that control when supplier's make take a sale as revenue and may impact what the supplier is willing to agree upon regarding buyer's rights of acceptance and especially how long buyer may have to accept or reject the product. They longer you have to accept the product, the longer it will be before they can take revenue on the sale. This impacts negotiations with US Based companied

Security interest. A method by which a supplier or financer can protect their interests in the equipment or goods until paid. It's similar to a lien against the title to that item. It puts other parties on notice of that interest and makes any subsequent sale also subject to that claim.

Setoff. (also sometimes referred to as offset). The common law right to deduct any receivables from the supplier from any payables due the supplier. Setoff complicates the accounting for both the buyer and

supplier and is frequently only used when the buyer has an aging receivable the supplier hasn't paid or the buyer is concerned with the creditworthiness of the supplier.
Supplier's market. A time in which there is excess demand for the available capacity.

Shipped product quality level (SPQL). A quality measurement usually expressed in terms of parts per million (PPM) that provides the buyer with the ability to accept or reject a lot or which may trigger other quality obligations on the part of the supplier. For example a PPM rate of 150PPM would mean that a statistical sample of a lot had a rate higher than 150PPM it could be rejected.

Six sigma. A quality management process that focuses on identifying the root cause of the problem causing the defects and implementing change to both correct it and prevent it from reoccurring in the future.

Standard of commitment. Every obligation has a level or degree of commitment associated. That degree can be a warranty, a material representation, an absolute commitment, a conditional commitment or an obligation to use certain types of efforts (best, reasonable, reasonable commercial) or a general obligation (such as to act in good faith). Each is a standard of the commitment being made.

Statute of frauds. State laws require that certain agreements and documents be in writing, such as real property titles and transfers (conveyances), leases for more than a year, wills and some types of contracts such as contracts that, by their terms, cannot be completed within one year and certain contracts for the sale of goods under the Uniform Commercial Code.

Statute of limitations. In most jurisdictions the laws will establish a specific period of time that an injured party has in which to bring an action against the party that injured them. These types of laws are referred to as statute of limitations and the time frames allowed will be different depending upon the type of action. For example there could be different time frames for contract actions, versus tort claims for personal injury or property damage, and for intellectual property infringement. Where statute of limitation are important in contracts is these set the period during which a third party could a sue you, so you want the supplier to be responsible to you for the same period if they are the cause of the action.

Subrogation. Most often used in the negotiation of insurance provisions where the concept of subrogation occurs when the insurance company pays under it's policy, it requires an assignment of claims to them should they want to pursue a claim against a 3rd party. That process is a subrogation of claims.

Subsidiary. A term used to describe a company in which the parties have over 50% control. A wholly owned subsidiary would describe a company that has 100% control by the parent company.

Supply chain. Supply chain describes all processes and activities starting from when a customer places an order for a product until they take delivery. Includes order administration, production, procurement, distribution and fulfillment.

Surety bond. These are financial instruments, usually issued by insurance companies that guarantee the supplier will perform certain task or make agreed payments. See the definition of bonds for examples of different types of surety bonds.

Survival. A provision in agreements that allows certain rights of the parties to survive the expiration or termination of the contract so those rights can be enforced at any time. For example as a buyer you would want the supplier's warranties and indemnities to survive. As a supplier you would want buyer's obligation of payment to survive.

Temporary injunction. This is a court order barring certain actions until a legal action can make a final determination. For example a third party who feels their intellectual property rights have been infringed by a supplier could seek a temporary injunction against the supplier and buyer to halt production, sale or distribution of the product in question.

Term. The specific period of time covered by the agreement. Terms could be in effect upon signing, they could be made to be retroactive to a prior date or they can commence in the future.

Termination for cause. The right to terminate the contract for certain causes, which remain uncured. In a termination for cause the party claiming the cause may terminate the contract and sue for damages. If buyer is terminating the contract for cause, it normally should also have the right to cancel any open orders without liability.

Termination without cause. As part of their contract the parties may agree in advance how the contract may be terminated without either party being in breach of the terms of the contract. Most termination without cause provisions have terms where if buyer exerts the right to terminate for convenience there will be certain costs that must be paid in conjunction with that termination to effectively make the supplier whole such as paying them for any unusable work in process, any custom materials or parts that must be scrapped and any costs of canceling any orders or contracts that are unique to buyer's products. Another difference between this and termination for cause is cause may require a notice period, where are terminating without cause may be immediate because you have agreed to make the supplier whole on any unique costs.

Terms and conditions. A set of conditions agreed between contract parties.

Third party. A person or company that is not a party to the contract.

Third party beneficiary. A person or company that is not a party to a contract but has legal rights under it by having been named as a beneficiary. They may enforce the contract directly, even if the party to the contract doesn't enforce them. For example, a contract between buyer and supplier could name a third party as a beneficiary of the buyer's rights. If the Supplier breached the contract, the 3rd party beneficiary could enforce the term of the contract against the Supplier irrespective of whether the buyer elects to enforce them.

Tiers. The structuring of customers within a channel where different customers are offered different pricing, discounts and terms depending on the tier they are in. Tiers may be established based on volumes or importance as a customer.

Time-to-market. The time required to deliver a product offering to the marketplace, starting with an action to respond to a customer need and ending with the worldwide availability of the product.

Title. Legal ownership in the product or equipment purchases.

Total cost. A method by which you allocate the costs of the supplier relationship. Total cost is the landed cost plus additions of deletions to the price based upon the impact the contract terms and supplier's performance.

Total cost of ownership or total life cycle cost. The total cost, plus all future costs associated with the purchase over the useful life of the item. As investments or cost are future, they will be calculated on a net present value or discounted cash flow basis. For example if you purchases a piece of capital equipment the total life cycle cost of that purchase would be the total cost plus the cost of things over the life of the product like spare parts, repairs, consumable supplies, differences in operating hours, yields etc.

Total supply or value chain cost. Adds the fulfillment cost parameters to the concept of cost. It looks at not just the cost of getting the items to you, but getting the item to the end user. This cost includes the total life cycle cost, plus the transactional costs for remainder of supply chain. For example, if one supplier could perform direct fulfillment and another couldn't the comparison of the total Supply chain costs between the two suppliers would include any incremental costs to the supplier that could perform direct fulfillment against any savings of direct fulfillment.

Transfer cost. The cost at which a supplier will sell their products to their subsidiaries that will then establish their own price and include their own overhead and profit. Transfer cost includes overhead and profit for the Selling entity.

Value based selling. A selling tactic where the supplier tries to focus the sale on the value the customer will receive and not the cost of the product. Traditional Value based selling models will use ROI models to show how much the customer will save so the cost of the product is paid for out of the savings in an attempt to take the focus away from what the product costs and whether that cost is competitive.

Value of money. The value you place on the investment you need to make. For example, your cost of money could be the rate you can borrow money at. The value of money is the rate you would expect to make versus competing investments for the same money. If you can borrow at 6% and would expect to get an 18% return on your investments, your value of money is 18%.

VAR (Value added reseller). A company that buys a supplier's product and then adds value to it before reselling to their customer. The key is the uniqueness they add makes them not be directly competing against the supplier in the marketplace and as such supplier will provide them discounts to help expand their markets.

Vendor managed inventory (VMI). VMI refers to the situation where a supplier manages a hub location where product can be pulled on an as needed basis and the supplier manages the replenishment of the inventory to the hub.

Waiver. The giving up of a legal right. The concepts is that if you have a right, and fail to enforce it, in the future you will not have that right as by your actions you have given it up or waived it. Most contracts have language that that failure to enforce a term will not constitute a waiver of any future rights.

Warranty. Warranties are a representation of a fact, which if untrue would subject the supplier to damages and termination of the contract if the breach is not remedied. There are legal warranties that are representations of fact such as they have title to the product. There is also a materials warranty against defects in the material and workmanship that is the traditional product warranty that allows return of the product for repair, replacement or refund.

Warranty exclusions. Warranty exclusions are a description of things that effectively void the warranty. Typical examples of requested supplier warranty exclusions are abuse, misuse, unauthorized modifications, etc.

Warranty of fitness for a particular purpose. If the end use of a product is made known to a supplier there could be a warranty that the product will work in that specific use or purpose. Most suppliers specifically try to exclude any warranties of fitness for a particular purpose. Whether you need this warranty will usually depend upon whether your specifications are sufficient to describe exactly what is needed such that you aren't relying on the Supplier to ensure that it will work in its intended purpose.

Warranty of merchantability. The warranty of merchantability is a representation that the products being sold are of "merchantable quality" and may be resold. Most suppliers specifically try to exclude any warranties of merchantability. Whether you need this warranty will usually depend upon whether your specifications are sufficient to describe exactly what is needed and whether you have sufficient other requirements to manage quality levels.

Warranty redemption. The process where you request defective product be replaced under the supplier's warranty against defects in material and workmanship.

Warranty types. Warranties fall into a number of basic general categories:

- Express – a warranty that is created in a contract by a statement of fact which is made about the object of the contract and which forms a basis of the bargain. A warranty that says that the product will comply with the specifications is an express warranty.
- Implied – a warranty that is not expressly stated in the contract but is recognized or imposed by law based on the nature of the transaction.
    - Warranty of fitness for a particular purpose – an implied warranty that the item being sold is fit for the purpose for which BUYER is purchasing it.
    - Warranty of merchantability – an implied warranty that the item being sold is merchantable (of the quality that is generally acceptable in the line of trade).
- Affirmative – a warranty stating that a fact or condition is true.
- Promissory – a warranty stating that a fact or condition is and will remain true.

Warranty types common in hardware

- Warranty period, warranty inclusions/exclusions
- Things warranted:
1. Right to enter into the contract

2. Performance complies with applicable contract obligations, laws, regulation or ordinance
3. No claim, lien, or action exists or are threatened
4. Products and services do not infringe any intellectual property right of a third party
5. Free of defects in design, material and workmanship
6. Product conforms to the warranties, specifications
7. Product safe for use
8. Products are new

Warranties Types Common in Software

- No third party code or disclosed third party code.
- Compliance with all licensing agreements applicable to such third party code;
- Deliverables and Services do not infringe any privacy, publicity, reputation or intellectual property right of a third party;
- Services will be performed using reasonable care and skill
- It will not engage in electronic self-help;
- Products or services contain no harmful code;

Warranty Disclaimer. A warranty disclaimer excuses the supplier from providing their warranties in certain events. One type of warranty disclaimer is usually to exclude implied warranties that may exist under law such as the warranty of merchantability or warranty of fitness for a particular purpose. Other traditional warranty disclaimers are usually for damages caused by someone other than the supplier to the item, such as damages in transit (where the supplier didn't own the responsibility for delivery) or abuse to the product in its use or handling, unauthorized changes or repairs, etc.

Warranty Redemption issues:

- Warranty Redemption Period And What Starts The Warranty Period
- Remedies available
- Who determines whether the defective item will be repaired, replaced, or the purchase price credit or refunded?
- Return Material Authorization ("RMA") process
- Responsibility for cost of returns
- Turnaround time for repair/replacement
- Self help rights
- Return location

Willful. An act that is done deliberately as opposed to an act that may be done inadvertently. The distinction between willful and inadvertent may be used to distinguish between acts that will have liability versus acts that may not have liability or the amount of potential liability. For example an inadvertent disclosure of confidential information may be excused if corrective action is taken to correct the problem. A willful disclosure of confidential information could be a material breach of the agreement and subject the party to major damages.

Work for hire. A situation where the author, creator or designer of a work that could be copyrighted sells all rights in that work to the buyer who could then copyright the work.

Work in Progress (WIP). WIP is most frequently used in change or termination provisions to address buyer's liability for work that has been started but not completed and which is either being cancelled or changed where some or all of the work may be impacted by the change. May also be referred to in the negotiation of lead-time or flexibility where it is important to understand what activities are being done at what points in the process.

Wrongful. The word wrongful is used to describe an act that: is a breach of a legal duty; is illegal; or would be contrary to equity; unfair; or would represent an injustice.

Yield. Yield is the measure of the output of a particular activity or process. In negotiations you would negotiate the yield when you are paying based on the processes performed rather than the finished products or services provided. For example, if you were purchasing the production of a semiconductor you could pay only for acceptable finished product or you could pay based upon all the processes performed that are required to produce the chip. As the output of good product from those processes could vary based on the processes used, complexity of the product, etc. you would negotiate the minimum acceptable output or yield that the supplier is responsible to provide.

Index

A
Acceptance: criteria · 28
Allocated cost · 207
Amendments to the agreement · 29
Assignment · 29
Authority · 65

B
Basic elements of a contract · 57
best efforts · 176
Best's reports" · 38
Bilateral contract · 58
Building knowledge · 4
Buyer instructions · 30, 244
Buyer's insurable interest · 38

C
Cancellation: cancelation rights and charges · 30
Changes:
Buyer's ability to require changes · 46;
Effective date of changes · 33, 246;
Product modifications · 44;
Supplier authorized changes · 48, 246
Supplier unauthorized changes · 49, 246
Choice of law and forum · 30
Commercially reasonable · 176
Commitment standards · 174
Common law · 58
Communicating in negotiation · 145
Condition precedent · 59
Condition subsequent · 59
Consideration · 57
Contract drafting:
  Appendix content · 240;
  Dates, date numbering conventions · 32;
  Defining days · 32
  Incorporating documents by reference · 35;
  Incorporating supplier documents · 36;
  Numbers · 41;
  Severability of terms · 47
Contracting parties· 31
Cost accounting terms · 195
cost and risk of delivery · 12
Cost in contract terms · 21
Cost models · 200
cost of inventory · 12
Cost of money · 11
cost of quality · 13
Cost of warranty · 13
Cost -understanding Cost · 7
Costs in a supplier relationship · 9

D
Damages · 31, 60;
  Actual damages · 252;
  Consequential or special damages · 252;
  Direct damages · 252;
  Expectation damages · 252;
  General damages · 252;
  Incidental damages · 252;
  Punative damages · 252
Deliverables: customer · 32, 250
Delivery:
  Delivery term · 33;
  On time delivery · 42
Discounts · 215
Dr. Chester Karrass. · 1
Driving behavior · 73

E
Effective date · 33
End-of-life:
  Supplier product withdrawl · 34
Enforceability problem costs · 151
Epidemic defects · 34
Equitable remedies · 61
Equity · 58
Errors and omissions. · 34
Exceptions and carve outs · 165
Exclusions to avoid doubt · 170
Excuse of performance · 65
Express contracts · 58

F
Force majeure · 34
Forecasts · 35
Form, fit, and function · 168

G

General Indemnification (Hold Harmless and Indemnity) · 35
"Getting to Yes" · 1
Glossary of procurement terms · 239

H

Harvard Negotiation Project · 1
Herb Cohen "You Can Negotiate Anything" · 1
How companies are organized · 86
How companies operate · 83
How suppliers sell · 84

I

Implied contracts · 58
Implied warranties · 178
Incidental and consequential damages · 59
Inconsistencies · See conflicts between documents
Infringement. · 36
Insurance:
   Automobile liability insurance · 37;
   Comprehensive general liability · 36;
   Naming buyer as additional insured 37, 264;
   Requirements for insurers · 38;
   Waiver of subrogation rights 37, 264;
   Workers compensation 47

K

Key ingredients of cost · 11
Knowledge · 167

L

Landed cost · 14
Lead-time · 38
Legal defenses · 65
Legal requirements for contracts:
Authority · 29, 276;
Right to enter into the agreement · 46, 276
Liability:
Buyer's management · 181;
Sellers manage liability · 163;
Nature of liability · 265;
Liability supplier personnel · 48
Life cycle costs · 17
Limitation of liability · 39
Limits of liability · 69
Liquidated damages · 59

M

Manage performance · 79
Material breach · 59
Material representations · 178
Materiality · 166
Merger of prior agreements · 40
Minor breach · 59
Mitigating costs.: Supplier's responsibility to mitigate · 40
Modifying templates to manage risk · 52

N

Negotiating concessions · 191
negotiating cost · 195
negotiating delivery · 221
Negotiating quality · 227
Negotiating using cost analysis · 205
Negotiation · 123
Negotiation basics · 113
Negotiation myths · 130
Negotiation process 4
Negotiation strategies · 114
Notices: Requirements for Notices · 41

O

Offer and acceptance · 57
Overhead · 207

P

Packaging and packing · 42
Payment: payment term · 42
Persuasion in negotiation · 191
Phases of negotiation · 115
Point in time language · 171
Price:
Competitiveness · 43;
Defining the currency · 31;
Taxes and duties · 49
price curve · 86
Prices: unit prices · 43
Privity · 43
Privity of Contract · 66
Procurement risks · 25
Product life cycles · 85

Q

Qualifying / softening language · 164

Quality:
   No defect found · 40;
   Responsibilities for managing quality · 45

R

Reasonable · 176
Remedies · 59
Rescheduling · 46
Resellers and distributors: Purchases from resellers 45
Resources substance to stand behind obligations. · 35, 247
Responsibility for costs associated with non-conforming product · See Compliance with Specifications
Rights and duties · 179
Rights of acceptance · 40
Rules of construction · 62

S

Sales channels · 90
Set-off · 42
Shipping: buyer's carriers · 47
Sources of liability · 64
Special or punitive damages · 59
standard terms · 97
Statute of frauds · 57
Statutory law · 58
Structuring contracts to drive behavior · 73
Supplier personnel:
   Acceptability of supplier personnel · 48;
   Responsibility for supervision, control · 48
Supplier Proposed Changes 186
Support:
  Spare Parts · 47;
  Parts, repairs, support · 39
Survival · 49

T

Tactics to negotiate cost · 210
Term of contract · 50
Termination: termination rights · 50
Third party personal injury, property damage · 51
Third party purchase · 240
Time value of money · 16
Tips for negotiating with sales people · 95
Total cost · 1, 14
Total life cycle cost · 14
Total supply or value chain cost · 14
Trade secrets misappropriation · 40
Transfer price · 88
Trigger events · 171
Trumping / precedence provisions · 169

U

Understanding contracts · 57
Unenforceable contract · 58
Unilateral contract · 58
Unreasonably withhold consent · 166
Using prequalification · 117

V

Voidable contracts · 58

W

Waiver · 51
Waiver of jury trial · 30
Warranties:
   Compliance with laws · 276;
   Products are new · 45;
   Warranty against IP infringement · 44;
   Warranty redemption · 277;
   Warranty: affirmitive · 276;
   Against 3rd party claims, liens · 39;
   Defects in design, materials or workmanship · 32;
   Exclusions · 51;
   Express · 276;
   Fitness · 276;
   Implied · 276;
   Merchantability · 276;
   Product safety · 44;
   Promissory · 276

ABOUT THE AUTHOR

John C. "Jack" Tracy has managed contracts and procurement organization for over forty years. He started his career in procurement as an Officer in the U.S. Air Force where he became interested in procurement contracts and the law. After the Air Force he attended law school and after graduating started his career in procurement and contract management. The majority of his career was spend in the high technology industry. He worked for Digital Equipment Corporation managing procurement contracting and operations over a broad range of administrative and production commodities. It was at Digital where he gained substantial international experience. Jack spent the last ten years of his career at IBM managing contracting for a variety of production commodities and managing procurement activities associated with a number of divestitures. In a brief departure from high technology Jack worked in banking for BankBoston. At BankBoston he managed the contracting to build the bank's on-line banking presence for a number of the bank's divisions. Jack holds a Bachelor of Science degree in Marketing from Syracuse University and a Juris Doctorate from Suffolk University Law School. He was admitted to practice law in the Commonwealth of Massachusetts.

Made in the USA
Lexington, KY
08 July 2011